A NATIONAL  TRUST GUIDE

# GREAT AMERICAN
# MOVIE THEATERS

IOWA THEATRE, CEDAR RAPIDS, IOWA

KIMO THEATRE, ALBUQUERQUE, NEW MEXICO

EASTMAN THEATRE AND SCHOOL OF MUSIC, ROCHESTER, N.Y.

# GREAT ☆ AMERICAN ☆ MOVIE THEATERS

DAVID NAYLOR

Foreword by Gene Kelly
Epilogue by Joseph DuciBella

GREAT AMERICAN PLACES SERIES
THE PRESERVATION PRESS

The Preservation Press
National Trust for Historic Preservation
1785 Massachusetts Avenue, N.W.
Washington, D.C. 20036

Printed in the United States of America
91   90   89   88   87      5   4   3   2   1

Library of Congress Cataloging in Publication Data

Naylor, David, 1955–
    Great American movie theaters

    (Great American places series)
    Bibliography: p.
    Includes index
    1. Moving picture theaters — United States.
2. Architecture — United States. 3. Architecture,
Modern — 20th Century — United States.
I. Preservation Press.  II. Title.  III. Series.
NA6846.U6N394   1987      725'.822'0973      87-6939
ISBN 0-89133-127-1

Edited by Diane Maddex, director, and Janet Walker, managing editor, The Preservation Press; editorial assistance provided by Paul Wolman.

Designed by Meadows & Wiser, Washington, D.C.

Composed in Vladim by General Typographers, Inc., Washington, D.C.

Printed on 70-pound Warren Patina by the John D. Lucas Printing Company, Baltimore, Md.

Front cover: Auditorium of the Russell, Maysville, Ky. (Lake County Museum, Curt Teich Postcard Collection)
Back cover: Impressions in the forecourt of Grauman's Chinese, Hollywood, Calif. (Lake County Museum, Curt Teich Postcard Collection)

# CONTENTS

■ ■ ■ ■ ■ ■  THE THEATERS  ■ ■ ■ ■ ■ ■

CORNER OF THE GRAND FOYER AZTEC THEATRE, SAN ANTONIO, TEXAS

GRAUMAN'S CHINESE THEATRE, HOLLYWOOD, CALIFORNIA

Theatre Row at Night
Dallas, Texas

■ ■ ■ ■ ■ ■ ■ ■ ■ ■ ■ ■ ■ ■ ■ ■ ■ ■ ■

# FOREWORD

I can remember a time when where we went to the movies was just as important as the movies we went to see. The picture palaces built in America in the 1920s, and even the small-town cinemas built across the land in the 1930s, helped transport us into other worlds. From the early days of the nickelodeons, motion pictures have exerted a magic over all of us. The movies are the quintessential 20th-century art form, and the structures created to show them are no less unique.

Fantasy, exoticism, extravaganzas — as such wonderful excesses played on the screen, these qualities also came to dominate the look of movie theaters. Picture palaces had to rival the movies in size and imagination just to keep pace with the larger-than-life images being shown on the screen. From the moment moviegoers arrived to buy their tickets, there was a sense of something special, a feeling that to step inside was to enter another time and place. The marquees, the ticket booths and even the tickets were seductive enticements. On entering the auditorium itself, the everyday world was left behind, to be replaced by the special magic that was the movies. And do you know what it used to cost to watch the movies for an afternoon or an evening? Sixty-five cents, and for that we got not only the movie but music and live entertainment as well.

The Wiltern, Los Angeles, in 1931.

Theater names alone spoke to us of grandeur (Majestic, Palace, Crown, Coliseum) and of faraway places (Alhambra, Granada, Elsinore, Nile). But for many towns and cities, the majesty is gone. Some of our greatest theaters are lost forever, torn down or destroyed by neglect. How could this happen to the places that once held our fantasies, theaters where by 1930 some 90 million people went to watch films each week? Certainly, a major culprit was a simple lack of awareness of the special place these landmarks occupy in our culture.

This book recaptures the spirit of the old movie theaters and, better yet, shows where to find and see the hundreds that remain. The pages that follow describe these architectural wonders in detail, providing irrefutable evidence of why the picture palaces and movie houses of the past now share a treasured place in our national memory.

For me, the memories are tangible. It was in the 1940s in Riverside, Calif., that I first saw myself, magnified 20 times, on screen in the premiere of *For Me and My Gal.* I then understood why movie theaters were designed on such a Brobdingnagian scale. Probably the most famous movie theater in the world, Grauman's Chinese in Hollywood, was the setting for *Singin' in the Rain* in 1952. What could top this flamboyant Oriental marvel as the site of the premiere of our movie-within-the-movie? *Singin' in the Rain* reached its grand finale on the stage of the Chinese, but the movies and the movie theater live on.

More than a quarter century after *Singin' in the Rain,* I

Opposite: Ushers from Grauman's Chinese (1927) in the early years of the theater's history. The theater continues to play a legendary role by attracting thousands of tourists each year to compare their footprints with those cast by Hollywood stars in the forecourt.

found myself filming in another great American theater. The film, *The Movie Palaces,* was produced by the Smithsonian Institution's Office of Telecommunications for broadcast on public television. The theater was the Wiltern on Wilshire Boulevard in Los Angeles. Nothing could match the klieg-lighted 1931 opening of this Art Deco "Garden of Eden," known then as the Western, but the Wiltern's grand reopening in 1985 gave hope to theater lovers everywhere. Five years after closing its doors in 1980, the Wiltern was carefully rehabilitated and refurbished by people who recognized that the theater had a future as well as a past. The Wiltern is one of a special group of cinemas that continue to dispense pleasure along with a dream or two. These theaters are as much a record of Hollywood and 20th-century America as the old movies themselves.

May your seats always be on the aisle — preferably in one of these great American theaters.

Gene Kelly

# PREFACE

As I write these words, a demolition is in progress directly across the road. "Progress" in this case takes the form of a highway interchange due to fill the site of the Edgemoor Theater (1941) in Wilmington, the only Delaware theater in this book. In 10 years of visiting theaters, and covering well over 100,000 miles, I have never witnessed a theater being torn down.

The Edgemoor sat in a quiet section, well outside downtown Wilmington. A nearby shopping center has been abandoned for years. Movie showings at the Edgemoor gave way to church sermons some 15 years ago. In truth, the Edgemoor never was much of a palace. The Warner (1931) in downtown Wilmington was the glamour theater of the area (razed in the 1970s). The slightly Moderne character of the Edgemoor was closer in appearance to the cinderblock shopping center movie houses of the 1960s than to the Rapp and Rapp–designed Warner of the 1930s. Far greater theaters than either of these have fallen with no one to mark their passing.

Demolition of the Edgemoor.

What keeps me here, as the Edgemoor crumbles before my eyes, are memories from my teenage years. Nights of running up the aisles to the concession stand come back to me, along with movies watched from the thickly upholstered chairs in the enclosed smoking room, above the back of the auditorium. I didn't smoke — I just enjoyed the high vantage point.

As a late product of the baby boom, I can only imagine the pleasures of moviegoing during Hollywood's golden era. Only through the eyes and spoken recollections of others can I experience the anticipation that came from watching a new picture palace being built and seeing the enticing ads in the newspaper for its opening. The one thing I can do is visit the grand old cinemas that remain. So many of these theaters have been saved in the past two decades that it seems as if the surviving palaces can now stand forever, unchallenged on their firm foundations. The reality is that there are constant challenges. Every day, people make great sacrifices to promote the use of these theaters, to operate them while they maintain their architectural integrity, to defend the buildings against high-rise speculators and parking lot barons. Not every picture palace has such champions. The fate of abandoned theaters is to lay dormant, until somebody else wants the land or the roof caves in.

Once the temporarily residing church departed, the Edgemoor had no purpose and no champions. And so it falls. For those of us who haunted the place in our youth, scattering popcorn amidst the rocking seats, memories alone must now suffice. For the theaters in this book, I hope the champions are more vigilant.

David Naylor

■ ■ ■ ■ ■ ■ ■ ■ ■ ■ ■ ■ ■ ■ ■ ■ ■ ■

# ACKNOWLEDGMENTS

Initial thanks go to Joan Dillon at the Folly Theatre in Kansas City, Mo., for suggesting the idea for this guide and to Virginia Wilbur Miller for bringing us together. A great many people — preservationists, theater owners and employees, as well as interested local citizens—helped pull together the materials necessary to produce this guidebook. At least a partial listing of those directly involved appears below. For information, photographs and general encouragement, thanks to:

Alabama: Alice M. Bowsher, Betty Hayslip, Jane Keaton, Michael Leventhal and Patricia F. Seitz. Alaska: Randy Juster. Arizona: Kay Benedict, Douglas E. Kupel and Linda Laird. Arkansas: Jeanie Gillespie. California: Herb Gunn, Gene Marchu, Allen C. Michaan and Laura Soble. Colorado: Dark Cloud, Beth Downs and Felicia Furman Dryden. Connecticut: John Hiddlestone, Randi Lemmon and Dawn Maddox. District of Columbia: Richard Longstreth, Jerry A. McCoy and Nancy B. Schwartz. Florida: Michael F. Zimny. Georgia: Colene G. Reed, Kenneth H. Thomas, Jr., and Emma Adler. Hawaii: Lowell Angell and Ralston H. Nagata. Illinois: Dorothy B. Cromie, Janice Curtis, Maureen E. Gustafson, Katherine Hamilton-Smith, Irvan J. Kummerfeldt and Karen L. Lincicome. Iowa: Larry S. Reed and Douglas S. Russell. Kansas: Martha Hagedorn, M. Meredith Hill and Bob Maes. Kentucky: Jason Fenwick. Louisiana: Robert B. DeBlieux, Michael K. Gorman and Charles F. Seale. Maine: Skip Baker and Earle G. Shettleworth, Jr. Maryland: Janet L. Davis, Orlando Ridout V, Jean Russo and Mary Louise de Sarran. Massachusetts: Margaret Adams, Webster Bull, Jane Carolan, Kathleen A. Cavanaugh, Le Grand David, Rick Heath, Carol Huggins, Kim Lovejoy and Paul Peabody. Michigan: Squire Jaros. Minnesota: Dennis Gimmestad, Alan K. Lathrop and Bonnie Wilson. Mississippi: Richard J. Cawthon. Missouri: Claire F. Blackwell, Jane F. Flynn and Tim Klass. Montana: Lon Johnson, Michael Koop and Edrie Vinson. Nebraska: John E. Carter, Joni Gilkerson and Don Robertson. New Hampshire: Linda Ray Wilson. New Jersey: Oswin Hadley, Terry Karschner and Gale Sasson. New Mexico: Bob Lockwood and Tina C. Van Dyke. New York: John H. T. Dow, Roseann Fitzgerald, Rodney C. Hensel, Quentin S. Jacobs, Randy Piazza, Lindley V. Pryor, Charles E. Rich, Lisa Schaeffer and Marie Vasaturo. North Carolina: Carol M. Blake, Diane H. Filipowicz and Beth Thomas. North Dakota: Daniel Cornejo and Marty Perry. Ohio: Patti Eddy, Steve C. Gordon, Sue Gorisek, Ronald Jaksic, Ted J. Ligibel, Samuel M. McKibben II, Mike Monk and David A. Simmons. Oklahoma: Bill E. Peavler. Oregon: Dan J. Eden, Toni McSwain, Elizabeth Walton Potter, Nancy W. Price, Robert K. Rothschild, Mark Siegel, John W. Southgate and Phyllis Sutter. Pennsylvania: Susan Cavenagh, Thomas W. Grbenick, Gordon Madison, Janet Potter, George Shelps, Charles R. Tranter and Steve Wiesenthal. Rhode Island: Pamela Kennedy. South Carolina: J. Tracy Power, David B. Schneider and Henrietta Wechsler.

South Dakota: Melanie A. Betz and John E. Rau. Tennessee: Joseph E. Hodges, Steve Rogers and Claudette Stager. Texas: Ed Allcorn and Roxanne Schroeder. Vermont: Gary Lemieux and Elizabeth Vinyard. Virginia: Sue Bachtel, David M. Barnett, Lynn Blakemore, Robert I. Foreman and Susie Peters. Washington: Bill Wood and the staff of the state preservation office. West Virginia: Rodney S. Collins. Wisconsin: Donald M. Aucutt, William Ryan Drew and Brad Faughn. With regrets to those whose names have disappeared from the files.

Special thanks go to National Trust representatives in the regions: Vicki Sendstead (Northeast), John Meffert and John Hildreth (South), Tim Turner (Midwest), Clark Strickland and Mary M. Humstone (Mountains/Plains), Libby Barker Willis and Christopher Slusher (Texas/New Mexico), and Kathy Burns and Lisbeth Henning (West).

The membership and the archives of the Theatre Historical Society were a major force in compiling and reviewing the entries for various regions of the country. My special thanks to Michael Miller (New York), Robert K. Headley, Jr. (Hyattsville, Md.), Bret Eddy (Detroit), B. Andrew Corsini (South Bend, Ind.), Joseph DuciBella (Chicago), Wallace Baumann (Knoxville), Irv Glazer (Philadelphia) and Terry Helgesen (Los Angeles). Additional thanks to the volunteer staff of the THS office in Chicago: Bill Benedict, George Quirk and the gang.

Related thanks to Preston J. Kaufmann and Tom B'hend of the American Theatre Organ Society for supplying information and photos from their archives. Also to the staff in the Prints and Photographs Division of the Library of Congress, including Mary Ison.

For substantial help through the doldrums and storms of day-to-day work on the book, my great appreciation to: Diane Maddex, Janet Walker, Carole Collins and the Michelles LaLumia and Wortham of the Preservation Press for revisions and packets; Paul Wolman for helping me collect my thoughts; Kathleen Costello Bar-Tur for safe navigation; David B. Schneider for sharing the fruits of his academic and professional labors; Richard F. McCann for the pages of the preserved; and Joseph Duci-Bella for the pages of the past.

I would also like to express my personal thanks to the following for one reason or another: Again to Joan Dillon and Ginnie in Kansas City; to FiFi Sheridan and Gail Wentzell for old times' sake; to Nancy N. Green and Irene Hoffman from back when; to Martin and Anna Sophia for getting me to Galesburg; to Walter and Sonja, Robin and Michael for living so far from the ocean; to friends and family for clips and photos — at the corners, Eskimo Dan in Alaska, Berenice in Vancouver, Bob in Florida, Jane in California and Linette in Connecticut and Grant in New York, as well as Mickey in Dallas and cousin Karen in Pennsylvania; to Brother Andrew for the encore; to the folks and Mary Margaret for helping me survive the rough spots; to Diane Maddex for unconventional wisdom in shepherding this project; and, ultimately, to Chantal for all time.

# THEATERS AND THE MOVIES

D epicting the history of the movie theater in America requires a canvas of epic proportions, sufficient to take in a cast of thousands. In many ways, the story is the kind of tale the old Hollywood loved to tell.

The drama begins at the dawn of this century, with the first nickelodeons built by a few visionary entrepreneurs. Here, patrons watched flickering black-and-white images — generally 10-minute silent melodramas or comedies. Although choppy and incomplete by today's standards, these brief moving pictures were often magical in effect, featuring stunts and tricks that were more awe-inspiring to early theater patrons than the current high-budget special effects are for customers today.

Historian David A. Cook, in his book *A History of Narrative Film* (1981), identifies the first use of the word "nickelodeon" with a Pittsburgh theater of that name completed in 1905. ("Odeon" is derived from the Greek word for theater; the nickel was the price of admission.) These plain-faced theaters usually contained just a few rows of chairs set up in long, narrow halls. The enclosing walls showed the simplest of decorations at most.

By the early 1910s, a decade after the first nickelodeon had opened, filmmakers had begun to produce photoplays — more developed narratives captured on celluloid. In this form the motion picture graduated from the cramped nickelodeons to established larger theaters with seats for hundreds or even thousands of patrons. Still, what we have come to know as the movies were not quite mature enough to go out on their own; instead, they supplemented vaudeville acts, then in their prime.

It was only after World War I that theaters built primarily to showcase silent motion pictures were opened in any great number. Vaudeville remained popular, but the theater marquees of the day showed that the "silents" had gained equal billing or better. This dual presentation policy was institutionalized by the so-called combination houses, equipped with a full complement of stage equipment as well as a screen and projectors. During the 1920s the most famous vaudeville promoters, Fanchon and Marco, kept pace with the burgeoning silent movie industry by developing their stage-show "Ideas." These individually choreographed and costumed shows were created and released at the rate of one production per week. For each new "Idea," a team of Fanchon and Marco's "Sunkist Beauties" would set out on a 50-week tour of duty, presenting the act in Fox theaters nationwide.

Vaudevillians were not the only live performers at the new motion picture theaters. The great organists of the day rose with their consoles from the depths of the organ pits before film presentations and during intermissions. As they rose, their stirring music poured forth from hidden chambers. Best known of the organ models was

Above: The Dumbarton (1913), once a nickelodeon in Georgetown, Washington, D.C. Below: Ascher's Palace (1921), Peoria, Ill., with its marquee advertising vaudeville, orchestral and organ performances as well as photoplays — plus "iced air."

Opposite: Denver in 1900, with nickelodeons lighting up the western night.

Wurlitzer from the Riviera (1926), North Tonawonda, N.Y., hometown of the pipe organ manufacturer.

the Wurlitzer, manufactured by the Rudolph Wurlitzer Company of North Tonawonda, N.Y. These magnificent instruments enabled organists to reproduce the effects of a full orchestra, along with such unlikely sounds as cuckoo clocks, train whistles and sleigh bells. The organ consoles were usually as elaborately decorated as the surrounding auditorium spaces. And the organists were often so talented that they could draw huge crowds no matter what was on screen. Among the best was Jesse Crawford, popularly known as the "Poet of the Organ." According to contemporary publicity reports, his fame led Wurlitzer to introduce a new model in his honor, the Crawford Special. Wurlitzer built five of the huge specials. Crawford himself played the original at the Paramount (1926, Rapp and Rapp; demolished) on Times Square. A four-manual/36-rank specimen at the Fox (1929) in St. Louis survived years of neglect, to be reborn with the theater in 1982.

### MOVIEGOING IN THE 1920S

By the mid-1920s the picture palace, with all its trappings, was an accepted and cherished part of American life. Theater openings and movie premieres drew crowds far in excess of the number who could actually see each show. On weekdays mothers could attend film showings without the added expense of hiring a babysitter; many picture palaces operated professionally staffed nurseries and supervised play areas. Weekend matinees were the province of schoolchildren. In later years, this segment of

Right: Children lined up for a promotional photo at the Rialto (1919), Tucson, Ariz. Below: The Main Street (1938) on Sinclair Lewis's own Main Street, Sauk Centre, Minn., in 1957.

the audience would be drawn back week after week by adventure serials and animated features.

The largest concentrations of grand-scale movie theaters were in the major metropolitan areas — Chicago, Los Angeles and New York. Yet theater patrons in less populous cities such as Buffalo, Minneapolis, Seattle and Denver could take their pick from among 10 or more palaces each. Even small towns generally could boast two or three fancy movie houses, clustered along Main Street or around the town square. This great boom in theater building was not spontaneous, however; it was highly dependent on how the movies shown at these theaters were made and distributed.

## ARCHITECTS AND MOGULS

The initial film exhibitors, the nickelodeon owners, had to purchase the two- or three-reel films they showed from whomever they could find. At first they paid for films by the foot. It was a number of years into the new century before the leasing of a motion picture to several theaters in succession became common practice.

Most successful among the early exhibitors were those who quickly expanded their operations to meet the increasing demand for and availability of films. By the early 1920s a few farsighted showmen had already secured places for themselves in movie theater history. In California, it was Sid Grauman who overshadowed the competition. From early success managing the Million Dollar (1918) and the Metropolitan (1923, demolished) in downtown Los Angeles, Grauman moved out to Hollywood. There he established his fame by building the exotic Egyptian (1922) and the world-renowned Grauman's Chinese (1927).

The young Sid Grauman, the West's renowned film exhibitor.

The most acclaimed showman on the East Coast was Manhattan's Samuel "Roxy" Rothapfel. His first big break came in 1914, far uptown in Harlem at the Regent (1913). Just a few years later he was comfortably ensconced as manager of the 4,000-seat Capitol (1919, demolished) in midtown Manhattan. Before the end of the 1920s he supervised the opening of the huge and impossibly opulent theater bearing his name, the Roxy (1927, demolished), just north of Times Square on Broadway.

Even as local exhibitors such as Roxy Rothapfel were reaching their peaks, the stakes in the film business were being raised far above the concerns of New York or Los Angeles. The great Hollywood studios had been born. Their overseers quickly realized the need to get the widest possible distribution for their new films. How better than by showing the movies in regional or national networks of theaters controlled by the studios themselves? Before the Depression forced a halt to such activities, the studios and their subsidiaries embarked on a binge of new theater building that put their predecessors to shame.

Crucial to the chain-building process was the participation of several architects who already had established themselves as masters of theater design. Because of the early ties between motion pictures and

Above: The Capitol (1920), Takoma, Wash., an early theater designed by B. Marcus Priteca. Below: Architect Thomas W. Lamb, who started his theater-designing career with classical buildings in New York and New England.

vaudeville, the pioneer theater architects built halls capable of housing both forms of entertainment. The bulk of commissions in the early 1920s came from vaudeville circuit owners. In the Northeast, architect Thomas W. Lamb built a sprawling network of theaters for acrobat-turned-vaudeville promotor F. F. Proctor. In the Northwest, B. Marcus Priteca stepped in as house architect for the circuit run by Alexander Pantages. Several of the early Orpheum theaters in the West were from the drawing boards of G. Albert Lansburgh. Perhaps the most successful partnership between early showmen and architects was made in Chicago. By 1921 Rapp and Rapp had built showplaces for the Balaban and Katz operation all around Chicago. At the heart of the Loop rose the Chicago (1921). To the northwest was the Central Park (1917), with the glorious Tivoli (1921, demolished) to the south.

As the Hollywood studios formed and gained power, the theater business changed dramatically. From the start, Metro-Goldwyn-Mayer was the force to be reckoned with. This studio, which would dominate movie-making in the 1930s, got its jump on the other studios by constructing a vast empire of theaters in the 1920s. "We sell tickets to theaters, not movies," was the motto of Marcus Loew, whose theater chain played MGM's pictures. The primary architect for the Loew's picture palace operation was Thomas W. Lamb. At the time of Loew's death, Lamb had just finished one of his finest theaters in the Loew's chain, the palatial Midland in Kansas City, Mo. (1927), and other grand showplaces were in construction in Syracuse, N.Y. (1928), and Columbus, Ohio (1928).

At about the same time in Chicago, Balaban and Katz joined its operation to a production group originally known as Famous Players. Subsequently renamed Paramount Pictures, this studio was set up as a chief competitor to MGM. Architects Rapp and Rapp benefited from the association between their old bosses and the new studio, expanding their horizons far beyond the shores of Lake Michigan. The Rapp brothers received the commission to build the Paramount flagship theater (1926) on Times Square in New York City, as well as the Paramount outposts in Seattle and Portland, Ore. (both 1928).

In addition to their work for Paramount, Rapp and Rapp designed theaters for Warner Brothers Pictures in West Chester (1930) and Erie, Pa. (1931). The Warner operation by then had already consumed the Stanley theater chain, whose major theaters had been built in Philadelphia (1921, demolished) and Baltimore (1927, demolished) to designs by architects Hoffman and Henon.

When Mary Pickford, Douglas Fairbanks and Charlie Chaplin formed United Artists Studios in the mid-1920s, yet another architect found his workload increased. After creating the principal showplace for the stars' partnership in downtown Los Angeles (1927), C. Howard Crane adapted this design for United Artists theaters in Chicago and Detroit (both 1928).

Crane also did some work for William Fox, one of the most interesting characters in the history of the movie theater business. Fox never wore a watch and reportedly always kept his office blinds closed to make time stand still. For this eccentric business wizard, Crane built not only the 4,000-seat Fox (1928, demolished) in Brooklyn but also twin 5,000-seat masterpieces in Detroit (1928) and St. Louis (1929). Fox was immensely proud of these theaters and of later Fox showplaces in Atlanta (1929) and San Francisco (1929, demolished). According to studio publicity the boss claimed, "No second of every 24 hours passes but the name of William Fox is on the screen in some part of the world." And in nearly every case, the screen in question was in a theater bearing the Fox name on its marquee.

Yet as the showpieces of the Fox empire were opening in 1929, the emperor was heading for disaster. In July of that year Fox was seriously injured in an automobile crash that killed his chauffeur. Returning to business a few months later, Fox found himself drastically overextended financially as the stock market took its famous tumble. Although the Fox film empire spread even farther in the 1930s and the studio survived to become 20th Century–Fox, William Fox was out of the business by 1932. He lived in relative comfort until he died in 1952.

Top: An example of C. Howard Crane's early work, the Capitol (1922) in Detroit, later known as the Grand Circus. Above: Movie mogul William Fox, Crane's client in Detroit and other cities.

### A NEW BUILDING TYPE

As moviegoing became an established practice across the country, patrons witnessed the birth of a distinctly modern and quintessentially American architectural creation: the motion picture palace. The decor of many of these theaters mirrored that of Old World palaces of the past. But the unique development and functional necessities of the film business demanded more than imitation. The architects of this new building type were faced with complex needs almost unrivaled in their day, requiring a vast collection of rooms under one roof and often situated on irregular plots of land.

These theaters were built essentially to serve a

purpose that was purely economic: attracting moviegoers to the box office. Their exteriors helped fill this role, using forms and styles that made them stand out from their surroundings. A broad canopy marquee, often accompanied by a towering vertical sign, announced the building's name and purpose. To make sure that nobody missed the message or the latest film, tracer and chaser lights were used to trim these often elaborate signs. Early nickelodeon theaters pioneered the use of outdoor electrical signage. Many of the early theaters outlined their arched and gabled facades with light bulbs. One nickelodeon even sported an electric butterfly. When the movies graduated from nickelodeons to vaudeville halls, they took this ingenious use of nighttime illumination with them, along with the screens and projection equipment. Designers of the new movie theaters built on the tradition, seeking to catch the eye of potential patrons by outlining exteriors in stud lights and topping them with illuminated billboards as well as painting marquees in light. To help sell tickets, marble-clad and bronze-trimmed box offices were introduced in the 1920s.

Inside, the architects sought to impress theater goers with an abundance of lobby space on several levels, accessible by staircases (occasionally an elevator as

Above left: Box office at the Garden (1915), Pittsburgh. Above right: Box office at the Mayfair (1915), Portland, Ore., added in the 1950s when the theater joined the Fox chain. Right: Rapp and Rapp's auditorium for the Paramount (1928), Portland, Ore.

well). The lobbies had to be spectacular, observed one of Rapp and Rapp's designers, "to keep the patron's mind off the fact that he is waiting." Adjacent promenades were filled with art and expensive objects. And awaiting within the auditorium were seats as plush as any, often wrapped in mohair or velvet. At the ends of each row of balcony seats, beneath the armrests, specially designed chair stands with concealed pinlights helped moviegoers navigate the balcony stairs. Chair stands were often tailored to match the decor of the theater, for example, the Egyptian scarab design used in the St. Louis Fox.

Overall, the auditorium lighting had to be sufficiently bright for patrons to find their seats, but otherwise subdued for proper atmosphere and film viewing. Cove lighting was one solution; concealed by ornamental surfaces, cove lights bathed the auditorium in a soft multicolor glow. Powering the lights was just part of the job required of the electrical systems inside the picture palaces. The tradition of summer afternoon movie matinees dates to the 1920s, when the first air-conditioning

Top: Auditorium of the Byrd (1928), Richmond, Va., whose stage was extended early in its history, eliminating the orchestra pit. Above: Rapp and Rapp's Ocean State (1928), Providence, with its cove-lighted auditorium.

Left: City officials on a 1930 tour of the Paramount (1930), Abilene, Tex. Right: Lighting control panel. Below: Ushers at Abilene's Paramount, posing in 1930.

systems were heavily tested in crowded Chicago and New York theaters.

Backstage equipment included the usual rigging and lighting for stage performers. Asbestos curtains were included to shield the audience in case of a fire onstage. Fanciful drapery arrangements bordered the screen during film showings. Organ consoles in the orchestra pit required great chambers filled with pipes and related paraphernalia on both sides of the proscenium. Dressing rooms were provided for actors as well as musicians.

Beyond the various theatrical spaces, lobbies and lounges for sitting or smoking, theater designers threw in operable waterfalls, thematically consistent children's playrooms and staffed emergency aid rooms. The Roxy in New York City even had its own barbershop. With several shows a day in most theaters, moving people in and out became a prime consideration. Architects developed circulation patterns to ensure safety and convenience. Aiding their efforts were the theaters' own traffic cops, the ushers, many of them uniformed and trained like a crack drill unit. It all added up to an amazing array of architectural and human engineering feats fitted together in a unique building type. And the decoration of these picture palaces made them still more unique.

## THE ARCHITECTURE OF FANTASY

Questions of stylistic integrity — and of simple good taste — have plagued movie theaters since they first entered the American architectural stage. "The architecture of the movie palace," suggested Ben Hall in *The Best Remaining Seats,* "was a triumph of suppressed desire." It was not suppressed enough for many architecture critics, one of whom complained in 1928, "No more pitiful degradation of an art has ever been presented than the prostitution of architecture that goes on daily in the construction of these huge buildings . . . taste and beauty abased to the lowest degree."

Theater architects saw their role differently, and the public agreed with them. These designers aimed to create showplaces with all the trappings of the rich — but accessible to all. George Rapp of the Rapp and Rapp firm called theaters "a shrine to democracy where the wealthy rub elbows with the poor." The resulting architecture of fantasy gave movie theaters a mass appeal never found in the grand opera houses that preceded them. Ultimately, it was all part of the show.

The decorative treatments of early nickelodeons matched the humble origins of the movie business as a whole. These theaters — for the most part, simple rectangular boxlike structures — were not based on any specific pattern. Creative owners took advantage of stock terra cotta ornament to embellish the fronts of their nickelodeons. As the audience for motion pictures grew, owners abandoned most of these nickelodeons for larger accommodations.

Many of the architects who designed the first picture palaces were born or trained in Europe. Their early designs reflect their familiarity with the opera houses and legitimate theaters of the Old World. Scottish-born Thomas W. Lamb began his career with a series of Adam-style theaters built throughout New York and New England. B. Marcus Priteca, based in Seattle, used his Beaux Arts background to develop wonderfully balanced classical designs for the Pantages chain. John Eberson, an immigrant from Austria, practiced an opera house style in his early theaters, although he embellished them with sets of rotating fans in an attempt to beat the summer heat in Texas and Kansas. Later, in the mid-1920s, Eberson devised the popular "stars and clouds" formula. These so-called atmospheric theaters simulated a romantic outdoor Mediterranean courtyard, with a conventional seating arrangement set beneath a blue plaster "sky" lit by hidden pinpoint "star" lights.

A second generation of theater architects helped Eberson loosen still further the confines of classicism, bringing a measure of exoticism and whimsy to the picture palaces of the 1920s. The Boller Brothers, a firm that worked mostly in Missouri, Texas and the Southwest, designed an array of Spanish Colonial Revival theaters. But they were also responsible for a Babylonian-Persian picture palace, the Missouri (1937) in St. Joseph, and the Pueblo Deco blend of ornaments of the KiMo in Albuquerque (1927). Style changes during this period

Architect John Eberson, whose atmospheric theaters captured the imagination of moviegoers.

Top: Proscenium arch and stage of the Orpheum (1922), Wichita, Kans., in the 1920s, an early Ebersonian design. Right: Auditorium of the Astro (1927), Omaha, showing Eberson's later use of architectural facades and sky patterns to create his noted atmospheric interiors.

The Persian-inspired Missouri (1927), St. Joseph, designed by the Boller Brothers.

were dizzying, as architects and designers ransacked the cultures of several continents for inspiration: East Indian, Dutch, Siamese, Tudor and Mayan rapidly joined the more conventional Italian baroque and French Second Empire as acceptable sources for ornamental treatments.

The trend toward using exotic designs for theaters is generally considered to have begun with the archeological discoveries of 1922 in Egypt. From the tomb of Tutankhamen and the great hall at Karnak, architects lifted elements to decorate new cinemas. Along with Grauman's mock temple in Hollywood, Egyptian theaters sprang up in small towns such as DeKalb, Ill. (1929), and Coos Bay, Ore. (1925).

Oriental design elements formed the basis for some of the most popular and flamboyant decorative schemes ever built. Grauman's 1927 Hollywood showplace was the best known, but the Fifth Avenue (1926) in Seattle was perhaps the most elaborate use of Chinese architecture in America. Architect R. C. Reamer and his designer, Gustav Liljestrom, were inspired by photographs of Forbidden City halls and temples published in a contemporary German volume. The end product of their efforts was a plasterwork palace that recalls the dynasties of ancient China in ways both faithful and fanciful.

At the end of the 1920s, both the baroque and the exotic gave way to the simplified lines and bright colors of Art Deco for new theater design. Two California architects were at the forefront of the aesthetic change: S. Charles Lee in Los Angeles and Timothy L. Pflueger in the Bay Area. Lee led the way with his zigzag geometry for the Fox-Wilshire (1930). For sheer versatility and overall mastery of the Art Deco style, nothing can top Pflueger's design for the Oakland Paramount (1931). All that remained to close out the golden age of theater building was the construction of Radio City Music Hall (1932). This radiant swan song took shape as Rockefeller Center struggled into existence in Manhattan against the tide of the Depression.

The Los Angeles (1931), designed for Los Angeles by S. Charles Lee before he embarked on a more experimental path with his Art Deco theaters.

## DECLINE AND FALL

Movies came of age in the 1930s, as enhanced sound effects meshed easily with the action flickering on the screen. Yet the boom of theater building had already passed. The heady rush to build ever-more elaborate theaters from 1927 to 1929 resulted in an overabundance of picture palaces with too many seats to fill. One ray of hope for theater owners was the higher quality of motion pictures coming out of Hollywood. The films of Capra, Lubitsch and others at least enabled the majority of theaters to remain in business.

The economic hardships of the Depression eventually fostered some commercial creativity on the part of theater owners. Extravagant promotional stunts were concocted in attempts to boost box office totals. Rarely able to bring in movie stars for Hollywood-style grand premieres, theater owners in the hinterlands resorted to offering free china to their patrons. Others held "Bank Night" money giveaways or other special contests sometimes sponsored by area businesses or charities. Some small-city theaters were lucky. Ronald Reagan and Pat O'Brien appeared in South Bend, Ind., for the world premiere of *Knute Rockne—All American*. In 1947 a Texas theater operation arranged for James Stewart and director Frank Capra to fly into Beaumont, Tex., for the local premiere of *It's a Wonderful Life* at the Jefferson (1927). For the duration of World War II, promotional displays in the lobbies were replaced by booths selling war stamps and bonds.

A few years after the war ended, theater going again began to slip with the advent of television. For all too many of the downtown picture palaces, the slide worsened in the mid-1950s. This decline left theater owners highly vulnerable when the twin demons of the 1960s arrived: urban renewal and movement to the suburbs. Built in profusion on valuable downtown city blocks, but too far from the new population centers, theaters incurred heavy losses and rising expenses. Thus, the overbuilding of the 1930s led directly to the theatrical demolition derby of the 1960s. For those downtown theaters hanging on, the options were limited. Once advertised as offering "an acre of seats in a garden of dreams," even the grandest picture palaces seemed to have become

Demolition of San Francisco's "Fabulous Fox" (1929) in 1963. Thomas Lamb's luxurious theater was designed as a western showplace for the Fox empire.

cavernous, empty spaces with fraying decor.

Again, theater owners responded with creative, although somewhat destructive, solutions to their problems. Some subdivided their auditoriums, occasionally piggybacking a screening room or two in the balcony area. More than a few owners chose to revive their long-dormant stage apparatus to put on rock shows, supplementing dwindling movie revenues. For all the abuse suffered by these theaters during rock concerts, at least the doors were kept open.

Too late for many theaters, in the 1970s the tide turned again for picture palaces. Scattered cries arose in many cities to save beloved old theaters. Downtown movie houses were just waiting to be reborn as the now-ubiquitous performing arts centers. The era of preservation had arrived in America.

A gallery of demolished theaters. Top left: The Esquire (1935) in Dallas. Top right: The State (1929) in Manchester, N.H. Above: The Oriental (1927) in Portland, Ore.

The modern-day United Artists (1985), San Diego, a multiplex built up to stand out.

## THE ART OF MOVIEGOING TODAY

For the first time in 60 years, film exhibitors are opening new 3,000-seat theaters in major towns and cities. Of course, the seats in these so-called multiplexes may be divided among as many as a dozen separate screening rooms. Yet contrasted to the characterless twin- and quad-cinemas of the 1970s, many of the newer complexes maintain at least a pretense of providing fashionable settings and comfortable seats for patrons. The eight-screen octoplexes of the 1980s often include architectural elements that seem to blend Art Moderne and high tech in what perhaps some day will be categorized as Deco Revival or, better yet, Re-Deco.

Among the more successful multiplexes is the new seven-screen Shirlington, located in a suburban Virginia shopping mall near Washington, D.C. The Shirlington has a fancy marquee above entry doors centered by a vertical Lucite pylon. The overall shape of the front facade is composed of glass blocks, massed in a ziggurat form last popular 50 years ago. Also opened near the end of 1986, the 10-screen Lloyd Cinemas in Portland, Ore., has a tall atrium corridor cutting through it, decorated with an impressive array of neon signage. First stop for all moviegoers is a box office executed in the style of the ocean liners of the 1930s. Angled red and black lines, apparently modeled after the quasi-Deco geometric patterns of Frank Lloyd Wright, decorate the gray fabric walls enclosing most of the screening rooms.

The trend of building these fashionable multicinemas has little direct bearing on the fate of the pre-Depression picture palaces that still stand, however. The vast majority of the downtown palaces currently in operation play host to some mix of live musical and theater performances. First-run movie screenings are almost entirely the domain of the suburban centers, with the huge movie multiplexes taking the lion's share of the best new movies.

What even the modern-day movie theater tycoons must admit is that although the multiplexes of the 1980s may approach the older palaces in scale and expense, the new complexes cannot replicate the sense of magic inspired by even the least elaborate small-town Fox or Paramount theaters of 50 or 60 years ago. Clearly not every one of these historic picture palaces can be saved as a movie theater or as a center for the performing arts. But we should preserve what we can. And when we sit in the reupholstered seats of a rescued theater, as the lights dim before a ballet or a theater performance, we can meditate for a moment about the ghosts of the silent screen or the master organists who once performed there. These palaces are vital links to the culture of our past.

Lloyd Cinemas (1986), Portland, Ore., a "Star Wars" design for the movies.

# ENCORES FOR OLD THEATERS

In retrospect, at least, adapting movie theaters for new theatrical uses seems like the most natural thing in the world. Now, a symphonic performance or a touring Broadway show is likely to fill a theater where, just a decade earlier, B-grade movies played to rows of empty seats. In small towns and big cities major performance groups are just as likely to work in a rehabilitated movie house as in a new concert hall. Yet just 20 years ago few would have dreamed such a thing possible.

The 1960s were perhaps the palaces' darkest hour. No theater was sacred — not even the "Cathedral of the Motion Picture," New York's Roxy (1927), which fell in 1961. Even after a few of the picture palaces were converted into performance halls, major cultural icons such as Radio City Music Hall (1931) and Grauman's Chinese (1927) were still threatened with death or dismemberment. Only through a slow process of adjustment did movie theaters regain the status of prized cultural monuments that they once held in the 1920s and 1930s.

To bring public recognition to, and often to save, historic theaters, many are now being added to local, state and national landmarks registers. Historic resource surveys increasingly are including theaters in their inventories, as the importance of these often fantasy-laden, eclectic and always fascinating structures is gradually being recognized. Landmark designation often provides design review over proposed alterations, but it is not a guarantee against demolition. Few movie theaters have been listed in the National Register of Historic Places, the official inventory maintained by the U.S. Department of the Interior's National Park Service, as sites have been restricted to those at least 50 years old. Many theaters, just past this age, are only now being considered for this historical status.

In addition to architectural significance, an important motivation for theater preservation has been economic: adapting the old was cheaper than building anew. After the first few palaces were renovated, more people recognized their intrinsic beauty and significance and sought to save other theaters. A prestige factor emerged for a time: a restored theater bestowed on its administrators a badge of civic merit. People believed, often rightfully so, that they had taken an abandoned piece of their town and turned it back into something special. As demands for more performance space put pressure on communities seeking to showcase the performing arts locally, unused or underused movie theaters proved excellent candidates. Gradually, theater reuse became a matter of simple good sense, almost part of the natural order of things.

To a large extent the issues facing any city or private group trying to save a theater are those that originally

Symphony performance at the Circle (1916), Indianapolis, one of many theaters now used for the performing arts.

Opposite: Grand foyer of Heinz Hall, Pittsburgh, one of the first theater conversions, carved out of Rapp and Rapp's Loew's Penn (1927).

The Tampa, Tampa, Fla., an atmospheric marvel from the hand of John Eberson, being restored for its 1977 reopening.

confronted the theater's builders: how to address the functional needs of the performers, the aesthetic delight of the patrons and the economic survival of the operators. Added to the list today are the cultural needs and historical interests of the community, as well as the architectural integrity of what have become community landmarks in many cases. In converting an old theater for modern use, the biggest challenge is adapting the theater to modern theater technology, present-day comfort requirements and building codes, while at the same time avoiding unalterable damage to the historic structure inside and out. Realistic, practical plans and feasibility studies are needed to save theaters based on economic and cultural needs, location, structural condition, safety and technical requirements, aesthetics, comfort and management concerns, as well as community devotion to and support for the structure itself.

Using a theater the way it was built — that is, maintaining the auditorium, stage and lobbies for the performing arts or film — is the most acceptable use and least harmful to the building's integrity. If it is not possible to maintain the same or a similar use, changes for other purposes, such as meeting halls or churches, should be sympathetic and avoid gutting interiors or making other radical changes to the building. Regrettably, many of the theaters in this book have been irreversibly altered to allow for multiple screens, enlarged stages or some other goal that took priority over the original character and detailing of the theater itself. While such unsympathetic handling of the theater may have appeared essential at the time to ensure survival, such changes are never the preferred preservation course.

Granted a preservation-minded management, decisions still must be made as to what can be restored and what can be adapted to fit current needs. Exacting restoration may be virtually impossible in all but a few cases. Most theaters have undergone a gradual evolution over half a century of hard use. Original details, structural and ornamental, may be lost forever. Architect Malcolm Holzman, who helped renovate the Ohio in Columbus, Ohio, has said that "any restoration is interpretive." Whatever is done — restoration, rehabilitation, adaptation — the work should follow the spirit of the original. Those involved must constantly keep in mind what it is that makes their theater special and how best to preserve that historical character.

In some cases, all that is needed to revive a theater, especially for continued use as a theater, is careful cleaning, repainting and perhaps some minor replacements — seats or some lighting fixtures, for instance. Other projects may involve major changes such as reducing seating capacity to improve patron comfort and sight lines, enlarging the stage and wings to accommodate today's larger stage productions, or constructing additional theaters in the building by altering lobbies or reducing the size of a balcony. Such a project might also include changing the lobby to improve traffic circulation and updating heating, ventilating, air-conditioning and electrical systems to meet code standards. Modernizing lighting and acoustical systems may also be necessary. Whatever alterations are made, the twin goals of preservation must be weighed against each other: to maintain as much as possible of the building's integrity and to make the project economically viable.

The Interior Department has issued a set of standards and guidelines that provide useful advice when preserving and rehabilitating old and historic buildings. The standards recommend that the new use of a building be compatible with its former use and that changes to a structure be made in such a way that they do not impair the building's original integrity. Other recommendations are to avoid removing original and distinguishing features; avoid alterations that have no historical basis in the building; recognize that changes made in the past may have a significance of their own; treat stylistic features with sensitivity; repair, rather than replace, deteriorated features; when making necessary replacements, match the originals as closely as possible and base them on evidence, such as photographs or drawings, rather than on conjecture; clean using the gentlest means possible, avoiding the use of sandblasting; include alterations and additions so they do not destroy original features and are compatible in size, scale, color, material and character.

Denver's Mayan (1930). Local citizens fought to save this theater, now converted into a triplex.

The recent history of theater renovations suggests that a clear understanding of preservation goals is essential to ensure that the efforts and monies expended serve, to the greatest extent practicable, the artistic, cultural and architectural heritage embodied by the theaters. The new challenge in the late 1980s is to determine exactly how renovated theaters can best serve the people of their towns and cities. Again, economic factors have exerted a strong influence on artistic decisions. Government fund-

The Michigan (1926), Detroit. Cars moved into the building in this garage conversion — one of the least sensitive uses of a theater short of demolition.

ing for operational purposes is now rare if not nonexis-
tent. Commercial ventures in national touring productions have run up against skyrocketing costs for travel
expenses, staging, technical payrolls and advertising
fees. Theater managers, lacking funds to produce and
promote their own shows, often find few traveling
productions coming to them. Performing arts centers
thus have opened up their programming to allow for the
widest possible range of events, not limited to those on
stage. Even hosting banquets in some of the palatial
grand lobbies has proved popular in recent years. In the
current theatrical climate, theaters with the greatest
flexibility built into their reuse programs have fared the
best. Still, there have been many roads to preservation.

What follows is a set of 10 case studies that, taken
together, reflect the history of theater renovation in its
many guises. The examples, which are also included in
the guide section, have been selected to highlight the
variety of paths taken by different public and private
groups and individuals to bring their theaters back to life.
As with the theater and the movies themselves, there have
been great successes and relative flops. The preservation
of at least a sizable fraction of our old movie houses
provides us with the opportunity to benefit from both the
triumphs and the failures.

## EARLY ORCHESTRA HALL CONVERSIONS

The managers and members of a few symphony orchestras were among the very first to recognize the value
of adapting movie palaces for new uses, probably
because the majority of theaters built in the 1920s
included room in the pit for an orchestra, even if only to
accompany the act on stage. As picture palaces became
concert halls, the orchestras moved up to center stage.

Symphony managers, like theater owners, had economic motives in promoting conversions. These managers discovered they could significantly lower costs by
electing to rehabilitate a decayed movie theater rather
than to build a new facility. The lavish Old World styling
of many picture palaces was an added inducement.

Aside from cleaning and repairing the lobby and
auditorium decor and, frequently, repairing and recover-
ing the seats, the most common concern in these concert
halls has been their acoustics. Most theaters were
designed for some live performances, so their auditoriums featured reasonably good acoustics. Still,
some minimal changes have been necessary to accommodate full orchestral performances. At one extreme, the
new tenants of the old Warner (1931, now Powers
Auditorium) in Youngstown, Ohio, enhanced sound
quality by placing an array of sound baffles along the
auditorium walls and ceiling. A more preservation-
oriented approach was taken in the Orpheum (1927) in
Vancouver, British Columbia. There, the orchestra is
backed by a bandshell fixed within the proscenium arch.
The only change to the auditorium proper was the
painting of a new mural, based on the original on the

surface of the Orpheum's oval dome. The work was supervised by Anthony B. Heinsbergen, the theater's original decorator, brought out of retirement.

For 40 years the St. Louis held down the north end of the Grand Boulevard theater district; the later Fox (1929) marked the south end. The midtown district, located well west of downtown, had become a rough neighborhood by 1966, when the last movie, *The Sound of Music,* played at the St. Louis.

Shortly before the theater closed, local philanthropist Oscar Johnson, Jr., endowed the St. Louis Symphony with a $500,000 gift toward the purchase of a new hall. Faced with estimates of $10–20 million for new construction, the Symphony Society chose instead to adopt the soon-to-be-abandoned St. Louis. The final cost of the conversion would approach $2.5 million, of which $1 million was a gift from the widow of Walter S. Powell, the eventual namesake of the hall.

The St. Louis Symphony had performed at the theater several times before acquiring it and came to recognize both its benefits and its flaws. The grand space provided by the mirror-lined main lobby was clearly among the former. The baroque-style auditorium was judged to have sufficient seating but not quite the sound desired for the planned performances. Acoustic specialist Cyril M. Harris was called in to remedy the perceived shortcomings. First, the shell of the building was insulated to shield the interior from the traffic noises of Grand Boulevard. Changes to the auditorium layout included placing cylindrical baffles inside the former organ screens. The stage area received an orchestra shell and a complete overhaul of the mechanical systems.

Years after its successful conversion in 1968, Powell Hall received the blessing of architecture critic Ada Louise Huxtable. She praised the conversion as a "triumph of suitable preservation" and described the product as "a concert hall of suave elegance, beautiful sound and stunning economy."

■ **Powell Hall
(Loew's St. Louis)**
St. Louis
Rapp and Rapp
1925

Above: Powell Hall's refined facade. Below left and right: Rapp and Rapp's sweeping auditorium and classical lobby.

■ **Paramount**
Oakland, Calif.
Miller and Pflueger
1931

The Paramount, with its spectacular Art Deco design, was probably the first of the concert hall projects to involve restoration rather than remodeling of a picture palace. In the early 1970s, the Oakland Symphony Orchestra was working to enhance its status as a small-city orchestra. Part of the symphony's plan was to find a new home for the 1973 subscription season. But after receiving estimates for a new concert hall in the range of $13 million, the symphony decided to purchase and relocate at the Paramount.

The Oakland Symphony Orchestra Association brought in Jack Bethards, previously business manager for an opera company, to oversee the move into the former movie theater. Bethards, in turn, hired former opera company colleague Peter Botto to supervise the restoration project. The two men and their staff labored at breakneck speed to meet the symphony's season deadline and yet to maintain the authenticity of the restoration. Begun on December 20, 1972, the $2 million job was completed just in time for the Oakland Symphony to go on as planned, September 22, 1973. Seating was reduced from the original 3,476 to 2,998. Otherwise, the Paramount was judged by patrons who had seen the theater in the 1930s to be as good as new.

A sad postscript to the restoration has been the recent disbanding of the Oakland Symphony Orchestra. Forced in 1975 to sell the Paramount to the city of Oakland for one dollar, the symphony finally declared bankruptcy in 1986. The management organization of the theater, Paramount Theatre of the Arts, Inc., has kept the reborn Art Deco masterpiece in business since the symphony's demise, with what had been supplementary events — stage shows, travel films and popular music performances.

Top: The Paramount's vertical sign with a 70-color mosaic by Gerald Fitzgerald, showing the god and goddess of cinema. Above: Spectacular Art Deco auditorium with an organ grille at right. Restoration of the theater included a thorough cleaning of the grillwork ceiling above the auditorium and foyer. Right: Workers restoring recessed panels in the vaulted ceiling of the mezzanine lounge.

## MULTIPURPOSE RESCUE OPERATIONS

The list of downtown picture palaces salvaged to become
centers for the performing arts currently runs to several
dozen theaters. These former movie houses may have one
or two major local performance groups as principal
tenants, but for the most part these centers thrive on
variety. Music concerts can range from chamber music to
New Wave, with dance matching that artistic spectrum.
Live theater may be the product of local talent or an
import from Broadway. Organ concerts remain a popular
attraction at many theaters, often in conjunction with a
classic film series.

Equal in their variety have been the means and
methods by which these theaters have been turned into
performance halls. More than a few picture palaces have
been saved largely through grass-roots efforts. Volunteer
groups then often continue to help operate the building
they helped rescue. Government funding, from all levels,
has been a significant factor in the turnaround of many
abandoned theaters (see examples of the Illinois state
legislature's support of theater reclamation in the last
section).

When William Fox went into partnership with the
Shriners, he envisioned this theater as the southern
stronghold of his picture palace empire. By 1973 the Fox
was showing low-budget movies, and its lease had to be
renewed on a yearly basis. The following year, Southern
Bell Telephone and Telegraph acquired an option on the
Fox, with the intention of demolishing the theater to clear
space for a planned office tower. The city of Atlanta
stepped in to postpone demolition for eight months and
to allow interested civic groups the chance to save the Fox
as a performing arts center.

■ **Fox**
Atlanta
Mayre, Alger and Vinour
1929

Auditorium of the Fox, the
exotic "Mecca on Peachtree
Street."

Incorporated as Atlanta Landmarks, this nonprofit
organization was able to borrow the necessary $1.8
million from a group of local banks to purchase the land
under the Fox. Southern Bell graciously agreed to
purchase only land adjoining the Fox building, deeding
the building to Atlanta Landmarks as part of the deal.

Having officially acquired the Fox in June 1975, Atlanta Landmarks began the difficult tasks of retiring its debt with the banks and taking care of pressing maintenance inside the theater. Financial need was addressed immediately with a surcharge of 25 cents on each ticket sold and fund-raising activities that led to federal grants and private donations (as much as $440,000 from one individual). The surcharge continues today to be an excellent source of renovation funds. To date, combined revenues have helped restore not just the Middle Eastern atmospheric auditorium but also three Fox ballrooms and the building's storefront areas along Peachtree Street. Among the grand events staged at the rejuvenated Fox was a screening of *Gone with the Wind*, which had originally premiered across town at Loew's Grand (1932, demolished).

■ **Ohio**
Columbus, Ohio
Thomas W. Lamb
1928

For adaptive use, no theater rescue has been more widely studied and acclaimed than that of the Ohio. The story in Columbus has unfolded gradually, as continual fund raising has carried the theater through more than a dozen years of piece-by-piece restoration, as well as construction of a lobby addition.

The Ohio's marquee at night, 50 years after the theater opened.

In a process similar to that later staged in Atlanta, demolition of the Ohio was warded off by a group of local citizens who banded together in 1969 to form the Columbus Association for the Performing Arts (CAPA). Within six months, CAPA had acquired the Ohio at a cost of $1.75 million. Funds were raised through private and corporate donations, supplemented by bank loans.

Under the guidance of CAPA's leader, Mary Bishop, a painstakingly detailed restoration of the 2,900-seat auditorium was undertaken. During the slow course of the restoration, the theater doors have been kept open for an incredible variety of stage events, from the annual Nutcracker performances to a screening of the resurrected silent film *Napoleon*. The theater, located across the street from the Ohio State Capitol, has been named the state's official theater and has joined the Atlanta Fox and the Oakland Paramount as designated National Historic Landmarks.

In the early 1980s, a long-term plan to expand the limited lobby space of the Ohio was realized with the opening of a six-story pavilion on the south side of the theater. Its walls composed largely of glass, the addition was the work of architects Hardy Holzman Pfeiffer.

After a decade of Kung-fu movies and rock concerts, the Fox was left for dead in 1978, just shy of its 50th birthday. The 5,000-seat showplace remained dark for three years, until illuminated by dim flashlights held by Leon and Mary Strauss. Leon Strauss joined with a few other prominent local developers to form Fox Associates, together purchasing the theater in 1981.

The process by which the Fox was brought back to life

■ **Fox**
St. Louis
C. Howard Crane
1929

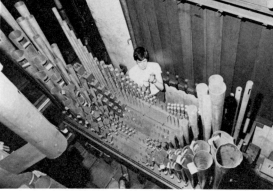

Above left: Staircase of the newly restored Fox in 1982. Above right: Restoration of plasterwork on one of the gigantic columns. Left: Organ pipes being prepared for the reopening of the Fox. The organ is one of the largest Wurlitzers in the country.

Top: The St. Louis Fox's auditorium minus more than 4,500 seats, removed for refurbishing. Above: Worker polishing brass trim.

resembled the rapid facelift of the Oakland Paramount. Under the direction of Mary Strauss, more than $2 million was spent in a largely faithful restoration of the absurdly spacious Fox interior. Plaster ornamentation was recast on site. Seats were reconstructed, and 7,300 yards of elephant-patterned carpet, replicating the 1929 original, were rolled out. The electrical systems and the stage equipment received a major upgrading.

Reopening in 1982, the Fox has been a phenomenal success story at the box office. The two-millionth patron of the restored theater arrived barely a year and a half after the Fox was back in business. To accomplish such feats, the operators of the Fox have staged just about every type of performance imaginable. The sole exception would be symphonic music concerts, left to its nearby neighbor, Powell Hall, renovated 14 years earlier.

## TWO NORTHWEST VENTURES

As a result of a chance meeting in the 1960s between an elderly theater architect and a young music student, the course of theatrical history in the Northwest was set for an exceptional period of revival two decades later. In training as a composer and performer, Richard F. McCann was introduced by a piano teacher to B. Marcus Priteca, who, nearly 50 years earlier, had begun to make his way in the theater world as the architect of the Coliseum (1916) in downtown Seattle. After completing his music studies, McCann apprenticed to Priteca. He inherited Priteca's office when his mentor died in 1971.

McCann then worked for a number of years as a consultant specializing in acoustics. After obtaining a degree in architecture, McCann set up a practice in his own name in 1978. The following year he was hired for a plum job, the restoration of Seattle's Fifth Avenue (1926), and his career in theaters was launched.

Since completing work on the Fifth Avenue in 1980, McCann has presided over the rebirth of two other theaters in Washington state. In California, work by his firm includes the renovation of the Pasadena Playhouse (1925), the Wilshire (1930) in Los Angeles and the Orpheum (1926, originally the Pantages) in San Francisco. As theatrical consultant, the McCann office also has played a part in work on the mixed new-and-old performing arts center in Portland, Ore. The most recently completed project by the firm is the Fox (1931) in Billings, Mont., which reopened in January 1987.

When the Fifth Avenue shut down its movie operations in 1978, there was some discussion about transforming this truly palatial Oriental theater into a Chinese restaurant. Instead, the heads of UNICO Properties, which managed the theater and the enclosing Skinner Building for the landlord University of Washington, orchestrated the formation of the nonprofit Fifth Avenue Theatre Association. By the end of 1979 a group of 43 corporate and individual sponsors had underwritten the loans necessary to finance the $2.6 million renovation of the theater. The loan was to be repaid from operating revenues once the Fifth Avenue was back on its theatrical feet. The economic stability of the venture rested with an annual subscription program designed to induce advance season ticket buyers to purchase five-show packages. The policy would prove successful, until the time when the managers had difficulty finding enough shows to put on.

Richard McCann was hired as project architect in September 1979. His plan for the Fifth Avenue called for rebuilding the theater and its equipment to serve as a "road house" for live theater, the heart of the five-show package. New production requirements involved wardrobe and dressing areas, a new stage structure and rigging, and reconstruction of the orchestra pit. Cosmetic repair to the Chinese-inspired decor came only after exhaustive research into the methods and materials used in both the 1926 design and the imperial model in Beijing.

The Fifth Avenue was reopened in 1980, a time when theatrical producers were working to develop a self-sustaining live American musical theater organization on a national scale. Riding the crest of a successful wave of touring productions, including *Annie, A Chorus Line* and *Sugar Babies*, the idea seemed promising. The Fifth Avenue tied its future to this venture, only to see it go sour in the mid-1980s as production budgets, travel costs and salaries of the technical staffs made the touring musical a scarce commodity. The few musicals that survived Broadway still traveled to Los Angeles and San Francisco, but rarely to Seattle.

The Fifth Avenue management was forced to retrench, opening itself up to rental for beauty pageants, special film showings and a variety of other one-night stands. Architect McCann has said that he wishes greater allowance had been made for flexible use of the theater, that "lighting, acoustics, and stage design could have been developed [to permit broader] commercial use of the facility." Although in no way to be judged a failure, the Fifth Avenue has provided a cautionary tale for other operations setting up business in renovated theaters.

■ **Fifth Avenue**
Seattle
R. C. Reamer
1926

Chinese detail from the auditorium wall of the Fifth Avenue.

The Fifth Avenue's stage, now host to a variety of spectacles, including film showings.

## ■ Pantages
Tacoma, Wash.
B. Marcus Priteca
1918

The Pantages during its heyday in the mid-1920s.

Created within the walls of the oldest surviving theater of the Pantages chain, the Pantages Center for the Performing Arts came into being primarily because of the efforts of some local citizens. The renovation process was instigated by these preservation-minded people who convinced the local arts commission and city council of the potential benefits. A rehabilitated Pantages would not only bring some life back to the downtown retail core of Tacoma, but the project also would enhance the city's image and bring in shows that bypassed Tacoma for Seattle. The Pantages Center, a nonprofit corporation, was formed by the city to arrange funding for the adaptation of the former vaudeville and movie theater.

The city of Tacoma completed purchase of the Pantages–Jones Building and the neighboring Illington Hotel in January 1979. The hotel property was critical to the project. Architect McCann used part of the hotel interior to add some needed depth to the Pantages stage, as well as to gain space for newly built dressing rooms and scenery-handling facilities. The problem of the severely restricted lobby space, related to the Pantages's original use as a vaudeville theater, was solved by installing a two-story glass-fronted entry lobby along the sidewalk in front of the theater.

Specific planning of additions to the Pantages was the province of Steve Rothman, a well-known theater operations consultant, theatrical director and producer. Along with constructing the additions and installing new mechanical systems (low-vibration HVAC equipment and new power and lighting setups), R. F. McCann and Company assumed the task of repairing and repainting the classical decor of the 1,100-seat auditorium.

Money needed to perform the reconstruction of the Pantages came largely from public funds secured by the individuals who originated the project. The funds included federal and state grants, for $1.5 million apiece,

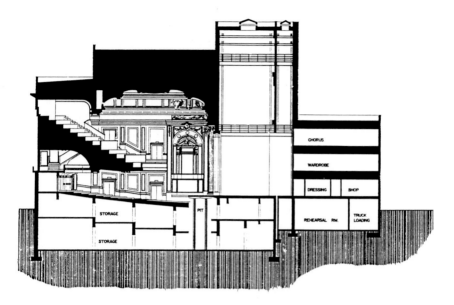

CHORUS

WARDROBE

DRESSING        SHOP

STORAGE        PIT

REHEARSAL  RM.        TRUCK LOADING

STORAGE

that were to be matched by an equal amount in private donations. The managing group was able to complete the restoration slightly under budget. Reopened in 1983, the Pantages has maintained an active presence in town, offering patrons a wide choice of music, dance and theater events on a regular basis.

Section drawing of the Pantages auditorium, stage and backstage facilities.

## STATEWIDE PRESERVATION IN ILLINOIS

Alone among states, the assembly of the state of Illinois virtually institutionalized a plan to develop arena and auditorium spaces in its towns and cities, with the exception of culturally rich Chicago. With the passage of the Civic Center Support Act in the early 1970s, the state authorized creation of regional authorities (originally eight or nine city and county groups) to assess the needs of their areas and to apply to the state for "brick and mortar" money. The state agreed to match local funds three-to-one with the state's share derived from a tax on racetrack betting.

Projects were not to be restricted to new construction, allowing for the restoration or adaptation of existing structures. To date, four new civic centers have been built statewide — in Peoria, Danville, Springfield and Rockford. Preservationists have matched this success with renovated theaters in Joliet, Aurora and DeKalb. A fourth Illinois theater, the Orpheum (1916) in Galesburg, is scheduled to reopen in early 1988.

Although the entertainment programs for these rehabilitated theaters have much in common, the processes by which the old-new centers came into being have varied as dramatically as the architecture of the different buildings (Art Deco, Egyptian Revival and French Renaissance). The processes and outgrowths are described below, with details courtesy of those involved in charting the course of their local theaters.

■ **Paramount**
Aurora, Ill.
Rapp and Rapp
1931

Exterior of the expansive
Paramount Arts Centre,
reborn with state and city
aid.

The Paramount and its 2,000-seat auditorium form just one part of a civic center complex, located on Stolp Island at the core of downtown Aurora. The major boost to the center was a $10.3 million grant from the Illinois State Assembly that enabled the formation of the Aurora Civic Center Authority in 1975. Only a year earlier the city had created the Aurora Redevelopment Commission to use the proceeds from a local bond issue to determine ways to revive the town center. Using a portion of the funds from these two groups, the city of Aurora purchased the Paramount Theater building in 1976 and began work on the $2.7 million restoration.

Under the supervision of the San Francisco–based ELS design group, various contractors worked to expand and revamp the stage housing and equipment, in addition to overhauling the lighting systems. Project work has included cleaning cloth panels that fill the auditorium side bays, replacing lost or broken pieces of the multitude of frosted-glass fixtures and constructing a new corner marquee that suggests the flavor of the stud-lighted 1931 original.

Since reopening as the Paramount Arts Centre in 1978, the theater has maintained a broad base in its entertainment program, offering music, dance and classic film series. According to preservation specialists Joseph Valerio and Daniel Friedman, just three years after the reopening the Paramount was able to take in "80 percent of operational expenses through ticket sales, rentals and other income." Overall, much of the success lies in the fact that the Aurora was remarkably well positioned to take advantage of the civic center legislation, passed just as the city was putting a brake on its downhill slide. Aurora's rebound has matched that of the Paramount, assuming a central role in the development of the high-tech corridor now known as the "Silicon Valley of Chicago."

■ **Egyptian**
DeKalb, Ill.
Elmer F. Behrens
1929

Envisioned at first as only the auditorium appendage of a new agricultural arena, the Egyptian has emerged as the self-sustaining star of both DeKalb County and the statewide civic center program as a whole. Its great success has been due largely to volunteer efforts provided by the nonprofit group Preservation of the Egyptian Theatre (PET). Formed the year after movie operations shut down at the Egyptian in 1977, PET immediately began negotiations with the DeKalb County Metropolitan Exposition, Auditorium and Office Authority (DCA) to restore the theater. By the end of 1982, the DCA was prepared to seek funding for the project. The state assembly agreed the following April to allocate $2.12 million against the $700,000 value of the theater building. The Egyptian again closed its doors in July 1982, but this time only to allow for repair of its fanciful interior.

The project required 14 months of work split among 17 separate prime contractors. Major portions of the restoration went to local businesses, including new electrical work and plumbing for a dressing room area once known as the "Swamp." The architect in charge of the project was Roland Killian of the AEC Group, an architectural engineering firm. To ensure the authentic restoration of the auditorium murals and plasterwork, PET hired Conrad Schmitt Studios of New Berlin, Wis.

The grand reopening in September 1983 included a full range of stage performances and an art exhibit mounted along the Egyptian's mezzanine level. Ownership of the building had passed by that time to the DeKalb County Authority, with the provision that PET was to manage and operate the Egyptian under a 99-year lease.

With its staff of around 100 volunteers, the operating board of PET prides itself that it takes "no operational

money from city, county, state or federal offices." All funding comes from rental fees and events sponsored by the Egyptian. Reports remain positive; the 40,000 attendance figure for 153 event days in fiscal year 1985 was surpassed by nearly 10,000 additional people for the same number of events the following year. The 1987 summer season supplemented weekend movies and concerts with a special pageant and the circus.

The Egyptian's multicolored auditorium, including its painted curtain and papyrus-like columns.

The most recent outgrowth of the Civic Center Support Act has been the $2 million grant to refurbish this 1,000-seat vaudeville house — issued just before the theater's 70th birthday. The agencies in charge—the Knox County Board and the related Civic Center Authority — decided at that time to hire Roland Killian, the architect for the Egyptian restoration in DeKalb. In the case of the Orpheum, certain design considerations requested by the board led to significant public involvement in the process, culminating in what might best be called the "Great Ceiling Debate."

Before the civic center legislation, the Orpheum had grown ever-more forlorn as the most neglected theater in

■ **Orpheum**
Galesburg, Ill.
Rapp and Rapp
1916

this town. A condition of the state grant was that the theater had to be self-supporting. In keeping with this provision, the county board hit upon the idea of food and drink concessions as a major source of operating revenues. The hitch in this plan surfaced only when the method for accomplishing this goal received a full public hearing in the summer of 1986.

The design proposed by the architect and accepted by the board called for the insertion of a false ceiling to divide the two-story entry lobby into two levels. The second floor was to house the concession and gallery area, to be called Critics Square, accessible by doors open on the mezzanine promenade. Opposition to this proposed alteration arose, headed by local author Martin Litvin and Anna Sophia Johnson, a rural Knox County farmer and environmental analyst. They argued that the board's plan would do irreparable damage to the entry lobby's special quality — its height. Lowering the ceiling would reduce the drama of entry to an act of simply crossing through a low-ceilinged ticket lobby, the two argued. They proposed a full restoration of the lobby, to include draped mirrors around the upper walls and a new central chandelier designed to enhance the space's former grandeur. But the Civic Center Authority and the board remained set on the Critics Square plan.

The question to lower or not to lower appeared destined for resolution in the courts. Before that happened, the issue turned on the statutes governing accessibility for handicapped persons. The designers had used the age of the Orpheum to circumvent the need to bring all aspects of the building up to this particular code. But if the theater is historic, and, therefore, need not be fully accessible, how to justify lowering the ceiling for another type of accommodation? Faced with a choice between installing a new elevator or maintaining the lobby in its current state, the board relented and chose the latter.

Lobby of the Orpheum, Galesburg, Ill., subject of an intense preservation campaign.

Having saved the lobby from alteration, the loosely knit grass-roots citizens group has diverted its efforts to finding money to restore the space to something approaching its original appearance — work beyond the scope of the $2 million already allocated for other parts of the project. Waiting in the wings to perform are such local organizations as the Knox Symphony Orchestra and the Prairie Players theater group. The road to the 1988 reopening was not the smoothest, but none can say he or she was denied a voice in the rebirth of the Orpheum.

## HAPPY ENDINGS

There is much to be learned from the past 20 years of theater preservation. Lessons can be found in the civic activism in Tacoma, Wash., and Galesburg, Ill., and the unmatched volunteer efforts to save the Egyptian in DeKalb, Ill. The wisdom of the diversified entertainment policy of the St. Louis Fox can be better understood in contrast to the initially narrow perspective held at the Fifth Avenue in Seattle. Still, such lessons are not to be taken as gospel. Each theater renovation must be dealt

with as a venture with its own unique set of circumstances. A project's direction should not be guided solely by a successful model in another city. And yet, a few key ingredients played roles in all the best revivals. These are persistence, clarity of purpose, a sense of necessary sacrifice, an awareness of the events of the past and an eye to the needs of the future. If the chemistry is right, there will be one more feeling held in common: the sense of triumph as the doors of the rescued theater swing open to welcome its new audiences. It seems fitting that these movie theaters, which hosted thousands for the wonderful tales spun by Hollywood, should have happy endings of their own.

Carpenter Center for the Performing Arts, Richmond, Va., once a Loew's designed by John Eberson in 1928. The atmospheric auditorium with its Moorish-style overtones was restored in 1982.

Note: The primary source for the descriptions of concert hall conversions was *Preservation of Concert Halls, Opera Houses and Movie Palaces,* Information Series No. 16, prepared by Robert Stoddard in 1981 for publication by the National Trust for Historic Preservation. Information concerning the trio of performing arts centers — the Atlanta Fox, the Ohio in Columbus and the St. Louis Fox — came, in part, from *Movie Palaces: Renaissance and Reuse* (1982, Educational Facilities Laboratories Division of the Academy for Educational Development), written by Joseph M. Valerio and Daniel Friedman. Details on the Northwest renovations managed by R. F. McCann and Company were provided by Richard McCann and his staff.

■ ■ ■ ■ ■ ■ ■ ■ ■ ■ ■ ■ ■ ■ ■ ■ ■ ■ ■

# GUIDE TO THE GUIDE

The theaters in this book represent just what the title implies: a selection of the greatest movie theaters still standing in big cities and small towns across the United States. Every theater in every town could not possibly be included in this one volume; thousands more can be found, perhaps in your own neighborhood. But this cross section shows what I think are the greatest left to be seen, all examples of the glorious era of theater building and all worth making a detour for when traveling around the country. The selection is a personal one, aided by suggestions of theater historians, preservationists, listings in the National Register of Historic Places and similar sources. Many of the entries show the grandest picture palaces remaining, about which there is nearly unanimous agreement on their place in history; others are important and interesting particularly to their own towns and local history. A few of the lesser theaters in big cities were omitted, while minor ones were included for small towns where only a single theater remains. Both the palace and the smaller theater are vital to the record of America's cinematic past.

Theater entries are organized into six regions, beginning with the Northeast and moving south and then westward. Within each region, states, cities and theaters are presented alphabetically. Theaters in several large metropolitan areas (e.g., New York, Chicago and Los Angeles) are included under the larger city names.

Each theater entry highlights key details at the left or right. First to appear is the name or names by which the theater has been known. If it had more than one name, the most recognizable or commonly used name appears first, with the other name(s) in parentheses. Below the theater name is the address. The next line gives the architect or architects, where this is known. In a few instances, the name listed is that of the builder, decorator or designer. The last line indicates the year in which the theater opened. Where the theater was altered to a substantial degree, or rebuilt, a second date may follow that of the original opening. The descriptive portion of each entry covers a variety of information, such as noteworthy architectural details and significant events in the theater's past. The letters "NR" that may appear before the closing information indicate that the theater, the building in which it is located or its general district is listed in the National Register of Historic Places.

All but a few of the theaters still possess at least some portion of their original character. Many have been restored, rehabilitated or somewhat sympathetically refurbished; many have not. The chief determinant for inclusion was that the theater still be standing and able to be viewed, at least from the exterior, without threat to life, limb or personal freedom. There are only two exceptions to this rule, at least to date. The Edgemoor in

Wilmington, Del., and the Warner in West Chester, Pa., have been demolished.

This last matter underscores a common problem involved in cataloging these buildings. Changes in ownership, use and physical status can occur overnight. Thus, the closing information, placed within the brackets at the end of each entry, is subject to change. The information lists, first, the owner or managing agency of the theater. This is followed by the current use of the theater as it could best be determined and described. Some theaters listed as in business may since be closed, while others may have just opened after years of dormancy. Deed to the property may have changed hands.

For those who wish to learn more about movie theaters and specific examples included in this guide, a section entitled Information Sources appears near the end of the book. You may also contact the appropriate organization or theater in question. If you believe that any noteworthy theaters have been omitted from this guide, the author and the Preservation Press would like to hear from you.

The Granada (1929), later the Fox, Emporia, Kans. During a 1948 promotion, an anxious audience wonders who will win the Chevrolet town sedan.

Washington Street, Boston. This street of theaters competed with Tremont Street for Boston's movie-goers.

■ ■ ■ ■ ■ ■   CONNECTICUT   ■ ■ ■ ■ ■ ■

## CANAAN

■ **Colonial**
Railroad Street
c. 1920

The Colonial is a simple Greek Revival structure of wood with stucco infill. Six Doric columns form the two-story entrance portico, which is capped by a pediment centered by a single oval window. Thanks to a 1947 remodeling, the lobby appears as a late Moderne venture in varnished wood paneling. When the Colonial opened, the theater filled only the main floor of the building, with a dance floor above it and a bowling alley in the basement. Frayed a bit by time and weather, the theater still has movies a few nights a week. [Privately owned. For sale.]

## NEW MILFORD

■ **Bank Street**
**(New Milford)**
46 Bank Street
Buckingham and Taylor
1920

A pair of modern viewing rooms, designed in an Art Deco mode, now fill this building first known as the New England House Hotel. As constructed in 1902, the hotel had a Renaissance Revival appearance. W. G. Mock, owner of the nearby Star Theater, hired the firm of Buckingham and Taylor to convert the hotel in 1920 into what became known as the New Milford. A facelift, performed in 1937, gave the theater the radiating geometry of its current facade, with a stepped roof and chrome-cornered marquee. Steven "Rocky" Barry, who purchased the building in 1976, matched the Art Deco character of the exterior in his colorful reconfiguration of the interior into two smaller spaces seating 126 and 260, reopened in 1982 as the Bank Street. [Privately owned. Movies — twin.]

## STAMFORD

■ **Palace**
61 Atlantic Street
Thomas W. Lamb
1927

The elegantly eclectic design of the Palace includes Italian marble, French stage drapery and a tilework creation in the lobby modeled after the fountain of a Spanish villa. The overall decorative motif was borrowed

The Palace's marquee medallion honoring the original owner, S. Z. Poli.

from the Adam brothers by Lamb, a fellow Scotsman who did his part to revive this 18th-century style. A privately funded restoration in 1983 brought back much of the original character of the auditorium and lobby spaces. New gold paint was applied to the band of ornament along the proscenium arch and to the equally ornate organ grilles. Notable on the exterior is the old marquee, updated to announce the refurbished Palace Theatre of the Arts. NR district. [Arts Management, Inc. Performing arts center.]

## TORRINGTON

The Warner possesses a bold Moderne look, particularly in the blocky massing of its limestone exterior. Inside, a marble grand staircase rises beneath wall murals depicting scenes of Torrington in the 1920s. The design of the

■ **Warner**
68–82 Main Street
Thomas W. Lamb
1931

2,000-seat auditorium is dominated by an immense eight-pointed star of gold and silver, filling the low ceiling. The Warner now presents performances by local and touring theater groups. NR. [Northwest Connecticut Association for the Arts. Performing arts center.]

Promotional event at the Warner in Torrington.

## WATERBURY

The Palace was built when Lamb was at the peak of his Adamesque period. The cast-stone arches of the main facade give the theater an imposing presence near the town square. Lamb used scagliola (a simulation of marble) to build the engaged columns along the lobby walls and around the grand staircase. The expansive auditorium, seating nearly 3,500, sits below an elliptical dome ringed by elaborate bas-relief panels. A balanced composition of plaster organ pipes masks the actual organ chambers, located on either side of the stage opening. The proscenium arch is crowned by a great cartouche. Among the largest of the theaters Lamb designed for New England impresario S. Z. Poli, the Palace was renamed Loew's Palace in 1934, when Poli sold his regional theater empire. After a partial renovation in 1978, the Palace served as an all-purpose hall until it closed in 1982. NR. [Privately owned. Closed.]

■ **Palace**
86–110 East Main Street
Thomas W. Lamb
1922

■ ■ ■ ■ ■ ■   MAINE   ■ ■ ■ ■ ■ ■

### BAR HARBOR

■ **Criterion**
35 Cottage Street
Bunker and Savage
1932

This Art Deco movie theater was built primarily to entertain well-to-do tourists who continued to visit Mount Desert Island even through the summers of the Depression. When the Criterion opened, the *Bar Harbor Times* reported, "It has the air of Broadway — of the Big Time." This was no delusion. Patterned raw silk fabric was used to cover the auditorium walls. The ceiling was designed to resemble a tent, its radiating beams converging in a multifaceted frosted-glass chandelier. Inside and out, geometric Art Deco patterns of chevrons and zigzags appear. In the Criterion's early years, Keith vaudeville circuit acts were a part of the show. The current policy is to screen recent releases, for no more than a few nights each, during the busy summer season. NR. [Criterion Theatres. Movies.]

Right: The Grand's Moderne facade. Far right: The Criterion's more subdued exterior.

### ELLSWORTH

■ **Grand**
Main Street
1938

With just over 500 seats, this streamline Moderne theater has a wonderfully comfortable interior. Its principal ornamental feature is a golden picture-frame proscenium arch, encircled at regular intervals by silver wooden "cooling rings." The Moderne styling extends to the streetfront, where the splashy marquee is topped by the theater name in huge block letters. Boxing matches were staged in the orchestra pit, before the theater's renovation in 1975. [Hancock County Auditorium. Performing arts center.]

■ ■ ■ ■ ■   MASSACHUSETTS   ■ ■ ■ ■ ■

### BEVERLY

■ **Cabot Street (Ware)**
286 Cabot Street
Funk and Wilcox
1920

Trumpeted at the time of its opening as the "Golden Theater Beautiful," the Cabot Street Cinema was known as the Ware until 1965. In the course of a general renovation, a new neon marquee was added above the entry doors declaring the change in the theater's name. The 1965 redecorations included neo-Georgian murals, painted on the organ screens and along the curved auditorium sounding board. The current owners, members of Le Grand David, a three-generation magic troupe that has appeared numerous times at the White House, keep the theater spotless. One addition of theirs has been

an antiques-filled parlor replacing the conventional balcony lobby. White Horse Productions brought the live magic acts to the renovated Cabot Street stage in 1977, promoting weekend performances that still alternate with weeknight movie screenings. [White Horse Productions. Movies and magic shows.]

The Cabot Street's auditorium and facade. Now magic shows and movies draw crowds.

The first theater in town with electric lights, the Larcom opened as a combination playhouse and motion picture theater. The exterior was clad in patterned brick, with a carved stone panel spelling out "Larcom Theatre" above the entry. President William H. Taft, who maintained a summer residence in Beverly, was known to have attended performances here. By 1984 the theater had been reduced to showing "adult films," but that year saw the theater converted for stage performances. Restoration work was exacting, including efforts to track down replacement panels for the pressed tin ceiling of the auditorium. The source was found in a 1909 catalog of W. F. Norman and Company, one of the original building suppliers still in business. A magical new house curtain now complements the stage shows of Le Grand David, which also has a part-time stake in the nearby Cabot Street Cinema. [White Horse Productions. Magic shows.]

■ **Larcom**
13 Wallis Street
George Swan
1912

## BOSTON

Keith's Memorial was unquestionably among the finest theaters designed by Lamb, along with his Loew's Midland (1927) in Kansas City, Mo., and the San Francisco Fox (1929). This Boston vaudeville palace was built in tribute to Benjamin Franklin Keith by his partner, E. F. Albee. Among the grand interior spaces is Memorial Hall, the central foyer. A marble staircase climbs from the main floor to a landing where a spotlighted bust of Keith was once displayed. The siting of the theater, replacing an earlier Keith's, created the need for two opposing entry halls. Principal entry was through a baroque terra cotta composition on Washington Street. An auxiliary entrance on better-traveled Tremont Street provided Lamb with the excuse to add a second marble-pillared lobby hall.

■ **Keith's Memorial
(Opera House)**
539 Washington Street
Thomas W. Lamb
1928

Keith's Memorial, Boston. Marble columns and mirrors line the walls of the entry hall. Right: Rococo ceiling in the auditorium.

Almost heart-rending in its beauty, the grand baroque auditorium is best seen from the balcony crossover. A Composite-order colonnade encircles three sides of the balcony. Overhead, resting on a ring of ornately rimmed lunettes, is a magnificent rococo dome open to a delicately shaded mural of heavenly Paradise. A 1928 issue of *Motion Picture News*, quoting a cost of $5 million, effused that "there is no gilt paint in the theater, every bit of gold work being of gold leaf."

With conductor Sarah Caldwell at the lead, the Opera House was born inside this splendid old theater in the late 1970s. A recent addition is a restaurant that now fills the old Tremont Street entry hall. NR district. [Opera House. Opera and stage shows.]

■ **Music Hall (Metropolitan/Wang Center)**
252–72 Tremont Street
C. H. Blackall
1925

Advertised as the "Public's Castle," the former Metropolitan is Boston's largest theater. Accordingly, it is even more grandiose in scale, if less fine in detail and proportion, than its baroque cousin, the nearby Keith's Memorial (1928). The great central hall, designed loosely after Garnier's Paris Opera, rises up through four tiers of encircling promenades. Partial credit for the immense, golden-walled auditorium is given to Detroit-based theater architect C. Howard Crane. Short on subtlety, the spaces within the theater remain incredibly powerful. The Music Hall was renamed the Wang Center in 1983, in appreciation for a multimillion-dollar donation from the Wang family to renovate the auditorium. NR district. [Tufts–New England Medical Center. Rock and stage shows.]

■ **Paramount**
549–59 Washington Street
Arthur H. Bowditch
1932

The design of this theater owes much to the Paramount (1931) designed by Rapp and Rapp in Aurora, Ill. The Boston Paramount, too, has a flattened Art Deco–French Renaissance hybrid interior, although its side wall fabric panels have dark blue backgrounds in place of the bright scarlet of Aurora's. In both houses (and in the 1930 Paramount in Denver) zigzag motifs are evident. The limestone facade is less derivative, although the blue and white vertical sign, with its bubbling wave pattern, might be more appropriate to Miami Beach. NR district. [Adams House Realty Company. Planned nightclub and restaurant.]

This stately Beaux Arts playhouse became a first-run motion picture theater only in 1956. The graceful arches of the auditorium have survived through the years, as have the lunettes in the lobby, attributed to William deLeftwich Dodge, who also painted some of the murals in the Library of Congress (1889–97) in Washington, D.C. Emerson College acquired the former Majestic in 1983 but failed in efforts to revive the building as a stage facility. City landmark status, granted in 1986, prompts hopes for new plans for the Saxon. NR district. [Emerson College. For sale.]

■ **Saxon (Majestic)**
219 Tremont Street
John Galen Howard
1903

## DENNIS

The austere New England colonial church architecture of the exterior disguises the flamboyant Art Deco dream scene inside the Cape Cinema. Local impresario Raymond Moore commissioned Poor to perform this deception, adding to the Cape Playhouse compound Moore started in 1927. The centerpiece of the theater design is an immense Moderne planetarium mural covering 6,400 square feet above the auditorium. In the mural, the Milky Way loops overhead. Incorporated into this design are symbols representing the constellations of the zodiac, while a comet flashes past the aqua-colored proscenium arch. Rockwell Kent and assistant Ellen Goldsborough painted this heavenly Art Deco canvas, as well as a smaller sky view in the lobby filled by wild white horses. Conservators from the Boston Museum of Fine Arts restored the murals in 1981. [Cape Playhouse. Movies.]

■ **Cape Cinema**
800 Main Street (Route 6A)
Alfred E. Poor
1930

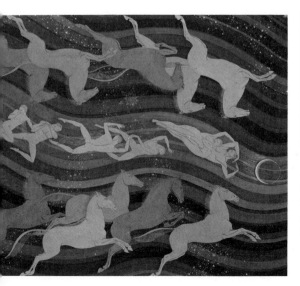

Above: Detail of the Cape Cinema's sunburst curtain. Left: Rockwell Kent lobby mural.

### GREAT BARRINGTON

**Mahaiwe**
14 Castle Street
J. McA. Vance
1903

The Mahaiwe is a late Victorian vaudeville house that has been the premier motion picture theater for this quiet town since the late 1920s. Over the past few years the stage has been refurbished to enable the theater once again to hold live stage performances in addition to movies. The classical ornamental details of the vaulted outer lobby have been given a fresh coat of paint. Further restoration has been planned. For now, with its old padded seats, the Mahaiwe makes for an extremely comfortable night at the movies. [Privately owned. Movies and stage shows.]

Above: The Mahaiwe's marquee with stud lights. Right: The Garden's marquee with stained-glass corner lights.

### GREENFIELD

**Garden**
353–67 Main Street
Mowll and Rand
1929

A marquee with fancy stained-glass corner lights and a stud-lighted vertical sign help promote the shows featured at the Garden. The auditorium is a painted variation of the atmospheric style, with side walls representing scenes of 19th-century New England. Dimly visible once the lights go down are painted streetlamps, a town hall with a working clock, a farm bordered by fieldstone walls and the town church with its tall white steeple. Conversion into a multiscreen theater was undertaken in 1986. NR. [Western Massachusetts Theatres. Movies — multiplex.]

### HOLYOKE

**Victory**
81–91 Suffolk Street
1919

A restrained classicism characterizes the exterior of this former vaudeville theater, located just a few blocks from the center of town. Its auditorium had to be rebuilt following a fire in 1942. Since its closing in 1979, the Victory has been the focal point of community efforts to rehabilitate the building as a performance hall. [Save the Victory, Inc. Closed.]

### NORTHAMPTON

**Academy of Music**
274 Main Street
William Brockton
1890

Brockton designed this showplace for silk tycoon Edward H. R. Lyman, who donated the theater to the city in 1892. Among the famous visitors to play here were Sarah Bernhardt, Pavlova, John Philip Sousa and Houdini. It

Above and left: The Academy
of Music, Northampton.
Below: The Paramount,
Springfield.

was another visiting stage artist, Jenny Lind, who
bestowed on Northampton the title of "Paradise of
America." The Academy's Victorian baroque brick facade is trimmed in terra cotta ornament with a musical
theme. Ceiling fans turn inside the auditorium, under-
neath the balcony. The town has the rare fortune of having
two surviving early theaters, with the Academy of Music
and the nearby Calvin movie theater both in operation.
Local performance groups still use the Academy's stage,
and infrequent rock concerts are held in-between
regular movie showings. [City of Northampton. Movies
and stage shows.]

### SPRINGFIELD

Carlson designed this picture palace within the shell of
the 1880s-vintage Massasoit Hotel Building. The decorative treatment of the high-domed auditorium follows
the classical lines of the Italian Renaissance. From the
early 1970s the theater program has bounced from
movies to live stage shows, back to movies and again to
live acts. [Western Massachusetts Theatres. Stage
shows.]

■ **Paramount**
1700 Main Street
Earnest Carlson, builder
1929

■ ■ ■ ■ ■    NEW HAMPSHIRE    ■ ■ ■ ■ ■

### MANCHESTER

The relatively unadorned entry to the Palace forms part
of the Athens Building in downtown Manchester. Marble
wainscoting lines the lobby walls. The 1,000-seat auditorium features a coffered ceiling and a classically
decorated proscenium, topped by statues depicting
theatrical muses. [New Hampshire Performing Arts
Association. Performing arts center.]

■ **Palace**
76–96 Hanover Street
Leon H. Lambert and Sons
1915

■ ■ ■ ■ ■    RHODE ISLAND    ■ ■ ■ ■ ■

## PAWTUCKET

■ **Leroy**
66 Broad Street
John F. O'Malley
1923

The last surviving theater in downtown Pawtucket, the Leroy was spared from demolition in 1970 by the prohibitively high cost of knocking down its solid structure. A partial restoration, carried out by local rock-show promoters, brightened the old Adamesque decor. Highlights of the 2,400-seat interior are baroque boxes hanging on either side of the stage and, to the back of the house, the bas-relief half dome hovering above the balustraded mezzanine promenade. Additional work to restore the interior began in 1982. NR. [Leroy Center for Cultural and Performing Arts. Performing arts center.]

## PROVIDENCE

■ **Ocean State**
**(Loew's State)**
220 Weybosset Street
Rapp and Rapp
1928

The restored interior of the Ocean State appears much as it did in 1928. As designed by Rapp and Rapp, the theater is a model of understated elegance, somehow right in every way. The brick exterior has just enough terra cotta trim to keep it interesting. The mirror-lined main hall has a full complement of marble and gilded plasterwork. The superbly balanced auditorium decor misleads patrons to underestimate the relatively large number of seats — 3,200. Opened as the new "Palace of Splendor," the old Loew's was reborn in 1976 as the premier showplace of its namesake, Rhode Island, the Ocean State. [Privately owned. Performing arts center.]

Above: The Ocean State's marquee. Right: Auditorium.

## WOONSOCKET

■ **Stadium**
329 Main Street
Perry and Whipple
1926

The Stadium has survived a turn as an X-rated movie house with most of its original decor intact. The street facade has a flattened Adamesque apppearance balanced around a 1950s-vintage marquee. The architectural highlights of the 1,400-seat auditorium are the broken pediments atop the organ grilles and the Stadium logo-cartouche centering the proscenium arch. Plans have been in progress since the 1970s to convert the theater for stage performances. NR. [Privately owned. Stage shows.]

# ■ ■ ■ ■ ■ ■  VERMONT  ■ ■ ■ ■ ■ ■

## BRATTLEBORO

The sons of Demetrius P. Latchis built this 1,200-seat theater as a monument to their late father. Architect Haynes hired internationally renowned artist Louis Jambor, a Hungarian immigrant, to paint murals based on Greek mythology. *The Reformer,* a local newspaper, reported that the artist had even painted his subjects following a Greek method, "using a combination of bees-wax that fixes the colors and at the same time gives them the appearance of being watercolors." The better-known gods in the murals, such as Apollo and Bacchus, are joined by sculpted figures of more obscure characters

**■ Latchis Memorial**
50 Main Street
S. W. Haynes
1938

including Thalia, the muse of drama, seated at stage left. The lobby of the Latchis has a lighted semicircular fountain supervised by Hebe, the goddess of youth and spring. The zodiacal pattern that once dominated the lobby floor is gone, survived by illustrated constellations painted on the ceiling inside the auditorium. The plaster buildings along the side walls are meant to suggest the Acropolis rising above the "agora" of the orchestra floor. Restoration of this fine late picture palace was in process in 1986. [Latchis Corporation. Movies.]

The Latchis Memorial's lobby and auditorium with Greek motifs.

## BURLINGTON

Vividly colored geometric stenciling, set against a bright golden background, is beginning to reemerge along the walls of the lobby and auditorium of the Flynn as a result of restoration under way since 1981. The painstakingly difficult process of stripping away layers of paint covering these floral patterns has been part of a $1.6 million effort to revive this showplace. Art Deco ornamentation visible inside the 1,400-seat auditorium includes floral designs along the organ screens and side wall pilasters capped by inverted chevron patterns. NR district. [Flynn Theatre for the Performing Arts. Performing arts center.]

**■ Flynn**
153 Main Street
Mowll and Rand
1930

Radio City Music Hall, New York City. The *Author of Life* mural by Ezra Winter fills the wall above the grand staircase.

■ ■ ■ ■ ■   DELAWARE   ■ ■ ■ ■ ■

## WILMINGTON

■ **Edgemoor**
Governor Prinz Boulevard
1941

Never a palace, the Edgemoor had the distinction of being Wilmington's last real picture show. Moviegoing in the long, narrow auditorium was similar to watching an in-flight movie aboard a slowly descending airplane. A crying room for patrons with infants was provided, behind glass, above the back of the main floor. The theater saw use as the Church for All People in the early 1980s, but was sacrificed for a freeway interchange in early 1987. [Demolished.]

■ ■ ■ ■   DISTRICT OF COLUMBIA   ■ ■ ■ ■

■ **Tivoli**
14th Street and Park Road, N.W.
Thomas W. Lamb
1924

A rare neighborhood house by Lamb, the Tivoli faces south toward downtown from its triangular city block. The Renaissance palazzo exterior features a semicircular glass and bronze canopy, bracketed by a pair of "Tivoli" vertical signs, all capped by a red tile roof. The interior has suffered from general neglect in recent decades. As built, the foyer was decorated with murals by New York artist A. Battisti. An elliptical dome covers the 2,500-seat auditorium. A lyre motif was incorporated into the design of the organ grilles. Despite its historical designation, the future of the Tivoli remains in limbo. NR. [Privately owned. Closed.]

Right: The Tivoli's facade and an interior wall. Below: The Uptown's facade. The letters light up each evening.

■ **Uptown**
3426 Connecticut Avenue, N.W.
John J. Zink
1936

The key architectural element of note at the streamlined Uptown is the patterned brickwork of its blocky street facade. The auditorium, with its great curved screen, is wrapped by yellow drapes. Now past its 50th birthday, the theater stands as the largest movie house in Washington. [Circle Theatres. Movies.]

■ **Warner (Earle)**
13th and E Streets, N.W.
C. Howard Crane, with Kenneth Franzheim
1924

In 1985 the Warner was designated a District of Columbia landmark. This honor came only after a long and celebrated battle waged against the theater's owners by the D.C. Preservation League. Had the preservationists failed, the District would have been stripped of

its sole remaining downtown picture palace, a block away from the revitalized Pennsylvania Avenue. Theater architect Crane gave the Warner a French Renaissance interior. The 36-foot-tall grand foyer is a draped rendition of the Hall of Mirrors at Versailles. The auditorium originally had seating for 2,240. Draped bays form the side walls, with a dome high above.

Initially known as the Earle, the theater ran both stage shows and movies until 1945. A franchise of the New York Roxyettes appeared during the last seven of those years. The Earle became the Warner only in 1947, even though Warner Brothers had assumed control of the theater just four years after it opened. Despite alterations in 1953 for Cinerama, the theater remains in good condition. [Privately owned. Concerts and stage shows.]

Above left: Lobby of the Warner. Right: Auditorium.

## ■ ■ ■ ■ ■   MARYLAND   ■ ■ ■ ■ ■

### ANNAPOLIS

Opened originally as a vaudeville house, this colonial-style theater was the work of an Annapolis architect who also designed several office buildings for the nearby Maryland House of Delegates. Intricate plasterwork and scenes of Maryland fill the walls. Movies eventually replaced vaudeville acts before the Circle closed in 1983. It was restored and reopened in 1986 to showcase new owners Wayne and Sandy Alan's "Bedazzled" magic act as the resident show. Its 700 seats also have welcomed live theater and performances for children. But the new Annapolis Theater of Magic had to put its prestidigitation skills to good use in 1987 to help keep the theater in operation: theater lovers were urged to buy a seat of their own to raise needed funds. [Annapolis Theater of Magic. Magic and stage shows.]

■ **Circle**
46 State Circle
Henry Powell Hopkins
1920

### BALTIMORE

This modest neighborhood theater has survived the ravages of time and the wrecking balls that destroyed the downtown picture palaces of Baltimore. Its style is streamline Moderne, with the bays of the theater front filled with glass blocks. A sunburst motif rules the fancy circular lobby. [Durkee Theaters. Movies.]

■ **Senator**
5904 York Road
John J. Zink
1937

## FREDERICK

**■ Tivoli (Weinberg Center)**
20 West Patrick Street
John J. Zink
1926

The Tivoli opened just in time for Christmas 1926. Inside the theater, past the fancy box office, a long Hall of Mirrors leads to an intimate inner lobby and the auditorium, with its flattened Palladian styling. The auditorium was flooded in October 1976 — so badly that water lifted the console of the Wurlitzer organ up onto the stage. Both the organ and the theater were refurbished, reopening in 1978 as the Weinberg Center for the Arts. [City of Frederick. Performing arts center.]

## HAGERSTOWN

**■ Maryland**
21–23 South Potomac Street
Thomas W. Lamb
1915

The Maryland was among the earliest full-scale theaters designed by Lamb for vaudeville and motion pictures. Local architect Harry Yessler supervised construction of the 1,350-seat neoclassical theater. Patrons originally entered the main lobby through a passage in a five-story apartment block. The apartments and the passage were destroyed in a 1974 fire that caused no major damage to the Maryland, which was converted for general perform-ance uses a few years later. NR. [Privately owned. Performing arts center.]

## SILVER SPRING

**■ Silver**
8619 Colesville Road
John Eberson
1938

The curving lines of Eberson's late Deco theater set the tone for the adjoining shopping center, considered ultramodern in its day. The entire complex has been threatened since 1984, considered an obstruction to the high-rise building boom of the past decade in this Washington, D.C., suburb. In the summer of 1984, the distinctively Moderne "Silver" vertical sign was pulled down in what was seen as an effort to demoralize local preservationists. Since that time, members of the Art Deco Society of Washington have obtained the original blueprints for the Silver from Eberson's son, Drew. Some hope remains that the theater will be saved and restored. [Privately owned. Closed.]

Facade of the Silver, before the loss of its vertical sign.

# ■ ■ ■ ■ ■    NEW JERSEY    ■ ■ ■ ■ ■

## JERSEY CITY

The Jersey, with its glorious 3,200-seat Italian baroque auditorium, was one of five Loew's "Wonder Theaters," so named because each was equipped with identical four-manual Robert Morton pipe organs (the "Wonder Mortons"). Of the other four in the New York metropolitan area, only Loew's Paradise (1929) in the Bronx still shows movies, albeit as a quad-cinema. Loew's Kings (1929) in Brooklyn has been closed for a decade. Loew's Valencia (1929) in Queens and Loew's 175th

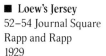

■ **Loew's Jersey**
52–54 Journal Square
Rapp and Rapp
1929

Loew's Jersey auditorium and facade.

Street (1930) in Manhattan were both transformed into churches. Like the Paradise, the Jersey was "multiplexed," with two minitheaters tucked under the balcony. Only patrons of the balcony theater were granted a view of the ornate main auditorium and its movie screen. One additional feature shared by the Jersey and its Bronx counterpart is a terra cotta clock tower crowning the front. Atop each clock, a life-size sculpture of St. George is set to slay a dragon, every hour on the hour.

The theatrical future of the Jersey is in jeopardy. A conglomerate purchased and closed the theater in August 1986, announcing its intention to save only the fancy facade and the three-story lobby rotunda as the front for its new office building. [Hartz Mountain Industries. Closed.]

At the time of its opening, the Stanley had a mighty Wurlitzer organ sitting on the left side of its orchestra pit in its 4,300-seat Italian-courtyard auditorium. A proscenium arch modeled after the Rialto Bridge in Venice crossed overhead. Out in the lobby were vast allegorical murals, painted in the manner of the Italian Renaissance by Hungarian-born artist Willy Pogany.

Today, a baptismal fount has replaced the old orchestra pit and biblical scenes cover the Pogany murals. The new owners, the Jehovah's Witnesses, brought in a cherry-picker to enable them to repair the damaged atmospheric

■ **Stanley**
2934–38 Kennedy Boulevard
Fred Wentworth
1928

The Stanley, Jersey City.
An early promotion and the
lobby entrance.

ceiling. More than 1,200 gallons of buff-colored paint were used to cover the side walls, with their faux stained-glass windows, and the mock-footbridge proscenium arch. Still in place are the foyer chandelier, reportedly salvaged from New York's old Waldorf Astoria, and the bronze vestibule entry doors. The copper marquee shines once again, as do marquee corner lights spelling out "Stanley" in stained glass. Regrettably, the giant electric roof sign proclaiming the Stanley to be "One of America's Great Theatres" was removed from the roof some time ago. A plaque to the right of the theater entry announces the availability of tours by request from 9 a.m. to 5 p.m., Monday through Friday. [Jehovah's Witnesses. Assembly hall.]

## NEWARK

■ **Newark**
195 Market Street
Thomas W. Lamb
1895, 1917

For the Newark, Lamb performed an Adamesque altera-tion within the shell of an old vaudeville theater, originally constructed in 1895. Further remodelings transformed the 1917 lobby design with an Art Deco look. Portions left unchanged included the triple-tiered opera boxes, a Lamb trademark at this stage of his career. The exterior still features the 1930s marquee and a Paramount vertical sign left from the Newark's days as part of that theater circuit. [Privately owned. Movies.]

## RAHWAY

■ **Rahway**
1601 Irving Street
David Oltarsh
1928

The Rahway was built with a fancy marquee and a vertical sign, both spelling out its name in flashing lights. The brick exterior is trimmed with a decorative linear pattern that appears to be Palladian in origin. Considera-ble support from the local community has led to recent efforts to restore the 1,450-seat auditorium to house a variety of stage performances. NR. [Rahway Landmarks, Inc. County arts center.]

# ■ ■ ■ ■ ■   NEW YORK   ■ ■ ■ ■ ■

### ALBANY

Eberson designed the Palace within a shell built from plans by another architect. The straightforward classical decor of the auditorium has received a monochrome coat of paint. The rounded corner space forming the entry lobby was completely covered over in the 1950s. Altered but relatively intact, the Palace now stands as one of the centerpiece properties in the officially designated Albany Theatre Arts District. NR. [Privately owned. Performing arts center.]

**■ Palace**
19 Clinton Avenue
John Eberson, consulting architect
1931

Above: Altered corner entry of Albany's Palace. Left and below: Elegant curves inside Shea's Buffalo.

### BUFFALO

Regional entrepreneur Michael Shea commissioned the Rapp brothers to build this particularly elegant French royal palace as the flagship of his theater empire. The beauty of the design relies heavily on the strongly modeled plasterwork ornament, ornate Tiffany chandeliers and rich draperies hanging in both the auditorium and the marble-lined grand lobby. Working with the city council, the nonprofit Friends of the Buffalo Theatre restored a substantial portion of the interior in the early 1980s. A second civic group, the Shea's O'Connell Preservation Guild, now leases and operates the theater. NR. [City of Buffalo. Performing arts center.]

**■ Shea's Buffalo**
646 Main Street
Rapp and Rapp
1926

## GENEVA

■ **Geneva**
**(Smith Opera House)**
82 Seneca Street
Pierce and Bickford;
Victor Rigamount
1894, 1929

The solid Romanesque Revival exterior of the Geneva houses a Spanish baroque atmospheric interior. A 1929 conversion by the Schine chain superimposed this new look over the old opera house interior (together with some Art Deco touches), as the 1,400-seat theater embarked on a movies-only policy that lasted nearly 50 years. Since 1978, however, the Geneva has played host to a mix of dance, opera and classical music. [Finger Lakes Regional Arts Council. Performing arts center.]

## ITHACA

■ **State**
109 West State Street
1928

The simple brick exterior of the State conceals an auditorium decorated in an English Gothic style, appropriate for this college-town theater. In contrast to the formally decorated auditorium, the lobby has the dimly lit feel of the banquet hall of a medieval castle, with plaster substituting for heavy stonework. A pair of lancet-arched stained-glass windows rests above gargoyle brackets over the doors leading to the auditorium. The Gothicized plaster ornament is most prominent above the theater organ screens, on either side of a coffered coat-of-arms sounding board. A second movie screen has been installed at the front of the balcony, walling it off from the main auditorium floor below. [College Cinema. Movies — twin.]

## NEW ROCHELLE

■ **Proctor's**
580 Main Street
Thomas W. Lamb
1927

In the mid-1920s Lamb designed most of a chain of theaters built by a former vaudeville acrobat, F. F. Proctor, who later sold his holdings to the larger RKO circuit. This Proctor's has the refined Adamesque plasterwork interior design that Lamb then favored, complete with the descending rows of opera boxes on either side of the balcony front. The main floor and balcony are now split in half, with the dividing wall slicing across the recessed bas-relief ornamental dome. A decorative band rims the dome. [RKO Theaters. Movies — quad.]

The Proctor's before conversion into a multiplex cinema.

## NEW YORK CITY: THE BRONX

Known in the planning stages as the Venetian, this theater was a high-priced piece of paradise, costing Loew's $4 million to construct and furnish. The baluster-lined Grand Concourse facade included a sculpted St. George slaying a dragon above a central clock face (the rider, alas, has been stolen). The outer lobby was designed to resemble a sheltered Spanish patio, with a mosaic-tiled floor and a deeply coffered ceiling. At some point, the Carrara marble fountain of the Italian baroque grand lobby was sacrificed to provide room for an enlarged candy counter. Eberson populated the court-yard atmospheric auditorium of the Paradise with an abundance of classical statuary, fake poplar trees and stuffed birds in flight. Nearly all this flamboyant detailing has been concealed by paneling and dropped ceilings built during the halving and subsequent quartering of the auditorium space. [Loew's. Movies — quad.]

■ **Loew's Paradise**
2413 Grand Concourse and
188th Street
John Eberson
1929

Historic views of the Paradise's stage and inner lobby.

■ **Prospect**
Prospect Avenue and
161st Street
E. C. Horn and Sons
1910

The 1,600-seat Prospect has operated continuously since its opening. Starting life as a legitimate playhouse, the theater shifted to Yiddish variety shows, eventually adopting a movies-only policy. The interior plasterwork is classical, complete with opera boxes. Caryatids hold up the boxes of the second balcony. [Loew's. Movies.]

### NEW YORK CITY: BROOKLYN

■ **Loew's Kings**
1049 Flatbush Avenue
Rapp and Rapp
1929

The location of the Kings, in a once-thriving shopping area along an as-yet ungentrified stretch of Flatbush Avenue, has proved a mixed blessing. Only in 1986 did anyone come along to push for demolition of the theater and development of the site. Yet concern that there is no ready audience at hand for the Kings has kept the theater dark for more than a decade.

The chief virtues of the Rapp and Rapp design remain intact. These include the rich terra cotta arch of the main face, the vaulted grand lobby with its mirrored walls and the densely ornamental French baroque auditorium. This last space, encircled by Corinthian columns and topped by a massive dome, contains seating for 3,600, almost all on the main floor. The arch-covered side bays are filled by murals depicting scenes from the royal court of the Bourbons. The stage hosted not just vaudeville but also high school graduations and beauty pageants. The young Barbra Streisand once worked as an usher here. A 1979 film documentary, *Memoirs of a Movie Palace,* by Christian Blackwood, traces the history of the Kings. [Flatbush Development Corporation. Closed.]

Auditorium of Loew's Kings with baroque ornamentation and the theater's terra cotta facade.

■ **Paramount**
Flatbush and DeKalb
Avenues
Rapp and Rapp
1928

Once the site of rock 'n' roll stage shows emceed by pioneering disc jockey Alan Freed during the late 1950s, the Paramount fell on hard times, ultimately passing into the hands of Long Island University in the early 1970s. The former lobby is now a cafeteria area, while classrooms fill the baroque plaster-walled balcony. The alterations are most dramatic where a gymnasium floor covers the former stage and orchestra seating, all beneath the intact French baroque sunburst proscenium arch. Lost in this unique conversion is a sense of the equally unusual semiatmospheric character of the old 4,100-seat auditorium. Views through the side bays were like arched visions into the formal gardens of French royal palaces in the late 18th century. The auditorium ceiling was formed by a recessed blue dome bordered by a perforated screen. This magical setting now bears witness to basketball games and other sporting events. [Long Island University. General university uses.]

Early views of the Paramount. The theater was stripped of its signs and some auditorium decor when it became part of Long Island University.

## NEW YORK CITY: MANHATTAN

Two years before the Beacon was built, Ahlschlager designed the Roxy (1927, demolished) for master show-man Samuel "Roxy" Rothapfel, who later operated this uptown theater. The Beacon is best known for its glowing golden auditorium. A polychrome sunburst plaster canopy projects above the stage, supported at the corners by two great lances. Seated golden lions on either side of the balcony are silhouetted against bright murals depicting caravans of traders.

A major flap arose in early 1986 when new owners announced plans to convert the Beacon into a disco-theque. The restructuring of the interior, intended to resemble the group's earlier Studio 54, would compromise the largest surviving picture palace in the city. Despite active community opposition, the city landmarks commission voted to permit the nightclub conversion of the 2,600-seat auditorium. As the legal battles proceed, a few concert dates have been booked by local rock promoters. NR. [Privately owned. Rock shows.]

■ **Beacon**
Broadway and 74th Street
W. W. Ahlschlager
1929

One wall of the Beacon's auditorium and the lighted marquee on Broadway.

Original Bunny facade.
A new overhang proclaims
the theater's later name, the
Nova.

■ **Bunny (Nova)**
Broadway and 147th Street
George H. Pelham
1913

Gilt-edged Corinthian columns in the sloping lobby are
the only noteworthy remnants of the original interior of
this theater. But outside, the stone-carved bunny
medallions topping the corners of the street facade
survive as a reminder of its origins. The Bunny opened as
a showcase for silent pictures, including those of its
namesake, silent star John Bunny. Now it has been
renamed for its current owner, Jesus Nova. [Privately
owned. Movies.]

■ **Loew's 175th Street**
Broadway and 175th Street
Thomas W. Lamb
1930

Boasting a "Rajah's Ransom in Furnishings," this was
the most thoroughly exotic of Lamb's creations. The last
to open of the five Loew's "Wonder Theaters" in New York
City, its Near and Far Eastern aura is attributed to
prominent Manhattan decorative specialist Harold Rambusch. The flamboyant lighting fixtures and polychrome
plasterwork came from the Rambusch Studios. The
mezzanine promenade, copied from Loew's State (1928)
in Syracuse, has views between ornate Hindu columns to
fanciful chandeliers above the foyer. The wall opposite
the promenade features plasterwork balconettes molded
to resemble brass grillwork. The foyer ends at a grand
staircase rising to a goddess-ruled Art Deco aurora
borealis done in silhouette. The golden walls of the
auditorium are formed by a perforated mass of Indo-
Chinese ornamentation, brilliantly colored by hidden
cove lighting. The massing of the theater's equally exotic
exterior has much in common with the Mayan Revival
temple form of Loew's Triboro (1931, demolished) in
Astoria, although Lamb maintained the Hindu flavor
along all facades. The domed shrine atop the northeast
corner of the building perhaps foretold the use of the
theater for the past decade as the home of evangelist
Reverend Ike. [United Church. Church services.]

This rare American piece of Art Nouveau architecture has been vacant for years as the various players involved in the redevelopment of West 42nd Street sort through proposals for the district. Lavish ornamentation inside the New Amsterdam matches the rich history of this famous showplace. In the first quarter of the century, Florenz Ziegfeld produced his Follies on the theater stage. These were followed by his Midnight Frolics staged in the roof nightclub perched above the theater building.

Attempts in 1982 by the Nederlander Organization to bring stage shows back to the New Amsterdam roof were halted once the supporting steelwork was shown to be badly corroded. Downstairs, the main auditorium seats have been removed, but the allegorical murals above the stage and the opera boxes are intact. Intricate vegetal patterns cover walls and columns, even blended into the staircase design. The bronze elevator doors in the outer lobby were cast with a sinuous Art Nouveau floral motif. NR. [42nd Street Development Corporation. Closed.]

■ **New Amsterdam**
214 West 42nd Street
Herts and Tallant
1903

Early views of the New Amsterdam's auditorium and facade.

New York City's answer to the glitz of Grauman's Chinese (1927) in Hollywood, Radio City has long been billed as the "Showplace of the Nation." Movies have always played second fiddle to live acts such as the organists at the twin Wurlitzers and, above all, the world-famous Rockettes. A full complement of the high-kicking dancers just barely spans the 144-foot-wide stage opening beneath the radiating arches of the auditorium ceiling. Art Deco themes predominate inside the Music Hall, with a few thematically matched medallions decorating the limestone exterior. Notable works of art include the Dancing Girl sculpture in the lower lounge, the floral-

■ **Radio City Music Hall**
Rockefeller Center
1260 Avenue of the Americas
Donald Deskey, designer
1932

Above: Radio City Music Hall's block-long stage below radiating arches. Right: The theater's corner entry at 50th Street.

motif murals in the upstairs ladies' lounge and the *Author of Life* mural by Ezra Winter rising above the grand foyer staircase. Designer Deskey was responsible for most of the furnishings, as well as for the coolly elegant color schemes and the geometric patternwork covering the interior walls.

Like the Chinese in Hollywood, the Music Hall has starred in movies as well as screened them. The auditorium is seen briefly in the film version of the stage show *Annie*. In Woody Allen's *Radio Days* a youthful surrogate for the filmmaker accompanies his aunt and her beau up the elegant grand staircase, as the off-screen narrator compares the experience to a trip to paradise. Occasionally threatened with demolition, Radio City remains a major survivor from the almost mythical past of New York City. [Radio City Music Hall. Stage shows.]

This Harlem showplace is widely considered to be the first full-sized theater built exclusively for viewing motion pictures. Samuel "Roxy" Rothapfel began his climb to the top of the New York theatrical world with his 1914 tenure as manager of the Regent. A church organization acquired the theater after RKO showed its final movie here in the late 1950s. Both the interior and the Venetian palazzo exterior have remained largely intact. [Church. Church services.]

■ **Regent**
116th Street and Seventh Avenue
Thomas W. Lamb
1913

### NEW YORK CITY: QUEENS

This Moorish–Spanish Renaissance palace — an atmospheric theater from the drawing board of Lamb rather than John Eberson — stayed in the hands of the RKO organization for more than 50 years. In 1976 the auditorium was split into three smaller screening areas. As a result, only the lobby, already stripped of its gloriously polychromed cherub fountain, received landmark protection. The business consortium currently holding title to the Keith's gutted the old 3,000-seat auditorium, without a permit, in early 1987. The group plans to build a shopping complex in the empty shell. [Privately owned. Closed.]

■ **Keith's Flushing**
129–43 Northern Boulevard
Thomas W. Lamb
1928

Keith's Flushing in 1944, now a shell.

Doctored view of Loew's Valencia showing how the clouds drifted above the atmospheric interior, now used as a church.

■ **Loew's Valencia**
175th Street and Jamaica Avenue
John Eberson
1929

Initial press releases for the Valencia described its auditorium as a "Spanish patio garden in gay regalia for a moonlit festival." When Loew's donated the atmospheric theater to a local religious organization in the 1970s, the nude statues filling the niches of the proscenium arch were robed and given wings, in an apparent promotion to angel first class. Crutches and casts shed by those who have been miraculously healed now line the lobby, amid the ornate plaster and tilework decorations. A startling addition inside the 3,440-seat auditorium is an immense crystal chandelier, imported from Greece, that hangs dead center from the old Ebersonian plaster "sky." Despite such major changes, the magical Venetian–Spanish baroque quality of the Valencia survives. [Tabernacle of the Prayer for All People. Church services.]

## NORTH TONAWONDA

■ **Riviera**
67 Webster Street
Leon H. Lambert and Sons
1926

In the hometown of the Rudolph Wurlitzer Pipe Organ Company, the three-manual organ here still plays a featured role in the life of this theater. Videotapes of televised concerts given from the brightly colored Wurlitzer console have been used by local preservation activists for restoration fund-raising purposes. The 1,200-seat auditorium has much to recommend it, including an expansive mural above the proscenium, a 15-foot chandelier and a pair of Spanish baroque organ grilles. The lounges and lobbies still contain some of their original light fixtures and furnishings. As a crowning touch, the brick baroque street facade is crested by a makeshift coat of arms braced by a pair of classical maidens. NR. [Privately owned. Movies, organ concerts and stage shows.]

The Riviera's "Mighty Wurlitzer," still used in conjunction with movies and live theater.

## ROCHESTER

Photographic film pioneer George Eastman envisioned a place to accommodate both popular film showings and classical concerts, all "Dedicated to the Enrichment of Community Life." This was to be no ordinary movie palace. The formal Italian Renaissance facade enclosing the theater space was the work of the renowned McKim, Mead and White architectural firm. The classically styled auditorium features opposing rows of murals, those on the right by Barry Faulkner and on the left by Ezra Winter. One balcony stair landing is graced with a painting by Maxfield Parrish. The coffers of the rounded auditorium ceiling foretold Hall's later work, the Florida (1927) in Jacksonville. In addition to the main auditorium, a 500-seat recital hall was built.

After 1930 motion pictures gave way entirely to concerts and stage performances. Before the switch, Eastman enlisted the services of artist Batiste Madalena to create with tempera a series of one-of-a-kind movie posters to fill the seven brass cases spaced between the theater entry doors. When Paramount assumed a brief lease on the theater in 1928, the management tossed the colorful posterboards on the trash heap, leaving Madalena himself to rescue this legacy of the movie years at the Eastman — a selection of which has recently been published in a monograph. [University of Rochester. Concerts.]

■ **Eastman**
26 Gibbs Street
R. E. Hall and McKim, Mead and White
1921

The Refurbished Eastman, now a concert hall.

## SALAMANCA

This 1,150-seat theater was a late Art Deco venture coproduced by the father-and-son team of John Eberson, the master of atmospheric picture palaces, and his son, Drew. Scheduled to reopen as the Cattargus County Living Arts Center, the Seneca interior has been adapted to include a 650-seat playhouse, art galleries, a dance studio and meeting rooms. [City of Salamanca. Performing arts center.]

■ **Seneca**
10 Main Street
John Eberson and Drew Eberson
1942

## SCHENECTADY

■ **Proctor's**
432 State Street
Thomas W. Lamb
1926

Access from State Street to this former vaudeville and motion picture theater is by way of a narrow shop-lined arcade lined with Italian marble. A local group acquired the building in the mid-1970s and restored its Adam-style interior. NR. [Arts Center and Theatre of Schenectady. Performing arts center.]

Above: The Proctor's low-profile exterior and spacious restored auditorium.
Right and below: The Landmark, Syracuse. Mural detail, the auditorium and detail of an interior column.

## SYRACUSE

Hindu, Persian and Oriental design motifs are blended in the colorful interior spaces of this mystical, grand-scale movie palace. A simple baroque arch in terra cotta decorates the entry. Directly inside the doors is the grand lobby, with its jeweled dome. One wall of this spectacular space incorporates a mural, between the fancy engaged columns, depicting a royal procession of Indian elephants. The golden grillwork auditorium still has its original valance lined by portraits of Hindu deities.

When the theater was threatened with demolition in 1977, local citizens began a volunteer drive to save their pre-Depression "Shangri-La." Proceeds from concerts and tours, donations and state funding enabled a newly formed nonprofit corporation to purchase the State and set it on the road to recovery. NR. [Syracuse Area Landmark Theatre. Performing arts center.]

■ **Landmark (Loew's State)**
362–74 South Salina Street
Thomas W. Lamb
1928

## TICONDEROGA

Entry to the State is marked by an Art Deco marquee attached to its original Greek Revival street facade. The theater was known as the Playhouse before a renovation in 1937 for movie showings. At that time, the classical decor of the interior was revamped along Moderne lines. Of special note were the new light fixtures, formed by strips of glass and illuminated in a variety of colors. Although the State was twinned in 1984, the current owner has announced plans to restore this last old theater in town to its 1937 appearance. [Privately owned. Movies — twin.]

■ **State (Playhouse)**
181 Montcalm Street
1916, 1937

Below left: The State in Ticonderoga. Below: The Proctor's in Troy.

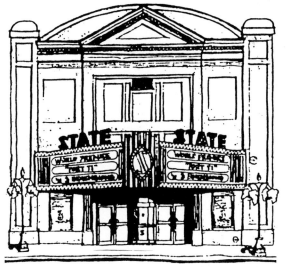

## TROY

A few Gothic-inspired details, including some parrot-faced gargoyles, highlight the brick and terra cotta street facade of the Proctor's. The auditorium, unused now for years, has standard Adam styling. NR. [Privately owned. Closed.]

■ **Proctor's**
82 Fourth Street
Arland W. Johnson
1914

## UTICA

■ **Stanley**
259 Genesee Street
Thomas W. Lamb
1928

Billed as the "Pride of Utica," the Stanley is the only survivor among a half dozen theaters in downtown Utica. Lamb called the decorative motif he used for this theater a "Mexican baroque" style. This hybrid theme is apparent from the outset with the twisting Moorish columns of the baroque arched terra cotta facade. The auditorium strongly resembles that of the Ohio (1928) in Columbus. The principal differences are the sunburst draperies of the Stanley organ screens and the cove-lighted dome in place of the star-pattern ceiling found in the Columbus theater. A Kung-fu epic on Christmas Eve 1974 closed out the Stanley's days as a movie theater. A local arts group spent four years raising funds and executing a splendid restoration. NR. [Central New York Community Arts Council. Performing arts center.]

Above: Interior doorway ornamentation at the Stanley. Auditorium decor was borrowed from the Ohio in Columbus. Right: Terra cotta facade with marquee.

■ ■ ■ ■ ■   PENNSYLVANIA   ■ ■ ■ ■ ■

### BALA-CYNWYD

Despite the name change in 1982, the Egyptian origins of the theater's prevalent decorative motifs remain clearly visible. The Egyptian Revival treatment of the theater facade, with its engaged lotus-capped columns, extends to the two side wings containing retail businesses. A royal barge floats below the flaring cornice of one wing, with a charioteer painted along the opposing face. High above the theater entry sits a carved vulture, its wings spread full. Despite this ominous creature, the former Egyptian is still alive and well. A mural of Cleopatra and her attendants appears worn but intact along the wall opposite the mezzanine promenade. Another vision of the Nile survives on one of the original stage curtains. [Privately owned. Movies.]

■ **Bala (Egyptian)**
157 Bala Avenue
Hoffman and Henon
1927

Original marquee of the Egyptian, later the Bala. The marquee is now gone.

### CHAMBERSBURG

The straightforward Classical Revival interior of the Capitol is substantially brightened by allegorical murals lining the walls of its auditorium and lobbies. Depicted are helmeted Roman warriors on horseback in pursuit of an exotic collection of zebras, leopards and gazelles. Under new management since 1980, the Capitol has had more than two-thirds of its original 900 seats repaired. Current entertainments include movies, concerts from the restored Moller pipe organ and weekly presentations of the Appalachian Jubilee, featuring traditional country music. [Privately owned. Movies and concerts.]

■ **Capitol**
163 South Main Street
1926

### EASTON

Grass-roots fund-raising efforts led to the purchase of the State for a modest $25,000 in 1981, thus saving the last theater in town. Since then, the volunteer Friends of the State Theater have been renovating the State in stages to serve as a full-time performance hall. A stud-lighted replica of the 1926 marquee helps draw attention to the preservation efforts, as repair work continues inside the Italian baroque auditorium. One local activist has an agenda that includes replacement of a sculpted goddess that once stood in a place of honor alongside the balcony stairs. NR. [Friends of the State Theater. Regional arts center.]

■ **State**
454 Northampton Street
William H. Lee
1926

## ERIE

■ **Warner**
811 State Street
Rapp and Rapp
1931

Tagged by one native son as "Erie's Very Own Xanadu," the Warner boldly announces its presence at the center of town. The arched terra cotta facade appears to exist solely to support the tall "Warner" vertical sign. Projecting from beneath this assemblage, the marquee features stained-glass corner lights and a spellbinding sunburst pattern traced in stud lighting. A solid bronze box office completes the composition. Inside, the Warner's grand lobby is styled as a Hall of Mirrors with a twist: Versailles meets Art Deco. Lines of classical decor are flattened in the golden plasterwork. Geometric patterning rules, not the French Sun King. A similarly eclectic auditorium is covered by a lacework ceiling, illuminated by concealed fixtures, as if open to the sky. The theater closed in the summer of 1977 but reopened two months later under city auspices as home to the local ballet and the Erie Philharmonic. NR. [Civic Center Authority. Performing arts center.]

## GLENSIDE

■ **Keswick**
291 Keswick Avenue
Horace Trumbauer
1928

The original character of the Keswick reflected the work for which Horace Trumbauer was best known: mansion architecture of Palm Beach, Fla., and Newport, R. I. Trumbauer designed only this one theater, set in the suburbs of Philadelphia. He gave its exterior a strongly articulated Tudor Revival appearance, a style seen often in fine houses but rarely in movie theaters. The interior had a more conventional Versailles royal treatment.

The French Renaissance auditorium was drastically remodeled in 1955, but its style is still visible in the decor of the Louis XV upper ladies' lounge. The lobby was changed as well, although the ornament of the vaulted ceiling survives above the dropped paneling that covers the space. The theater enjoyed a brief resurgence as a performance hall in the early 1980s, before the management ran into financial difficulties. Local preservationists are working to find new theatrical uses for the Keswick. NR. [Privately owned. For sale.]

## LANSDOWNE

■ **Lansdowne**
29 North Lansdowne Avenue
William H. Lee
1927

Ornate balconettes projecting from the corner towers of the Lansdowne facade tip off visitors to the overall Spanish styling of this 1,400-seat suburban theater. Lee was a Philadelphia architect who designed many other Delaware Valley showplaces, including the State (1926) in Easton and the Norris (1921) in Norristown. Spanish courtyards inspired Lee's design for the Lansdowne foyer and inner lobby, prompting the inclusion of a tilework fountain on one side of the lobby. The elaborate fixtures and painted ceiling of the auditorium show influences of Spanish baroque architecture. Plans were set in motion in 1986 to renovate the theater as a center for the performing arts. The proposed restoration will include repair of damaged features and improvements to the facility for a broad variety of performance uses. [Privately owned. Closed.]

## NORTHAMPTON

Clearly not a palace, the 600-seat Roxy still possesses its share of architectural delights. Much of the glamour attached to this Lehigh Valley showplace comes from an Art Deco remodeling carried out in the 1930s. Bands of repeating geometric stencil patterns decorate the auditorium ceiling. Light is provided from what a local writer called the "tiered China-meets-Art Deco lanterns." The chief lure of the Roxy is its glittery marquee, with multicolored stud lights and neon trim. This spectactular bit of machinery was repaired from a derelict condition in the 1970s by new owner Richard Wolfe. Showmanship has returned to the operation of this small-town movie house. [Privately owned. Movies.]

■ **Roxy**
2004 Main Street
E. R. Bitting
1921

Simple brick exterior of the Roxy with flamboyant signs.

## PITTSBURGH

This northside theater was maintained in top condition for more than 50 years by its devoted manager, Bennett Amdursky (later shortened to Amdur). In 1973, three years after Amdur's death, first-run feature films gave way to "adult" movies. What portions remain of the original Beaux Arts interior decor can be attributed to Amdur's efforts. Now operated as the New Garden Theatre, Amdur's showplace still has its neoclassical terra cotta street facade, largely unaltered. [Privately owned. Movies.]

■ **Garden**
10–14 West North Avenue
Thomas H. Scott
1915

In 1972 Loew's Penn joined the Orpheum (1927) in Omaha and Powell Hall (1926, originally Loew's St. Louis), also by Rapp and Rapp, as one of the first performance hall conversions in the country. Adaptation of the Penn preserved only a few portions of the auditorium's original decor. Illuminated coves surrounding the recessed central dome were retained. More typically, the baroque ornament of the side bays and organ screens was replaced by acoustic panels decorated with painted baroque-inspired motifs. In one of the firm's richest re-creations of Versailles, Rapp and Rapp gilded the tall Corinthian columns of the grand foyer. The arched street entry to this space has been filled by plate-glass windows, with new canopied entries cut into a

■ **Heinz Hall (Loew's Penn)**
600 Penn Avenue
Rapp and Rapp
1927

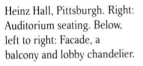

Heinz Hall, Pittsburgh. Right: Auditorium seating. Below, left to right: Facade, a balcony and lobby chandelier.

lobby fashioned inside a former storefront next door.

Notable dates for this theater include the opening, scheduled for September 5, 1927, but postponed a day because of the death of Marcus Loew, owner of the national chain of picture palaces. A period starting in the mid-1970s marked another significant time for Heinz Hall, when concerts conducted by André Previn were taped in the theater auditorium for airing by the Public Broadcasting System. [Pittsburgh Symphony Society. Concerts.]

### ■ Stanley
207 Seventh Street
Hoffman and Henon
1928

This late addition to the Stanley-Warner chain was among the most grandiose designs ever constructed by Philadelphians Hoffman and Henon. Its rich baroque ornamentation was surpassed only by the French Renaissance interior of the Mastbaum (1929, demolished), the finest of the center-city Philadelphia theaters built by this firm. The baroque treatment of the Stanley extends to three decorated bays on the principal facade. The side bays are fashioned conventionally from glazed terra cotta. A fanciful electric sign with a baroque motif fills the central bay. Efforts to renovate the 3,900-seat Stanley as a performance hall got under way in 1985. NR. [Privately owned. Performing arts center.]

The Victoria's auditorium, looking more like a 19th-century opera house than a movie theater.

## SHAMOKIN

Before his successful run of suburban Philadelphia movie theaters, all built during the 1920s, Lee designed this Beaux Arts showplace for the town in which he got his start as an architect. The Victoria opened as the flagship of the Chamberlain Amusement Company chain, for whom Lee would build many of his 200 other theaters. The 1,600-seat auditorium includes a horse-shoe balcony fronted by panels of Adamesque ornament. A shallow dome overhead has at its center a bulbous chandelier, ringed by smaller fixtures of matching design. The exterior of this downtown theater has its own flourishes, with bronze plaques announcing the name of the building just below the terra cotta cornice. The Victoria has been in continuous operation since its opening, with only minor alterations. NR. [Privately owned. Movies.]

■ **Victoria**
46 West Independence Street
William H. Lee
1918

## WARREN

Local philanthropist Thomas Struthers erected this unusual complex for his town, with the library book stacks on the middle floor between the lower-level theater and the top-story lodge hall. In its first incarnation, the theater was a late Victorian opera house. Cast-iron columns supported the delicately ornamented rim of the horseshoe balcony. This space was gutted in 1919, then rebuilt to accommodate motion pictures and Keith vaudeville acts. The last movie was shown here in 1980.

By mid-1982 the volunteer Friends of the Library Theater had raised nearly a half million dollars in private donations to repair and reopen the building. The softly shaded floral stencils of the 1919 design, painted over years ago, have been replicated along the walls and ceilings of the Library's 1,000-seat auditorium. The crystal chandeliers now hanging in the mezzanine foyer came to the theater from the Erlanger (1927, demolished) in Philadelphia, by way of Cincinnati's Palace (1918). The Library's backstage area has been upgraded to allow for a full variety of performance uses. [Thomas Struthers Trust. Performing arts center.]

■ **Library**
302 Third Avenue, West
David K. Dean
1883, 1919

## WEST CHESTER

**■ Warner**
120 North High Street
Rapp and Rapp
1930

Located near the primary intersection of this small college town, the Warner has just barely escaped demolition in recent years. Clearly, on seeing the interior, one might conclude that the Warner is among the least elegant of the theaters designed by Rapp and Rapp. Yet it is unquestionably among the most crazily flamboyant Art Deco theaters by these or any other architects. The design, most of it in its original state, starts out in a calm but colorful way with the electrical signage along North High Street. The blue and yellow sunburst marquee is slightly more restrained than the one gracing the Warner (1931) in Erie, at the opposite corner of Pennsylvania. The West Chester Warner has the splashier lobby, with gold and silver linings.

The outer spaces are tame in comparison to the Warner's auditorium — kitsch at its debatable best. Stenciled Art Deco hieroglyphics cover the modified Egyptian arch atop the proscenium. Except for the organ screens, the entire wall surfaces are filled with frantically detailed stencilwork. Squiggles and dots decorate the outer rim of the ceiling. The recessed central panel of the ceiling is a wildly abstracted celestial vision, as if seen in a planetarium run by an artistic three-year-old.

Preservation efforts were undertaken on behalf of this unusual theater in 1977, with stage shows replacing movies. The Warner closed in the early 1980s, however, possibly for good. NR. [Privately owned. Closed.]

## ■ ■ ■ ■ ■  WEST VIRGINIA  ■ ■ ■ ■ ■

### CHARLESTON

**■ Capitol Plaza (Plaza)**
123 Summers Street
P. Norwood Wiggins
1912, 1924

Construction of a $160 million hotel-mall-civic center complex three blocks down Summers Street helped bring about the reopening of the old 1,100-seat Plaza, which had been sitting empty for three years. A local developer, aided by public funds, spent $700,000 and five months refurbishing the former vaudeville-movie house, known since 1924 as the Capitol. Painter Bob Harmon and his crew required an estimated $13,000 in pale gold paint alone to retouch the highlights of the vines and rosettes of the auditorium ceiling. The theater's principal decorative effects are Classical Revival, particularly along the facade, where seated figures adorn the central pediment above the third story. One major alteration left untouched is the entry lobby, redone in 1956 in late Moderne wood paneling. Reborn in 1985 as the Capitol Plaza, the theater has been used for jazz and bluegrass concerts, ballet and a mix of local and traveling performances. NR. [Renaissance Productions. Performing arts center.]

### CLARKSBURG

**■ Grand (Rose Garden)**
444 West Pike Street
1913, 1940

A vaudeville theater that turned photoplay house in 1915, the Grand was the 13th theater in the country equipped to show the new "talkies" in 1927. Originally operated by the

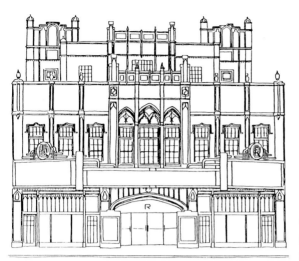

The Grand's exterior with its Gothic Revival details.

Robinson family, the theater was popularly referred to as the Robinson Grand. When fire gutted the interior in 1939, the family spent $600,000 to rebuild the theater. In addition to a curved Moderne auditorium, a Spanish ballroom was added at that time above the main-floor theater entry. The brick and terra cotta exterior, designed in a particularly fine Gothic Revival style, retains its 1913 appearance. A "Robinson Grand" vertical sign, suspended from the front in 1940, was removed during the recent conversion into the Rose Garden. [DeCarDe Inc. Stage shows and concerts.]

## HUNTINGTON

The old copper-clad "Keith-Albee" vertical sign still hangs from the tile-roofed cupola above the third story of the Keith-Albee Theatre Building. A marble and bronze box office sits directly below, between the sidewalk and the polished bronze theater doors. Inside is a theatrical rendition of the Spanish baroque period. The grand

■ **Keith-Albee**
929 Fourth Avenue
Thomas W. Lamb
1928

Ornamental flourishes embellishing the Keith-Albee's proscenium opening.

lobby is dominated by twisting black and gold columns and a trio of multicolored glass chandeliers. Featured in the men's lounge is a stone fireplace ornamented with various coats of arms and a fleet of sailing ships. The 2,000-seat auditorium of the Keith-Albee is a rarity, one of only six atmospheric theaters credited to Lamb. Anyone familiar with Loew's Ohio (1928) in Columbus would feel at home in the Keith-Albee. It is as if the Ohio had been moved to Huntington, but with its roof removed and left open to the night sky.

The Keith-Albee auditorium has been subjected to subdivision, but one respectful of the atmospheric design. Two new 300-seat theaters have been created on the main floor beneath the balcony; the upper-level seats share with the front rows of the main floor a view of the main screen. Each of the main-floor theaters possesses one of the stained-glass star light fixtures originally included in the decoration of the balcony soffit. A fourth cinema space is housed in an adjacent storefront directly off the grand lobby. [Privately owned. Movies — quad.]

The Keith-Albee, Huntington. Stage and auditorium. The theater's interior, like that of the Stanley in Utica, N.Y., is cousin in style to the Ohio in Columbus.

## MARTINSBURG

■ **Apollo**
128 East Martin Street
Reginald Geare and
Chapman Kent
1914

The Apollo was one of the first theaters in the state built primarily to show motion pictures. Built within a solid three-story brick office block, the theater seats just over 1,000 on its main floor and balcony, beneath a ceiling of pressed tin. Geare, from Washington, D.C., created the Apollo in association with Kent, a local architect. Geare later designed the ill-fated Crandall's Knickerbocker (1917) for his hometown. The collapse of the Knickerbocker's roof in 1921, caused by 30 inches of snow, killed 98 people and injured 150. The tragedy led to court proceedings against Geare, who ultimately took his own life. The Apollo survives intact. NR. [Berkeley County Civic Theatre. Stage shows.]

### MORGANTOWN

The street facade of the Metropolitan has a symmetrical five-bay arrangement with a flattened Classical Revival appearance. The original capacity of the auditorium was 1,300, with 800 seats on the main floor and the remainder in the horseshoe-shaped balcony. A fire in 1930 melted the four Czechoslovakian crystal chandeliers in the auditorium and necessitated a partial rebuilding of the interior. [Privately owned. Stage shows.]

■ **Metropolitan**
371 South High Street
Charles W. Bates
1924

### PARKERSBURG

The Smoot Amusement Company erected this theater directly across an alley from the old city hall in Parkersburg. The street facade of the Smoot has an Ionic temple front, executed in terra cotta, set within the brick box housing the theater. The Smoot became the principal showplace in town when the competing Camden fell to a fire in 1929. NR. [Privately owned. Movies.]

■ **Smoot**
213 Fifth Street
1926

### SPENCER

The present Robey was the last of the theaters set up in Spencer by local entrepreneur Hamond Robey. His first venture in the film exhibition business was the Dreamland, opened in 1907. At the time, movies were such a novelty that the townspeople would show up two or three times a week, often requiring Robey to hold five shows a night. This popularity prevailed despite a stiff admission price of 10 cents, "on account of the heavy expense [for] installing an electric plant." A year later Robey moved his enlarged operation to the new Wonderland. Finally, in 1911, Robey built the Auditorium in conjunction with the local Knights of Pythias Lodge. The current name and modest neoclassical appearance of the theater date to a 1926 remodeling performed by Carmichael and Millfaugh of Columbus, Ohio. The theater remains in the hands of the family of the original owners, giving the Robey a right to claim itself as the oldest American movie theater in continuous operation. [Privately owned. Movies.]

■ **Robey (Auditorium)**
314 Main Street
Carmichael and Millfaugh
1911, 1926

### WHEELING

The opulence of the Beaux Arts period of American architecture is fully evident in the design of the principal facade of the Capitol. Oval windows with inset lyres and paired Composite columns frame an elaborately decorated archway above the theater entry. The terra cotta composition is capped by a pair of maidens holding a medallion inscribed with a logo for the theater, and the words "Capitol Theatre" are cast into the entablature above the archway. The Capitol auditorium was remodeled in an Art Deco mode, but the exterior remains as built with storefronts on each side of the entry. The theater currently promotes country-and-western music shows as the Capitol Music Hall. [Privately owned. Stage shows.]

■ **Capitol**
1015 Main Street
Charles W. Bates
c. 1926

The Alabama, Birmingham.
Candy counters such as the
Alabama's were a big part of
the show by the 1940s.

## BIRMINGHAM

**■ Alabama**
1811 Third Avenue, North
Graven and Mayger
1927

Headlines in the *Birmingham News* just before the theater's opening on December 26, 1927, announced, "Birmingham gets $1,500,000 Christmas gift in Alabama Theater." The Alabama's Spanish baroque elements represent a departure from the more restrained classicism of Graven and Mayger's earlier theaters in Detroit (1927) and Minneapolis (1928), both demolished. Included among the original furnishings were objects from a castle in Spain, which the Alabama shared with Paramount-Publix chain flagships in New York and Los Angeles. Spain was not the only country to lend its decorative character to the Alabama. Lounges recall "a Chinese tea room, a medieval English manor hall, and an English hunting lodge." The Hall of Mirrors grand lobby is topped by a cove-lighted plaster ceiling molded in an intricately coffered pattern. The 2,100-seat theater fronts Third Avenue with an elaborate terra cotta facade modeled after a Moorish original.

Clockwise from left: The Alabama's lobby, facade and auditorium.

The Alabama came complete with a Publix 1 Model Wurlitzer organ. Now affectionately known as "Big Bertha," the four-manual / 20-rank organ has been maintained over the past 18 years by volunteers from the local chapter of the American Theatre Organ Society. The auditorium of the Alabama received a major refurbishing in 1972, and further restoration has been scheduled by the new owner. NR. [Alabama Landmarks. Movies and organ concerts.]

Entry hall and original exterior of Mobile's Saenger.

## MOBILE

This 1,895-seat theater recalls the classical lines of the Renaissance. Originally part of the Saenger chain spanning the deep South, this former combination vaudeville and movie theater now functions as the University Theater for the Performing Arts. [University of South Alabama. Performing arts center.]

■ **Saenger**
6 South Joachim Street
1927

## TUSCALOOSA

The Depression-era Bama was built with WPA funding as part of a municipal complex for Tuscaloosa. The first air-conditioned building in the city, the Bama combines a Moderne exterior with an Italian Renaissance auditorium, whose design is derived from the Davanzati Palace, in Florence, Italy, and included twinkling stars and a cloud-making machine. Art Deco elements embellish the downstairs and upstairs lobbies. The 1,000-seat Bama made an immediate hit with an opening night attraction of *Bringing Up Baby.* NR. [City of Tuscaloosa. Performing arts center.]

■ **Bama**
Sixth Street and
Greenshore Avenue
D. O. Whilldin
1938

Left: Moderne exterior of the Bama. Above: Atmospheric auditorium.

## EL DORADO

■ **Rialto**
117 East Cedar Street
Kolben, Hunter and Boyd
1930

A conventional facade arrangement of cast-stone pilasters, entablature, cornice and recessed parapet disguises the Rialto's ornate interior. Its Renaissance Revival decor reaches a grand climax in the grillwork organ screens framing the fanciful cartouche-topped proscenium arch. Little has changed inside the theater, empty now for more than a decade. NR. [Privately owned. Closed.]

## LITTLE ROCK

■ **Arkansas (Kempner)**
516 South Louisiana
H. B. Herts
1910

Alterations to the Kempner Opera Theater in 1921 and 1929 brought movies and then a new name to this showplace. In the process, the original Sullivanesque facade was replaced by a simpler Art Deco front of stucco with ceramic tile highlights. The Arkansas ended its days as a motion picture theater in 1977 and hit the skids. Plans to save the theater as a performance space have failed, apparently consigning the theater to demolition. NR. [University of Arkansas at Little Rock Foundation. Closed.]

## PINE BLUFF

■ **Saenger**
West Second Avenue and
Pine Street
Emile Weil
1924

The Saenger rose from the ashes of the Hauber (1912), a store-turned-theater that burned in 1922. A new Florentine-style picture palace was designed for Pine Bluff by Weil, the Saenger chain's regular architect. The theater opened under the restriction that no shows were permitted on Sundays. A legal test, prompted by a Sunday screening of *Strong Boy* in June 1929, ended with the acquittal of all those charged, much to the delight of many in attendance at the trial. Empty since 1975, the Saenger has become the subject of recent efforts to renovate it for stage performances. [Heckatoo Heritage Foundation. Closed.]

The Saenger's classical facade. The theater has been closed for more than a decade.

■ ■ ■ ■ ■ ■    FLORIDA    ■ ■ ■ ■ ■ ■

### FORT MYERS

A tropical vision in green and beige, the Edison is a handsome example of streamlined styling. The round-edged marquee and the vertical sign, with its neon cooling rings, hang suspended above the Hendry Street sidewalk. The Edison was *the* place for weekend dates in the 1940s and 1950s. In its current role, the theater dispenses fast food. [Privately owned. Restaurant.]

■ **Edison**
1533 Hendry Street
c. 1939

### JACKSONVILLE

In 1955 the Florida gained the distinction of being the first theater to host Elvis Presley on stage. The performer's rise to fame—or notoriety—was so rapid that for a return engagement two months later, Elvis was handed a court order to "tone down" his act.

■ **Florida**
128–34 East Forsyth Street
R. E. Hall and Roy Benjamin
1927

The theater is contained within a seven-story building, designed by Roy Benjamin to be clad with buff-colored brick and highlighted by terra cotta ornament. Reputed to be the first theater in the city with air conditioning, the building also boasted a rooftop ballroom for hot summer nights. The lobby of the Florida has the atmosphere of a Spanish garden, with twisting Moorish columns, star-shaped light fixtures and flowered trellises. A similarity to the main lobby of the Tampa (1926) by John Eberson is perhaps explained by the employment here of Michel Angelo Studios of Chicago. This firm was frequently used by Eberson, the master of the atmospheric style. The auditorium is more in keeping with Hall's earlier design for the Eastman (1921) in Rochester, N.Y. Yet, like the lobby, the 3,200-seat auditorium displays Moorish influences in its green and gold antiqued plasterwork. Of particular note are the stencil patterns of the ceiling's heavy beamwork and the coffered sounding board. Interior woodwork includes native cypress and oak. Rehabilitation as a performance space was completed by the local firm of KBJ Architects in 1983. NR. [Arts Assembly of Jacksonville. Performing arts center.]

### KEY WEST

The colorful terra cotta–trimmed facade of the Strand sits on Duval Street like the entrance to a grand carnival. The effect is enhanced by the roaring-lion medallion decorating the pediment above the lighted rainbow-arch entry bay. The theater name is spelled out in large letters above the front of the canopy marquee. Only a few events have been staged at the Strand in recent years. [Privately owned. Closed.]

■ **Strand**
529 Duval Street
1924

### MIAMI

The Olympia was among the earliest Eberson theaters to be fully imbued with the romance he sought to create in his courtyard atmospheric designs. A few opera boxes along the right side of the auditorium face a palace setting

■ **Gusman Center (Olympia)**
174 East Flagler Street
John Eberson
1926

The Olympia, Miami. This early view shows plants enhancing the atmospheric setting.

on the left straight from the Alhambra in Spain. Trelliswork shelters the upper balcony from a "night sky." Imitation Renaissance masterworks line the plaster rooftops and fill every niche. The lobby spaces include a gloriously detailed Moorish mezzanine. The main entry to the theater is through the base of a 10-story office tower. Around to the east are entry doors leading directly into a side lobby of the four-story theater wing. Above these doors runs a string of wrought-iron balconies reached through fabulously ornate quatrefoil window openings.

Vaudeville became part of the show at the Olympia in 1929 and remained until 1954. The last movie was shown in 1971. The next year, local philanthropist Maurice Gusman purchased the theater for use by the Miami Philharmonic Orchestra. Miami Beach architect Morris Lapidus took charge of the changeover. John Eberson's son, Drew, served as a consultant. In 1975 the theater was deeded to the city and rechristened the Maurice Gusman Cultural Center. NR. [City of Miami. Performing arts center.]

## PALM BEACH

■ **Paramount**
145 North County Road
Josef M. Urban
1927

With its aquarium-inspired panels of silk on the side walls and its ceiling of contoured cypress, the Paramount auditorium was appropriately posh as the 1920s entertainment center of this resort town. Architect Urban was celebrated for buildings in Egypt, Russia and his native Austria, and he also moonlighted as a set designer for the Ziegfeld Follies in New York during the 1920s. The Paramount followed the unusual policy of presenting just an afternoon matinee and a single evening show, for the winter season only. For the wealthy theater patrons, Urban provided a shelf balcony of 26 boxes above the

back of the fan-shaped auditorium. Seats in this so-called Diamond Horseshoe went for $1,000 per season. The entrance to the theater was marked by a large copper-sheathed dome. A ring of shops, opening onto an interior patio courtyard, served as a buffer from the street. A tall, arched entry was added at the corner in 1948, in front of the domed lobby.

By the 1970s the theater was seeing only sporadic use, and it closed for good in 1980. The shops were returned to mint condition and reopened in 1983, but a recent remodeling of the auditorium as office space has left little of the old theater interior intact. [The Paramount Limited. Shops and offices.]

The Paramount, Palm Beach. The exterior of this showplace was restored, but the interior has been converted for office use.

## PENSACOLA

The opening of this "magnificent edifice . . . a shrine to art, music, and drama" was page-one news for the *Pensacola Journal* in 1925. Elements of Spanish baroque architecture decorate the theater entry, located just a few blocks from Pensacola Bay. Inside the 700-seat auditorium, matching ornament is clustered around the organ screens. When the theater was renovated in 1981 under the auspices of the University of West Florida, the Saenger's Robert Morton organ was put back in working order. NR. [City of Pensacola. Performing arts center.]

■ **Saenger**
118 South Palafox Street
Emile Weil
1925

## SARASOTA

■ **Edwards**
57 North Pineapple Avenue
Roy A. Benjamin
1926

The Edwards was designed by Jacksonville architect Benjamin in what has become known popularly as the Florida Mediterranean Revival style. Rehabilitation of the fancy plasterwork auditorium and the adjoining shops and apartments was carried out in 1985. NR. [Asolo Opera Guild. Performing arts center.]

## TAMPA

■ **Tampa**
709–11 North Franklin
Street
John Eberson
1926

Theater historian Ben Hall pronounced this intimate Spanish-courtyard atmospheric picture palace "an Andalusian bonbon." Wondrously romantic, the interior overwhelms patrons with its fabulously ornate, polychrome plasterwork. Both the lobby and 2,000-seat auditorium feature tiled parapets, grand balustrades, urns illuminated by hidden lights and thin columns with tightly twisting shafts. Wrought-iron balconies hang from just below the organ grilles. John Eberson described the inspirations for his style to the *Tampa Tribune* on the theater's opening day:

My idea for the atmospheric theater was born in Florida. I saw the value of putting nature to work and so have borrowed the color and design that are found in the flowers and the trees. The inhabitants of Spain and southern Italy live under the sun and enjoy the happiness nature affords them. So I decided their architecture probably would provide the firm foundation for a theater.

Enhancing the atmospheric effects of the auditorium's make-believe buildings were hanging vines, potted

Above: The Tampa's marquee.
Right: Postcard view of the auditorium.

palms and stuffed birds along the tops of the encircling walls, beneath the blue plaster "sky" with its electric stars. A faithful restoration of the Tampa in 1977 has been followed by a decade of successful presentations of varied performance events. NR. [City of Tampa. Stage shows, concerts and classic films.]

Full view of the Tampa's auditorium.

■ ■ ■ ■ ■ ■    GEORGIA    ■ ■ ■ ■ ■ ■

### ATLANTA

The fabulous Fox is by far the most celebrated theater in the South. Previewing its 1929 opening, the *Atlanta Sunday American* praised the theater's "minarets, glittering domes, towers, and crowning battlements." And that was just the inside. The ribboned brick exterior is no less magical, if somewhat incongruous in its setting just north of the downtown business district. The threatened demolition of the theater in the late 1970s rallied local citizens to "Save the Fox." A $1.8 million rescue operation proved successful to keep alive what a reporter for the *New York Times* was moved to call "the Xanadu of Dixie." Clearly, the Fox is capable of stirring both the pens of writers and the emotions of those who attend the theater.

The construction history of the Fox is as exotic as its decor. The complex was originally designed to house shops along Peachtree, beneath an Egyptian ballroom, along with the lodge hall of the local Shriners. The building was to be called the Yaarab Temple of the Ancient Arabic Order of the Nobles of the Mystic Shrine. Financial difficulties forced the Shriners into partnership with movie mogul William Fox. Their arrangement called for the Shriners to enter through an archway beneath a copper onion dome just off Ponce de Leon, while theater patrons would use the mini-mosque box

■ **Fox**
660 Peachtree Street, N.E.
Mayre, Alger and Vinour
1929

The Fox, Atlanta.
Clockwise from top left:
Theater complex including
shops and offices, auditorium,
brick detail and an
ornamental urn.

office of the Fox located on Peachtree. The Shriners lost their lease at the outset of the Depression, and unpaid taxes put the Fox group out of business in 1932. Other organizations ran the theater with varying degrees of success until the crisis and subsequent rescue in 1978.

An inventory of the theater decor would require a large volume. The lobbies and lounges contain what seems to be an endless variety of Egyptian and Arabian design elements — throne chairs, lotus lamps, sphinx light-stands, Sun-god scarabs and an unusual keyhole door. Inside the auditorium, a 3,000-pipe Moller organ rises on its lift before the jewel-encrusted house curtain, inspired by tales from *The Arabian Nights.* A striped tent spreads above the balcony seats beneath the plaster "sky," with its projected dawns and dusks. Inside and out, the Fox remains awe-inspiring as the reborn "Mecca on Peachtree Street." NR. [Atlanta Landmarks. Stage shows, concerts and movies.]

## AUGUSTA

With just 850 seats divided among the main floor, mezzanine and two balconies, the Imperial bears a greater resemblance to the classical concert halls of Europe than to later picture palaces in America. Huge crystal chandeliers and equally magnificent wall sconces illuminate floral motifs decorating the auditorium. The five-bay exterior features masks of Comedy and Tragedy in terra cotta. The Imperial nearly fell to the wrecker's ball in 1981, only to be reborn four years later as a home for local ballet, opera and live theater groups. Decorator Colene Reed supervised the renovation of the interior, now brightened by a rich peach color scheme. [Imperial Partners. Performing arts center.]

■ **Imperial**
745 Broad Street
Lloyd Preacher
1917

Facade of the Imperial.

## SAVANNAH

Newspaper accounts of the day reported that, although far from complete, the Lucas opened on time. Patrons were treated to the sight of a great ornamental dome above the auditorium illuminated by more than 620 incandescent lights of red, white and blue. Most of the original Adamesque decor remains intact. The tiered side boxes have been removed, reducing seating to 1,100. A cafe-restaurant has filled the former lobby area since movie showings ended in the late 1960s. A local nonprofit organization has been working to adapt the theater for use as a performance hall. [Lucas Theater for the Arts. Closed.]

■ **Lucas**
Abercorn and Congress Streets
C. K. Howell
1921

■ ■ ■ ■ ■ ■    KENTUCKY    ■ ■ ■ ■ ■ ■

## ASHLAND

This modestly scaled theater was constructed from plans developed by the Paramount home office for a "model" theater at the 1932 World's Fair. The exterior is plain, aside from crisscross brick patternwork. Bright colors in a commedia dell'arte mural and bands of floral ornament enliven the Paramount's 1,300-seat auditorium, including the wingspread form of the proscenium arch. Various local groups, including the Greater Ashland Area Cultural and Economic Development Foundation and the Paramount Women's Association, have worked to restore portions of the theater since movies ceased in 1972. NR. [Paramount Arts Center. Stage shows.]

■ **Paramount**
1304 Winchester Avenue
1931

## BOWLING GREEN

■ **Capitol (Crescent)**
416 East Main Street
1925

The classical decoration of this theater extends to the fluted pilasters of the blocky stone exterior. The facade takes on a semblance of Art Deco styling thanks to the flashy lines and lettering of the Depression-period marquee. Built as the Crescent, the Capitol shut down its movie operation in 1976. Using a mix of state and local funding, the county arts commission was able to reopen the theater in 1981 as a regional performance center. [Bowling Green-Warren County Arts Commission. Performing arts center.]

## HOPKINSVILLE

■ **Alhambra**
501 South Main Street
John T. Waller
1928

The theater shares a block-long structure with the Christian County Courthouse. In like fashion, the Moorish atmospheric auditorium coexists with a lobby given an Art Deco update in 1943. Opened as a setting for talking pictures, the Alhambra was also equipped with full stage facilities. [Alhambra Committee. Planned performing arts center.]

## LEXINGTON

■ **Kentucky**
208 East Main Street
Joseph and Joseph
1922

The Kentucky's auditorium. Stained-glass domes ring the large central dome.

Louisville architects Joseph and Joseph decorated the brick facade of the Kentucky with tile highlights in salmon and white. Only the upper portion of this facade remains intact. The Adamesque interior was also altered in the 1950s, to suggest what *Box Office Magazine* called a "Southern Colonial character." Floral murals and ornately framed mirrors fill the walls of the vaulted lobby. The first theater in town to show "talkies," the Kentucky even had a private railroad siding next to it, to accommodate traveling theater and vaudeville groups. NR district. [Privately owned. Movies.]

## LOUISVILLE

The beautifully balanced main facade is centered by a tall Moorish spire that doubles as a vertical sign. Photographs of this polychrome spire from different periods of the theater's life reflect an ongoing identity crisis. A 1930s photo indicates joint ownership by Loew's and United Artists. A 1970s view shows the tower names boarded over. The house was then operating as the Penthouse–United Artists, with a piggybacked balcony theater. By 1980 the main floor had been terraced to serve as a dinner theater. Finally, 1986 photographs reveal tower faces reading "Palace," as yet another makeover proceeds. For all the alterations, the Palace remains one of the finest of Eberson's Spanish-courtyard atmospheric

■ **United Artists (Palace)**
625 South Fourth Avenue
John Eberson
1928

Clockwise from left: Facade of the United Artists, lobby with vaulted ceiling relief portraits and auditorium.

theaters, with a full complement of Renaissance statuary. Unique to the Louisville theater is the medallion-covered, vaulted grand foyer ceiling. Among the theatrical and political portraits in plaster on the medallions is a solemn profile of Eberson himself. Most prominent among the scattered plaster statuary is a copy of Donatello's *David* above the foyer entry doors. NR. [Louisville Palace. Performing arts center.]

## MAYSVILLE

■ **Russell**
9 East Third Street
Frankel and Curtis
1932

The overall design of the Russell shows a Spanish Colonial Revival influence, mixed with Moorish and baroque elements. The decorative effects are most pronounced along the brick exterior, with urn-topped towers framing a baroque crested loggia. The loggia bays are divided by terra cotta columns molded with twisting shafts. Both this fanciful exterior and the interior remain virtually unchanged after 54 years of continuous operation. [Privately owned. Movies.]

■ ■ ■ ■ ■ ■    LOUISIANA    ■ ■ ■ ■ ■ ■

## EUNICE

■ **New Liberty**
200 West Park Avenue
Duncan and Barron
1924

The renovated interior of this former vaudeville and movie theater has a freshly painted neoclassical character. The columns and archways of the auditorium side walls are a colorful caricature of classical architecture. The beautiful new stage curtain is the work of local

Detail of the new Alphonse Mucha–inspired curtain in the New Liberty.

artists Charles Seale and Alvine Hinjose and is painted in the manner of the Art Nouveau. The theater has been reopened as the Liberty Center for the Performing Arts. NR. [City of Eunice. Performing arts center.]

### NEW ORLEANS

The Orpheum shows Lansburgh at his Beaux Arts best. A polychrome terra cotta frieze runs nearly the length of the main facade of this former vaudeville house, just above the marquee. The upper portion of the facade is a classical five-bay scheme. Figures of cherubs and angels add an ethereal touch to the interior. The focal point of the auditorium design was the plasterwork "Orpheum" cartouche, in cream and gold, atop the center of the proscenium arch. Spared from demolition for a hotel, the theater received a $3.1 million restoration, reopening in 1982 as the home of the New Orleans Philharmonic. NR. [New Orleans Philharmonic. Concerts.]

■ **Orpheum**
129 University Place
G. Albert Lansburgh
1921

Above: The Orpheum's classical facade. Left: Auditorium ceiling detail.

■ **Saenger**
1111 Canal Street
Emile Weil
1927

This theater was Emile Weil's grandest foray into atmospheric-style interior design. The stately auditorium has walls that re-create buildings of the Florentine Renaissance. Plaster imitations of quarried stone blocks are massed to frame bubbling fountains and support statue-filled side balconies. Flagship of the Saenger chain, the theater was launched by a parade down Canal Street led by Adolph Zukor and F. P. Lasky, heads of the Paramount–Famous Players Studios, partners of the Saenger owners. In the course of a $2.5 million renovation in the late 1970s, all but one of the 12 original grand lobby chandeliers were sold to pay for an escalator from the main foyer to the upper lobbies. Only later was it reported that those chandeliers had come from Versailles by way of the Chateau de Pierrefonds D'Oise. Since its conversion, the Saenger has welcomed a broad mix of live theater and popular music concerts. NR. [Saenger Theater for the Arts. Performing arts center.]

Right: Auditorium in New Orleans's Saenger. Below: Shreveport's Strand.

### SHREVEPORT

■ **Strand**
619 Louisiana Avenue
Emile Weil
1925

The dominant feature of the Strand's exterior is its wonderful neobaroque dome, set above the corner entry doors. The space beneath this dome is filled by an equally ornate marble-floored lobby rotunda. A major overhaul of the interior, undertaken in 1957 for a brief fling with Cinemascope, cost the Strand its original opera boxes. Still present along the column-framed proscenium arch are a pair of winged cherubs holding a great plaster cartouche. A trio of fanciful murals fills the Palladian arches lining each side of the balcony. The Strand was revitalized in the early 1980s for its grand reopening in 1984 as a home for live theater, dance and symphony performances. NR. [Strand Theater of Shreveport Corporation. Performing arts center.]

■ ■ ■ ■ ■ ■   MISSISSIPPI   ■ ■ ■ ■ ■

## BILOXI

Florida architect Benjamin built this neoclassical vaudeville and movie theater for the New Orleans–based
Saenger chain. Engaged Ionic pilasters of cast stone
frame three central bays on the main facade. At the
corners, the brickwork suggests stone quoins. Gilt
plasterwork inside the Saenger matches the quiet classicism of the exterior. The backstage facilities of the theater
are considered the best in the area. NR. [City of Biloxi.
Performing arts center.]

■ **Saenger**
416 Reynoir Street
Roy Benjamin
1929

## CLARKSDALE

The Marion was among the first theaters anywhere
designed primarily to feature motion pictures, with stage
acts appearing only occasionally. Arched entryways
reminiscent of early nickelodeon designs lead through
lavish appointments to an auditorium seating well over
1,000 patrons. The focal point of the auditorium design is
the huge cartouche decorated with a single letter "M" at
the center of the proscenium arch. The Saenger theater
chain took over the Marion in the 1930s, renaming it the
Paramount. Three decades later, still showing movies,
the theater was twinned. By 1986 the building had come
into the hands of a local arts organization. It has been
resurrected for general performance uses as the Larry
Thomson Center for the Fine Arts, named for a native son
who now ranks among the leaders of the Hollywood
entertainment industry. [Mississippi Delta Arts Council.
Performing arts center.]

■ **Marion (Paramount)**
200 Yazoo Street
John Gaisford
1918

## CORINTH

The narrow arched entryway of the Coliseum is mislead-
ing. Inside awaits a wealth of ornament. A lobby of gilt
plasterwork with a floor of mosaic tile leads to a white
marble staircase serving the two balcony levels. Simplified baroque elements inside the auditorium brighten
the side bays and the proscenium sounding board. The
huge circular leaded-glass dome of the auditorium
ceiling is illuminated from above. Long the theatrical
heart of Corinth, the Coliseum was closed in 1978. NR.
[Privately owned. For sale.]

■ **Coliseum**
404 Taylor Street
Benjamin Franklin Liddon
1924

## HATTIESBURG

Hints of the newly popular Art Deco style appear in the
arrangement of bright tiles and terra cotta trim of the
Saenger's otherwise classically modeled brickwork exterior. The ornamental effects of the main lobby are
similarly mixed. Two frosted-glass fixtures hanging
above the lobby area are smaller versions of the main
chandelier in the auditorium. The successful restoration
of the lobby spaces, begun in 1976 by the city government, prompted later work to repair the Art Deco motifs
that highlight the organ grilles and the decorative

■ **Saenger**
Forrest and Front Streets
Emile Weil
1929

The Saenger, Hattiesburg.
Ornamental brick above
the entry.

stencilwork along the auditorium ceiling. Renovation of
the adjoining storefront spaces as art galleries is planned
to coincide with the final restoration of the Saenger
interior. [City of Hattiesburg. Performing arts center.]

## MERIDIAN

■ **Temple**
2318 Eighth Street
Emile Weil
1927

In a chain of events destined to be reenacted a few years
later with the Atlanta Fox (1929), the interior of this
building stood incomplete for years until a major motion
picture exhibitor came to the rescue. Originally designed
for the local chapter of the Shriners, the blocky Moorish
shell of the Temple was constructed in 1924. The 1,700-
seat auditorium space was not completed until 1927,
finally opening as the Saenger Temple under management of the Saenger chain. The Islamic archway hovering
behind the marquee is reminiscent of Louis Sullivan's
elaborate facade for the Transportation Building at the
1893 World's Columbian Exposition in Chicago. Stylistically related terra cotta trim runs along the cornice
line of the front and sides of the theater building. NR.
[Hamasa Building Association. Performing arts center.]

■ ■ ■ ■ ■   NORTH CAROLINA   ■ ■ ■ ■ ■

## CHARLOTTE

■ **Carolina**
224–32 North Tryon Street
Charles C. Hook and
R. E. Hall
1927

The odd Beaux Arts entry facade of the Carolina is
wedged between adjoining fronts decorated in Spanish
Mission and Tudor-Flemish styles. Local architect Hook
is credited with this eclectic exterior, while Hall, a New
York architect, designed the Carolina's Spanish at-
mospheric interior after the model popularized by John
Eberson. The original organist for this Paramount-
Publix theater was Fae Wilcox, who was trained by the
legendary Jesse Crawford at the Paramount flagship on
Times Square in New York. Accommodations made for
Cinerama in 1961 required changes to the Carolina's
interior. The theater went out of business in 1978. NR.
[Privately owned. Closed.]

## DURHAM

Originally known as the Durham Auditorium, the Carolina became part of the Paramount-Publix theater chain in 1929. The exterior has a formal Beaux Arts arrangement, with carved stone Corinthian capitals atop the pilasters dividing the central entry bays. Over the last few years the classical interior has been renovated as part of a new downtown civic center project. [City of Durham. Performing arts center.]

■ **Carolina**
211 Roney Street
Milburn and Heister
1926

Far left: The Carolina in Durham. Left: The Carolina in Greensboro.

## GREENSBORO

Ionic pilasters divide the bays of the Carolina's Greek Revival temple facade. Inside the 3,000-seat auditorium, engaged clusters of three columns each separate the organ screens from the proscenium arch with its plaster frieze. The richly draped Classical Revival interior has been renovated twice, first in 1980 and again after a fire the following year. Throughout its history, the Carolina has played a central role in the cultural life of Greensboro. [United Arts Council. Performing arts center.]

■ **Carolina**
310 South Green Street
Workman and DeSibour
1927

## WILSON

The predominant decorative theme of the Wilson is neoclassical, carried out in brick along the exterior and painted plaster inside. Envisioned as an opera house, the Wilson opened as a vaudeville theater, with movies soon added to the bill. During the 1970s the Wilson showed X-rated features. A turnaround occurred in 1984, as work started toward a 1987 grand reopening as the Wilson Theater of the Arts. [City of Wilson. Performing arts center.]

■ **Wilson**
108 West Nash Street
S. B. Moore
1919

## WINSTON-SALEM

This Palladian-inspired theater was built within the lower floors of an 11-story apartment building. The large classical urns decorating the niches below the Carolina's organ screens were removed during alterations in 1949. Local newspaper publishers donated the building to the North Carolina School of the Arts in 1977, with the richly

■ **Carolina**
407 West Fourth Street
Johnson and Bannon
1929

The Carolina, Winston-Salem. The auditorium, before conversion for performance use.

appointed theater to be converted for use as a training facility and performance hall. The school raised $9.6 million to do the work, including funds to preserve a 12-foot Tiffany chandelier. The former Carolina reopened in 1983 as the 1,400-seat Roger L. Stevens Center for the Performing Arts, named to honor the well-known Broadway producer. [North Carolina School of the Arts. Performing arts center.]

■ ■ ■ ■ ■   SOUTH CAROLINA   ■ ■ ■ ■ ■

## CHARLESTON

■ **Garden**
371 King Street
C. K. Howell and D. B. Hyer
1918

This one-time vaudeville house was the site of the first talking picture to play before the citizens of Charleston, *The Jazz Singer.* Federal financing, provided in 1977, enabled the city to lease and restore the interior to its brightly colored original state. Since then, performances of the Spoleto Festival have been held on the Garden's stage. [Pastime Amusement Company. Performing arts center.]

■ **Riviera**
225 King Street
Charles Collins Benton
1939

Built during a period when theaters received little if anything in the way of ornamental flourishes, the Riviera is an exceptionally attractive example of Art Deco design. Wave motifs highlight the windows on the principal stone facades of the building. Moderne lettering spells out the theater name atop the outer block of the hybrid Deco-Mayan temple-form exterior. The crowning feature of this design is a carved mask of Comedy at the center of the recessed upper block of the east facade; a similar mask was placed above the covered entry on the south side. Inside, a relatively simple lobby leads to the more fanciful 1,200-seat auditorium. Benton, best known for his church designs, gave the Riviera's auditorium a squared-off form, with only a slight raking to both the main and balcony floors. Exotic birds and butterflies fly in murals along the side walls.

Closed in 1977, the Riviera was leased in 1979 for two years of church meetings held by the Community Baptist Fellowship. Recently, plans were announced to fill the

The Riviera, Charleston.
Left: Facade detail. Below:
The Riviera in 1942.

auditorium with a mix of shops and offices. This idea met with substantial community opposition, led by the Friends of the Riviera, who still hope to keep the building as a theater. [Pastime Amusement Company. Closed.]

## COLUMBIA

After three decades as the State, this theater got a new name, together with a Fox marquee and matching neon signs. The hybrid style of the building is simplified Classical Revival, strongly influenced by Art Deco. This blend is visible on the exterior in the Deco renditions of classical masks located at the upper corners of the facade. [Privately owned. Movies.]

■ **Fox (State)**
1607 Main Street
c. 1935

## DILLON

A 1935 edition of the local *Herald* boasted that the 700 seats of the new Dillon were "stream-lined seats [and] the very latest type," giving this movie house "the distinction of being the first theater in the United States" to be so equipped. The stucco exterior was not so novel, executed with light touches of the Spanish Colonial Revival. In recent years the Dillon has been leased to the United World Out Reach Church. [Privately owned. Church services.]

■ **Dillon**
114 MacArthur Street
H. H. Anderson, builder
1935

## GAFFNEY

**■ Hamrick**
306 North Limestone Street
Charles Collins Benton
1930

The springtime 1930 unveiling of the Hamrick was a scaled-down version of the glittery picture palace openings of the 1920s. A staff of eight welcomed the 780 opening night patrons to this theater filled with "the atmosphere and splendor of Romantic Spain." The exterior mixed classical and Art Deco motifs in a balanced presentation. After the Hamrick closed its doors in 1968, years of neglect left the auditorium a shambles, with gaping holes in the ceiling. Enough of the original interior ornament remains, however, to make recent performance hall renovation plans seem plausible. [Privately owned. Closed.]

Right: The Hamrick's hybrid Moderne facade. Below: The Palmetto's mint-green and black facade.

## HAMPTON

**■ Palmetto**
108 Lee Avenue
c. 1925

The Palmetto is notable primarily for its mint-green ziggurat billboard facade, with its thick black borderlines. The dizzying marquee patterns are colored like a mint Oreo cookie in matching black and green against a background of cream white. This small-town theater still holds regular movie screenings. [Privately owned. Movies.]

■ ■ ■ ■ ■ ■    TENNESSEE    ■ ■ ■ ■ ■ ■

## CHATTANOOGA

**■ Tivoli**
709 Broad Street
Rapp and Rapp
1921

The Tivoli is an attractive 2,300-seat rendition of the elegant French baroque treatment that Rapp and Rapp worked to perfection during the 1920s. It resembles their slightly more elaborate Memphis Orpheum (1928). The Tivoli is largely unchanged from its early days. Surviving additions include the flashy marquee and vertical

"Tivoli" sign. Conversion of the theater for performance uses came early in the preservation era when the city leased and rehabilitated it for a March 1963 reopening. NR. [Privately owned. Performing arts center.]

The Tivoli, Chattanooga. Facade and auditorium in 1963.

## CROSSVILLE

For 40 years this theater thrived at the center of downtown Crossville, but the construction of a new mall cinema complex forced the Palace to close in 1978. As the 50th anniversary of the theater's opening approached, efforts got under way to restore it for some new use. The Palace is notable for its unusual Art Deco exterior of patterned stonework, built using what is locally known as Crab Orchard stone. The blocky Moderne auditorium, with seats for 600, has a series of bull's-eye wall sconces running along both side walls. The future of the Palace remains in limbo. [Cumberland Heritage. Closed.]

■ **Palace**
212 South Main Street
Eston Smith
1936

Deteriorated facade of the Palace.

## KNOXVILLE

■ **Bijou**
803 South Gay Street
1909

The Bijou was attached to the back of the Lamar House (1816), an elegant 15-room hotel. This little "jewel" opened auspiciously with George M. Cohan on stage in *Little Johnny Jones*. Just three years later, changes were made to enable the theater to show motion pictures, although Keith vaudeville acts were included as part of the show. Surviving to this day are the two triple-tiered box arrangements, each topped by a cartouche-and-muses sculpture group at the center of a broken pediment. The delicately colored interior, with seats for 1,100, was restored by a local preservation group in time for the theater's 70th anniversary. NR. [Knoxville Heritage. Performing arts center.]

■ **Tennessee**
600–04 South Gay Street
Graven and Mayger
1928

The Tennessee was constructed as part of the Burwell Building, an 11-story Renaissance Revival office block. The theater was billed as a "Moorish Movie Palace," although the decor more closely follows classical models. The oval-shaped auditorium seats close to 2,000, with its walls curving overhead to form the rim of a colorful dome. Movie showings ended at the Tennessee just one year shy of its 50th anniversary. The current owners purchased and refurbished the theater and its equipment to coincide with the 1982 World's Fair in Knoxville. The fancy three-manual Wurlitzer pipe organ still speaks through the cartouche-topped organ screens on either side of the stage. NR. [Dick Broadcasting Company. Performing arts center.]

Elliptical dome over the Tennessee's auditorium in Knoxville.

## MEMPHIS

Rapp and Rapp rendered this masonry vaudeville house, located at the southern edge of downtown Memphis, in the style of the Italian Renaissance. Overall, the decorative effects are fairly restrained, particularly on the exterior. The elegance of the lobby and 2,800-seat auditorium relies heavily on delicately modeled plasterwork, colored in rich golds and greens. For 40 years beginning in 1935, the theater operated as the Malco, a first-run movie house. General repairs carried out in 1969 kept the original Wurlitzer pipe organ operational. A $5 million restoration led to a grand reopening in 1985, with the theater once again bearing the name Orpheum. NR. [Memphis Development Foundation. Performing arts center.]

■ **Orpheum (Malco)**
197 South Main Street
Rapp and Rapp
1928

Left: The Orpheum's auditorium in Memphis. Below: Nashville's Tennessee.

## NASHVILLE

This 2,000-seat theater was designed in the early 1930s, but left unfinished until 1952. The Tennessee is housed within the Sudekum Building, an 11-story Art Deco office tower. As first envisioned, the structure was to be known as the Warner Building. The start of the Depression caused both the change in name and the suspension of plans to include the theater. When the auditorium was finally completed, a "Tennessee" vertical sign, capped by neon cooling rings, was attached to the side of the building. Inside, the dazzling lobby has an elegant mixture of curving metal strips and polished mirrors. NR. [Privately owned. Performing arts center.]

■ **Tennessee**
535 Church Street
Marr and Holman
1932, 1952

■ ■ ■ ■ ■ ■ ■    VIRGINIA    ■ ■ ■ ■ ■ ■ ■

## CHARLOTTESVILLE

The interior of the 1,300-seat Paramount has a flattened French Renaissance appearance in keeping with the larger urban theaters designed by Rapp and Rapp. The street facade has a monumentally overdone Greek Revival appearance, possibly in deference to the classical influence of Charlottesville's Thomas Jefferson. The theater was closed in the late 1970s, with shops temporarily filling its lobby. [Privately owned. Commercial uses.]

■ **Paramount**
215 East Main Street
Rapp and Rapp
1931

Balconies at the Wells,
Norfolk, with stencil patterns
and plaster ornamentation.

## NORFOLK

■ **Wells**
Tazewell Street and
Monticello Avenue
E. C. Horn and Sons
1913

Built within a brick box masquerading as an Italian palazzo, the elegant Wells has rows of thick brackets supporting a tile roof above the corner entry tower. Diamond-shaped terra cotta light mounts decorate the lower portions of the exterior. Inside the Wells, molded Rubenesque figures mingle with plasterwork Victorian women of more refined character. Two tiers of three boxes each step down the auditorium side walls. The Wells was renovated for live theater performances in 1980. NR. [Virginia Stage Company. Playhouse.]

## PORTSMOUTH

■ **Colony**
430 High Street
c. 1942

This late Moderne theater seats fewer than 1,000 in an auditorium decorated only by sweeping horizontal bands of color. Its chief architectural feature of note is the Art Deco horseshoe proscenium arch. [Privately owned. Closed.]

## RICHMOND

■ **Byrd**
2908 West Cary Street
Fred Bishop
1928

Restrained in its decor, the Byrd seems less a movie palace than a formal hall along the lines of the Eastman (1921) in Rochester, N.Y. Rich baroque ornamentation, crystal chandeliers and fine draperies decorate the interior spaces. Movie screenings at the Byrd are accompanied each night by performances on the original Wurlitzer pipe organ. NR. [Privately owned. Movies.]

Left: The Byrd's auditorium in 1929. The organ continues to be an integral part of the theater. Below: Early view of the Carpenter Center's Moorish exterior.

At the time of its opening, the atmospheric interior of the Loew's was reported in the local *Times-Dispatch* to be "appointed in a manner suggestive of a Spanish Castle of the first order — at least as Spanish Castles are described by the fancy fictionists." The blue-domed 2,000-seat auditorium is indeed impossibly romantic. The delicately colored and antiqued plasterwork is massed in striking Moorish-derived forms to match the ornate terra cotta trim of the curved-front brick exterior. The auditorium design culminates in the devilish curves of the proscenium arch. Classical statues bear silent witness before the organ screens. The theater was rescued in 1983 after being vacant for a decade and a half, to be reborn in 1985 as the Carpenter Center. NR. [Carpenter Center for the Performing Arts. Performing arts center.]

■ **Carpenter Center (Loew's)**
600 East Grace Street
John Eberson
1928

# MIDWEST

The Plaza, Kansas City, Mo.
Its lobby resembles a Spanish
patio and once came
complete with serenading
musicians.

■ ■ ■ ■ ■ ■ ■   **ILLINOIS**   ■ ■ ■ ■ ■ ■

## AURORA

■ **Paramount**
23 East Galena Boulevard
Rapp and Rapp
1931

Even in the age of Art Deco, Rapp and Rapp had difficulty giving up their preferred French royal style. As a result, the Paramount is a seamless blend of late Versailles and early Art Deco design. The time compression is particularly startling in the graphically modern murals of the auditorium featuring aristocratic nobles in scenes of the old royal court. Dividing the predominantly scarlet fabric panels are Art Deco versions of engaged

The Paramount's marquee, hybrid Art Deco auditorium and column detail.

Corinthian columns, each topped by illuminated capitals of frosted glass. Interior bay divisions are mimicked by color patterns in the theater's brick side facing the Fox River. A modified mansard roof, in hexagonal form, caps the corner entry rotunda.

The city of Aurora acquired the Paramount in 1975 and set aside $3 million to restore the theater, an outlay deemed preferable to the $20 million projected for a new facility. Restoration workers from Conrad Schmitt Studios not only replicated damaged side bay fabric panels and repaired the auditorium's central sunburst chandelier, they also very nearly matched the stud-lighted sunrise motif of the original corner marquee. Since its 1978 reopening, the Paramount has played host to everything from classic film series to classical music concerts, all part of ongoing efforts by the Aurora Civic Center Authority to keep the rehabilitated showplace in use. NR. [City of Aurora. Performing arts center.]

## CHAMPAIGN

Visible in the layout of this small-town vaudeville theater are traces of the French palatial style Rapp and Rapp would bring to full flower in the Chicago (1921). Eighteen ornate loge boxes ring the upper level of the 800-seat auditorium. The original decor included blue velvet drapes and ivory-colored plaster ornament. The Rapp brothers used this auditorium arrangement as the basis for the Versailles-inspired Ringling Memorial (1917) in Baraboo, Wis. While its cross-town competitor, the Virginia (1921), still shows first-run pictures, the Orpheum has been closed. [Privately owned. Closed.]

■ **Orpheum**
346 Hickory Street
Rapp and Rapp
1914

The Orpheum, a prelude to Baraboo's Ringling Memorial.

## CHICAGO

■ **Avalon**
1645 East 79th Street
John Eberson
1927

This exuberantly patterned brick and terra cotta Moorish "mosque" sits in the Avalon Park district, near the southern edge of Chicago. The inside of this atmospheric theater is even gaudier than the exterior. Here Eberson outdid his earlier Mediterranean courtyard schemes in composing an array of brilliantly colored domes and minarets in the make-believe temple walls. A spear-supported asbestos awning juts out above the proscenium to "protect" the performers from the simulated desert-night sky. The walls of the lobbies match the auditorium in rich textures and patterning, all with a Middle Eastern flavor.

The almost-holy character of the interior neatly fitted the second use of the building. In 1980 the blue plaster "sky" was painted a simple gray, and the Avalon was rechristened the Southside Miracle Temple and Church. In early 1986, however, Mayor Harold Washington announced that the Avalon would be reborn again, this time as the New Regal Theater for live theater and concert performances. [New Regal Theater Foundation. Planned performing arts center.]

The Avalon's auditorium. The theater now hosts live performances.

■ **Belmont**
1635 West Belmont Avenue
W. W. Ahlschlager
1926

This north side theater, which once boasted the most beautiful lobby rotunda in the city, was gutted in the 1960s during conversion into a bowling alley. A fire scorched the former lobby area in 1972, and since then the Belmont has seen only infrequent use as a staging area for flea markets. The glazed white terra cotta exterior, with its golden capitals atop engaged Corinthian columns, was meticulously cleaned in 1973. It stands in stark contrast to the derelict interior. [Privately owned. For sale.]

Left: The Belmont before conversion into a bowling alley. Below: The Chicago's French royal marquee.

In the Chicago, Rapp and Rapp created the first true downtown motion picture palace. The rich French royal treatment of this Loop showplace begins with the terra cotta triumphal-arch facade. Outlined by bright stud lighting, the arch supports a four-story vertical sign and a broad marquee with its famous branched "C" logo, taken from the city's coat of arms. Below the marquee, French-style bronze doors lead to a low-ceilinged carriage lobby from which patrons pass into a towering faux-marbre-columned grand lobby. Opposite the entry, a twisting

■ **Chicago**
175 North State Street
Rapp and Rapp
1921

Early views of the Chicago's auditorium and elaborately contorted staircase.

staircase (the one climbed by *Sun-Times* movie critic Roger Ebert at the start of his televised movie review program) rises to two promenade levels that encircle the 60-foot-tall grand lobby. A vaulted inner foyer, recently liberated from a false ceiling, has its own upper view-points from the mezzanine and balcony levels. Designed by the architects to provide overflow lobby circulation areas, these elaborate spaces create sheer aesthetic delight for moviegoers.

If the peripheral regions of the Chicago are glorious, the 3,800-seat auditorium is nothing short of flawless. Barely started on their prolific way, the Rapps here struck archetypal balances: opulence rendered with subtlety, capacity without the sacrifice of intimacy, lighting that is colorful yet subdued and ornamentation detailed on an architectural backdrop of grand proportions. The cove lighting of the ceiling dome and proscenium arch and the decorative treatment of the organ screens set design standards for all the palace architects. The four-manual Wurlitzer organ installed here was top of the line.

Originally built for midwestern showmen Balaban and

Katz, the Chicago was one of America's most durable downtown movie houses. Only in 1984, after protracted negotiations among the owners (Plitt Theaters), civic groups and city officials, did the Chicago close its doors, to reemerge in 1986 as a host for live stage performances. Even with fresh paint and overly bright lighting, the Chicago retains the feel of an old picture palace. For Chicago moviegoers, the popcorn is gone, but the memories linger on. NR. [Chicago Theater Restoration. Stage shows.]

The immense auditorium ceiling dome, coated with bas-relief plaster ornament, is the dominant feature of this one-time vaudeville house. Equally ornate are the picture-frame proscenium arch and projecting organ grilles that seem borrowed from St. Peter's in Rome. The sense of grandeur is enhanced by the manner in which the ornamentation was designed to wrap fully around the 2,900 seats of the auditorium and its shelf balcony. Pendulous light fixtures hang from the walls between the bays encircling this broad space. Renamed the Cine Mexico in 1977, this so-called Cathedral of Spanish Theaters runs a mix of movies and stage productions. [Valmar Azteca Management Company. Spanish-language movies and stage shows.]

■ **Congress (Mexico)**
2135 North Milwaukee
Avenue
Friedstein and Company
(1926)

Plasterwork dome of the Congress, covering a 2,900-seat auditorium.

The first of four large theaters built by this firm on Chicago's near-north side, the Diversey was by some accounts the least successful. No matter; the interior was gutted in 1973, and a shopping mall now inhabits the shell. The mall features a continuous seven-level ramp that wraps around a central atrium, with caged stud lights running the length of the ramp edge. A glass-paneled skylight tops the Century Shops, a pastel-colored

■ **Diversey (Century)**
2828 North Clark Street
Levy and Klein
1925

poor relation of New York's Guggenheim Museum. Blue, gray and pink banners hanging inside the building are matched by similar ones along the nearly unchanged main facade. [The Century Shops. Retail stores.]

■ **Esquire**
58 East Oak Street
Pereira and Pereira
1937

The exterior of this classy, streamline Moderne movie house was built with rich materials used in a restrained fashion. Above the long, low marquee, shiny marble panels cover the main facade. The lobby and 1,400-seat auditorium have broadly curvilinear shapes, matched by their globe-form light fixtures, common in the later stages of the Art Deco period. Film critic Roger Ebert has reported that the interior is due "to be gutted and turned into a multiplex — a collection of four or five shoebox theaters." The exterior, at least, is protected by city landmark status granted in 1986. [Plitt/Cineplex Odeon. Movies.]

Exterior of the Esquire, with its streamline Moderne marble facade.

■ **Gateway**
5216 West Lawrence Avenue
Rapp and Rapp
1930

The Gateway and the Paramount (1930, demolished) in Toledo, Ohio, were the only completely atmospheric-style theaters designed by the Rapp brothers. The low walls of the 2,000-seat auditorium are lined by statuary and arched bays drawn from the Italian baroque. The exterior is a marked contrast, a stepped Moderne design similar to the Rapps' Warner (1931) in Erie, Pa. A Polish-American cultural association purchased the Gateway in 1986, redesigning its interior along the lines of a 17th-century palace in Warsaw. The organization altered the exterior of the theater building, using materials far more costly than the originals. [Copernicus Center. Community auditorium.]

Located near the lakefront on the north side of Chicago, the Granada sports a terra cotta facade crested by rich baroque ornamentation. A colorful medallion centers a tall arched window, flanked by two smaller arched bays. Levy and Klein reproduced this arrangement with an even more elaborate cornice line across town at the Marbro (1927, demolished). The Italian baroque treatment of the Granada's 3,400-seat auditorium is credited to local designer Edward Eichenbaum, who later established himself as one of the foremost theater decorators. The side bays and coffered ceiling dome were painted in no fewer than 12 colors. [Privately owned. Closed.]

■ **Granada**
Sheridan Road and
Devon Avenue
Levy and Klein
1926

The Granada's sweeping baroque facade.

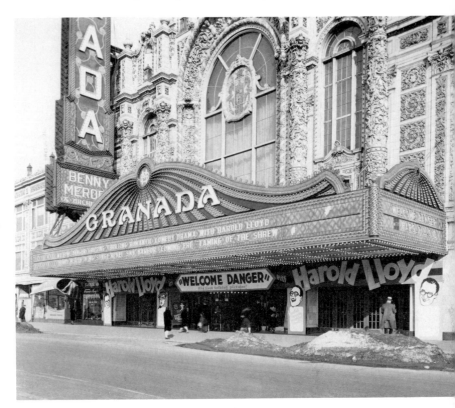

This 1,900-seat theater was one of the many neighborhood theaters designed by big-name architects but seldom seen in the major architecture magazines of the period. The principal theater facade, as well of that of the adjoining store and apartment complex, has terra cotta trim suggesting a baroque model, typical in much of Ahlschlager's work. [Privately owned. Church services.]

■ **Grove**
7620 South Cottage Grove
Avenue
W. W. Ahlschlager
1926

Moorish and Renaissance designs enliven the front of the modestly scaled Music Box. Inside, an Italian–Spanish colonial atmospheric-style auditorium awaits, with room for 769 patrons. After 50 years as a second-run movie house, the Music Box embarked on a series of programs as eclectic as the architecture, showing Spanish- and Arabian-language movies and finally X-rated films. Ultimately, theater buffs took over and restored the building to show classic films in repertory. [Privately owned. Movies.]

■ **Music Box**
3733 North Southport
Avenue
Louis I. Simon
1929

### ■ Nortown
6320 North Western Avenue
J. E. O. Pridmore
1931

Theater historian Ben Hall characterized the Nortown interior as "King Neptune Gothic Atmospheric." The architecture of this cinematic Atlantis is more Spanish baroque, but Hall was close enough. Sea horses, mermaids and mermen decorate the organ screens, with a ship's prow jutting from the center of each screen. A lighthouse brightens one wall. Signs of the zodiac cover the lobby ceiling. In the mid-1980s the balcony of this unique movie house was walled off and the main floor sliced amidships into two small theater spaces. Little of the original decor can be seen with the current arrangement. [Plitt/Cineplex Odeon. Movies — triplex.]

The Nortown's exterior and auditorium, now subdivided.

### ■ Oriental
20 West Randolph Street
Rapp and Rapp
1926

Theater goers of the late 1920s, by then used to the conventional European-style picture palaces, began to demand something more exotic. As a result, architects of the early movie theaters were pressed to diversify their styles. As the story goes, the Rapps were forced virtually at gunpoint by impresarios Balaban and Katz to design this cross-cultural concoction of Cambodian chimeras, Indian elephants and Thai-inspired temples. Completing the heterogeneous effects, the upper portions of the 22-story Oriental Building were once filled by colonial-style Masonic lodge halls. In the early 1980s the Oriental was mugged, or so a police report might have read. Stabbings in the balcony, arson and general vandalism made attending the theater as dangerous and suspenseful as the Kung-fu epics showing on the screen. Water damage was the final blow to the auditorium, closing the theater in 1982. An electronics shop now operates in the old lobby. NR. [Chicago Building Maintenance Corporation. Closed.]

This theater was a particularly fine example of the standard French Renaissance treatment Rapp and Rapp used for nearly all their designs for the Orpheum vaudeville circuit. The theater adjoins an early Art Deco hotel, the Bismarck. Although all seats remain in the balcony, the orchestra level of the old Palace has been converted by the hotel into a terraced banquet hall. Marble pillars line the luxurious lobby spaces, which are now used to supplement the banquet hall. [Bismarck Hotel. Banquet facility and meeting hall.]

Soon after completing the Central Park (1917, demolished) for Chicago entrepreneurs Balaban and Katz, the Rapp brothers were called on here to help a second Balaban and Katz house make a transition from vaudeville to moving picture palace. The interior is a variation on the Rapps' French Renaissance theme. The Riviera was reopened with its decor intact as a trendy discotheque in 1986. [Privately owned. Nightclub.]

The Southtown opened on Christmas Day 1931 with a newspaper ad proclaiming the theater to be "Like a Trip to Sunny Spain." By the autumn of 1958, the 3,200-seat Spanish delight had been closed. The Southtown was destined to spend the next two decades as a department

■ **Palace**
**(Bismarck Pavilion)**
157 West Randolph Street
Rapp and Rapp
1926

■ **Riviera**
4746 North Racine Avenue
Rapp and Rapp
1919

■ **Southtown**
610 West 63rd Street
Rapp and Rapp
1931

Left: Historic view of the Southtown. Above: Lobby with flamingo pool in background.

The Southtown's flamingo pool.

store, its colorful baroque plasterwork subject to the harsh glare of fluorescent lights.

A 1930 issue of *Motion Picture News* promoted the forthcoming theater, designed as the Paramount for impresarios Balaban and Katz, as "an unusual modernized treatment" of Italian and French baroque. The completed theater was actually a vast Spanish colonial palace, with strong Art Deco overtones. The hybrid Spanish and Deco treatment was carried over into the grand lobby, with its red and black tile floor, although traces of French design elements appear here as well. The lobby design culminated in the wildly flamboyant Flamingo Pool, backed by a tiled Art Deco fountain with a neon border. French baroque designs dominated the Southtown's auditorium, although also with an Art Deco twist. Semiatmospheric in style, the auditorium has views "out" through the side bay arches and is covered by a tentlike stenciled ceiling.

In 1986 the department store, too, abandoned the Southtown, the last big picture palace built in Chicago. [Carr's, Inc. Closed.]

■ **United Artists (Apollo)**
47 West Randolph Street
Holabird and Roche;
C. Howard Crane
1921, 1927

Originally a 1921-vintage Greek Revival legitimate theater, designed by Chicagoans Holabird and Roche, the hall was converted for motion pictures just six years later. Crane left the Corinthian-columned exterior essentially unchanged. The classical interior of the theater was replaced by a Spanish Gothic treatment, similar to Crane's United Artists (1927) in Los Angeles, but overlaid with colorful Moorish detailing. A plasterwork thatched auditorium ceiling centers on a cove-lighted dome, ringed by 10 smaller portholes. The lobby has a similar Middle Eastern flavor, executed in black marble and polychrome plaster. [Plitt/Cineplex Odeon. Movies.]

■ **Uptown**
4816 North Broadway
Rapp and Rapp
1925

In planning the Uptown, motion picture exhibitors Balaban and Katz are reported to have told their architects to "leave patrons awestruck." To do so, the Rapp brothers gave their largest palace (4,381 seats) an atypical Spanish treatment, risking a departure from

their traditional, polished French Renaissance design. The experiment was a huge success. The architectural show begins with a monumental terra cotta facade in baroque style. Inside was a grand lobby "larger than anything before attempted and decorated with a lavishness never before attempted outside of Spanish and Italian palaces," as the in-house magazine gushed. The Uptown's auditorium was equally impressive, with its 46,000 square feet of space covered by a triple-inset dome. Included in an impressive array of show machinery at the Uptown was one of the "marvelous freezing plants that have made 'B&K' theaters divertingly cool in the hottest summer," an air-conditioning system quite advanced for its day. [Privately owned. Planned concerts]

Left to right: The Spanish-style Uptown, the French baroque Tivoli and the Spanish baroque DuPage.

### CHICAGO AREA: DOWNERS GROVE

This 1,500-seat theater and the adjoining hotel, located in the suburbs southwest of Chicago, were well placed to take advantage of the commuter rail lines that run alongside. The Tivoli design is a simple French baroque, richest on the exterior in the terra cotta composition above the theater marquee. Although damaged during a 1950s conversion for Cinemascope, the interior bas-relief plasterwork is being repaired. [Tivoli Enterprises. Movies.]

■ **Tivoli**
5201 Highland Avenue
Van Gunten and Van Gunten
1928

### CHICAGO AREA: LOMBARD

The terra cotta Spanish baroque arch above the DuPage's entry is echoed by the plaster organ screens in the courtyard atmospheric auditorium. A second-run movie house since 1977, this designated city landmark shut down in 1986. [Ownership contested. Closed.]

■ **DuPage**
109 Main Street
R. G. Wolff
1928

### CHICAGO AREA: OAK PARK

This late-vintage Lamb movie house has a striking Moderne exterior, surmounted by a bright neon vertical sign. The broadly curving lines of the auditorium walls and ceiling look much like the designs popular in the British Odeon theater chain of the same period. Chicago

■ **Lake**
1020 Lake Street
Thomas W. Lamb
1936

Exterior and auditorium
of the Lake, Oak Park.

**■ Pickwick**
5 South Prospect Avenue
Zook and McCaughey
1929

The Pickwick's interior, with
Mayan-like features.

designer Joseph DuciBella performed the 1985 conversion into a triplex movie house, retaining much of the 1930s appearance. [Tivoli Enterprises. Movies—triplex.]

### CHICAGO AREA: PARK RIDGE

The Pickwick, with its blocky Moderne tower and flanking pylons of Indiana limestone and Minnesota granite, is a high-toned elder relation of Depression-era palaces such as Thomas W. Lamb's Warner (1931) in Torrington, Conn. Much of the interior decoration, including the zigzag organ grillwork and the knockout fountain sculpture composition in the main foyer, was the work of sculptor Alfonso Ianelli. The blocky insets of the auditorium ceiling, reminiscent of Mayan temple architecture, were designed to focus attention on the stage.

This effort seems superfluous when one sees the wildly colorful asbestos curtain that could well be a forerunner of Abstract Expressionism. The entire console of the three-manual Wurlitzer organ was originally painted in the same abstract patterns. Regrettably, this is the only theater attributed to Zook and McCaughey, known primarily for English cottage-style residences. NR. [Privately owned. Movies.]

Blocky tower and pylons of the Pickwick.

## DeKALB

Twin images of Pharaoh Ramses II, executed in polychrome terra cotta, bracket a scarab stained-glass window atop the main facade of the Egyptian. The courtyard atmospheric auditorium has painted scenes of the pyramids at Giza below its flat blue plaster "sky."

■ **Egyptian**
135 North Second Street
Elmer F. Behrens
1929

Ramses figures guarding the Egyptian's main facade.

Winged pharaohs' masks, in gold and black, rest above the lotus capitals ringing the walls. Golden pharaohs sit on either side of the proscenium opening. This spectacular tribute to Egypt was the work of the same architect who built the Pekin (1928, demolished), a Chinese pagoda picture palace in downstate Pekin. The Egyptian closed in 1977 and sat empty until a civic group restored the theater under the direction of architect Roland Killian of Springfield, Ill. Since its grand reopening in 1983, the 1,500-seat theater has been self-supporting, playing host to a mix of local and touring productions. [Preservation of the Egyptian Theatre, Inc. Performing arts center.]

## EDWARDSVILLE

■ **Wildey**
100 St. Louis Street
1909, 1937

Silent films, vaudeville and Cinemascope have filled the seats of this theater, built by the local Odd Fellows chapter. Originally decked out with lavish opera boxes, the Wildey has been the object of community restoration efforts since the last film was shown in 1984. [Madison County Arts Council. Planned performing arts center.]

## GALESBURG

■ **Orpheum**
57 South Kellogg Street
Rapp and Rapp
1916

On the day of its opening, the Orpheum was heralded as "a veritable house of enchantment" by the local *Republican Register*. This sentiment was inspired most likely by the beautiful proportions of the plasterwork walls, which curve around to form the ceiling of the auditorium. The modest-sized Orpheum is an elegant intermediary between the Rapps' former Majestic (1910, now the Five Flags) in Dubuque, Iowa, and the overwhelming palaces they built in Chicago during the 1920s. The Second Empire facade of the Orpheum is capped by a pea-green mansard roof, pierced by five porthole windows. The double-height entry lobby was designed as a Hall of Mirrors in miniature. This lobby became a community battleground in 1986, as state-funded renovation plans called for the insertion of a floor that would have cut the space in two. The preservationists prevailed and are currently seeking a chandelier to illuminate the lobby. [City of Galesburg. Planned performing arts center.]

The Orpheum's early Rapp and Rapp exterior and the auditorium, with its curving plasterwork walls.

## JOLIET

Thanks to the efforts of the Rialto Square Arts Association, this theater was the beneficiary of a restoration by Conrad Schmitt Studios in 1978. On reopening in 1981, the Rialto sparkled with old gold highlights in the predominantly crimson and ivory French Renaissance design. Entering the Rialto Square brings patrons to a voluminous rotunda ringed by paired faux-marbre columns. Off this space is the esplanade, a Hall of Mirrors roughly the size of one of the huge railroad station waiting rooms of the early 1900s. The auditorium is no less grandiose, with Greco-Roman ornamentation mixed in with the predominant French. The rehabilitated theater once again is packing them in as the "Jewel of Joliet." [Joliet Metropolitan Exposition and Auditorium Authority. Performing arts center.]

■ **Rialto Square**
102 North Chicago Street
Rapp and Rapp
1926

Section of the Rialto Square's auditorium and the theater's organ.

## PEORIA

The last remaining picture palace in Peoria, the Madison was an early design by the architect who concocted the Coronado (1927) in upstate Rockford. Classical-style bas-relief plasterwork decorates the high domed ceiling of the auditorium. An oval dome also opens from the main lobby up through the mezzanine promenade. Balconettes reminiscent of Italian Renaissance design decorate the east facade of the exterior. NR. [Managed by Knoxville Associates. Planned performing arts center.]

■ **Madison**
502 Main Street
Frederic J. Klein
1920

## ROCKFORD

With its cove-lighted Golden Dragon organ screens, Persian balconies hanging from the mezzanine promenade and towers and turrets inside the 2,400-seat Spanish-castle atmospheric auditorium, the Coronado is a magically blended vision. Klein even threw in two Art Deco Birth of Venus figures as the centerpieces for a

■ **Coronado**
312–24 North Main Street
Frederic J. Klein
1927

Exterior of Rockford's Coronado and its dragon organ grille.

diamond-patterned half dome hovering over the grand lobby. Unlike most palaces, Rockford's "Wonder Theater" has been well maintained all through its history. The white and gold dragon-encrusted Barton pipe organ is in the tender care of the Land of Lincoln Theatre Organ Society. NR. [Kerasotes Theatres. Movies and stage shows.]

■ ■ ■ ■ ■ ■ ■　INDIANA　■ ■ ■ ■ ■ ■ ■

### ELKHART

■ **Elco (Lerner)**
410 South Main Street
K. V. Vitchum
1924

The style of this theater is Classical Revival — simple on the front, exuberant inside. More than a thousand colored lights were used to highlight the Adamesque bas-relief auditorium dome, from which a bulbous plaster chandelier hangs. The street facade of the Elco has a restrained Second Empire appearance dominated by a row of monumental engaged columns. The stud-lighted marquee has additional rows of bulbs along its underside. NR. [Privately owned. Movies.]

### FORT WAYNE

■ **Embassy (Emboyd)**
121 West Jefferson Street
A. M. Strauss, with
John Eberson
1928

The walls of this theater feature an unceasing array of bas-relief plasterwork. The influence of Eberson is most noticeable in the lobby spaces, particularly the tile-floored outer lobby. The Embassy was rehabilitated in 1985 as the home of the Fort Wayne Philharmonic. A skybridge connects the theater with a new convention center–hotel complex across the street. NR. [City of Fort Wayne. Concerts and stage shows.]

■ **Paramount**
121 East Wayne Street
A. M. Strauss
1930

A dizzying blend of geometric patterns decorates this former member of the Paramount-Publix theater chain. A sunburst pattern caps the main entry facade. Pilasters in the lobby are a hybrid of Corinthian and Art Deco.

Stylized ornament, meant to suggest a geometric jungle, decorates the multilayered golden picture-frame proscenium arch, surrounded by masklike organ screens. The theater closed some years ago, and the lobby was converted for use by a retail operation. [Privately owned. Closed.]

The Paramount's marquee and interior, defined by geometric patterns.

## INDIANAPOLIS

A prominent downtown location led the designers of the Circle to give it a suitably dignified Classical Revival appearance. The interior leans heavily on Adam styling, with its painted bas-relief plasterwork. The Monument Circle facade is a bright white terra cotta Greek temple front. Following a $9.2 million rehabilitation in 1983 by Cleveland architects Dalton, van Dijk and Johnson, the Circle became the home of the local symphony. NR. [Indianapolis Symphony Orchestra. Concerts.]

■ **Circle**
45 Monument Circle
Rubush and Hunter
1916

Promotion of a Harold Lloyd film at the Circle. Lloyd figure cutouts scale the Circle's wall, but local patrons appear unimpressed.

### ■ Indiana
134 West Washington Street
Rubush and Hunter
1927

Just a block away from the Indiana State Capitol grounds, Rubush and Hunter put up this exotic blend of Spanish baroque, Moorish and East Indian ornamentation. Russian-born sculptor Alexander Sangernebo was entrusted with the terra cotta frontispiece, with its ruffled arch topped by medallion busts of King Ferdinand and Queen Isabella of Spain. A marble staircase in the grand lobby leads up to a mural depicting a distant view of the Taj Mahal. Inside the auditorium, imitation ashlar blocks set off the densely ornamented proscenium arch, in turn capped by a row of plaster urns and finials. Only slightly less spectacular, the grilles for the Grand Barton organ were more of the same. Even the Cosmetic Room on the mezzanine level recalls old Castile. A writer for the Historic American Buildings Survey has speculated that the model for the Indiana was the Court of the Ages at the 1915 Pan-Pacific Exhibition in San Francisco.

Kangaroo bracket detail from the Indiana, the exterior and the auditorium.

During a 1979 conversion for live theater performances, the balcony was removed to allow creation of a second-level auditorium. Not to be overlooked is the recently restored Indiana Roof, an atmospheric Mission-style ballroom that the architects positioned atop the theater. NR. [Indiana Repertory Theatre. Playhouse.]

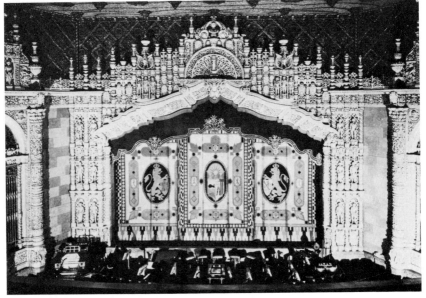

## SOUTH BEND

Polychrome elements decorate the exterior of this one-time vaudeville and movie theater, styled to suggest a Spanish castle. The Renaissance decor of the auditorium includes tiered sets of boxes that slope downward as they approach the proscenium opening. The designer of the Palace interior was Edward Eichenbaum, who later assisted architects Levy and Klein with the Granada (1926) and Marbro (1927, demolished) in Chicago. Renamed the Morris Civic Auditorium in the late 1970s, the theater has been renovated, and its lobby and auditorium once again sport a clean-lined elegance for patrons. NR. [City of South Bend. Performing arts center.]

■ **Morris (Palace)**
211 North Michigan Street
J. S. Aroner
1922

Left: Grand lobby of the Morris. Right: The Iowa's corn cob sign.

■ ■ ■ ■ ■ ■   IOWA   ■ ■ ■ ■ ■ ■

## CEDAR RAPIDS

Seating in the Iowa's Italian Renaissance auditorium is down from 1,800 to fewer than 600 following a 1983 remodeling for intimate stage productions. Sadly gone from the exterior is a one-of-a-kind vertical sign, with the name "Iowa" against a field of stud lights patterned as a gigantic ear of corn. Despite the playhouse conversion, the original Barton organ console remains in the orchestra pit. [Cedar Rapids Community Theatre. Playhouse.]

■ **Iowa**
102 Third Street, S.E.
1928

This vaudeville house had a change in both name and programming (to show Paramount pictures) before it was a year old. The auditorium is roughly Adamesque in decor, with plaster Grecian urns framed by Corinthian columns visible in the balcony. With just under 2,000 seats, the auditorium is illuminated by torchères bracketing the organ screens and cove lighting that fills the

■ **Paramount (Capitol)**
123 Third Avenue, S.E.
Peacock and Frank
1928

Right: Interior of the
Paramount, Cedar Rapids.
Below: The Capitol's ornate
marquee in Davenport.

vaulted dome recessed above the balcony. A group of
townspeople rescued the theater from gradual decay in
1976. NR. [Cedar Rapids Symphony Orchestra. Performing arts center.]

### DAVENPORT

■ **Capitol**
326 West Third Street
Rapp and Rapp
1920

The Rapp brothers built this theater within the 10-story
Kahl Building as a showcase for movies and vaudeville.
Alterations to the interior of the Capitol have reduced its
seating from 2,500 to about 2,000. The last remodeling
in 1968 included the restoration of landscape murals that
fill the three bays of a half dome above the front of the
auditorium. Under the current management, the theater
features occasional organ concerts from its original
Wicks pipe organ. [Dubinsky Brothers Theatres. Stage
shows, rock concerts and movies.]

■ **Orpheum (Adler)**
136 East Third Street
Rapp and Rapp
1931

This theater, originally built for the Orpheum vaudeville
circuit, is less a picture palace than a forerunner of the
streamlined performance halls of the mid-20th century.
In 1931 the *Davenport Democrat* called the theater "a
stunning example of modern decorative art." Its square-
edged proscenium arch expands out, accordion-fashion,
from the front of the hall. The underside of the balcony
flares upward to its front edge in an equally expansive
manner. Frosted-glass fixtures in the auditorium match

The Orpheum's Moderne
auditorium.

the grand lobby chandeliers. Paired lobby fixtures are set within a geometrically patterned coffered ceiling. The lobby and much of the original decor of the 2,750-seat auditorium were restored during a $4.2 million renovation in 1985. The theater was renamed the Adler to honor the memory of local newspaper publishers E. P. Adler and his son, Philip D. Adler. [River Center for the Performing Arts. Stage shows and concerts.]

### DUBUQUE

The earliest known theater by Rapp and Rapp, the old Majestic is a Second Empire design executed in brick and terra cotta. Inside, it is a rich Beaux Arts example with gilded boxes and a steep upper balcony. The theater's varied history can be followed by charting the changes in its name. Opened for vaudeville as the Majestic, it became a movie house, the Spensley, in 1929. Four years later it was renamed the Orpheum, showing RKO pictures exclusively. Since a 1970 rehabilitation the theater has been known as the Five Flags, in tribute to Dubuque's equally varied course of history from the days of Marquette and Joliet. NR. [Five Flags Center. Performing arts center.]

■ **Majestic (Five Flags)**
405 Main Street
Rapp and Rapp
1910

The Majestic's brick facade and Beaux Arts interior.

■ ■ ■ ■ ■ ■   KANSAS   ■ ■ ■ ■ ■ ■

## EMPORIA

**■ Fox (Granada)**
809 Commercial Street
Boller Brothers
1929

The main face of this theater, which opened as the Granada, is true to its name, recalling in stucco the Spanish Colonial Revival period. Finial-topped towers rise at either end of the tile roof. Just above the marquee, four slender arched windows are set within the facade, divided by vulture-capital columns. A corbeled parapet above the windows incorporates a set of five terra cotta clown figurines. A fire in 1959 destroyed the original Robert Morton pipe organ, in addition to the proscenium ornamentation and stage equipment. Remaining plaster ornament in the lobby and auditorium has a Moorish flavor. Closed since 1982, the Fox may yet reopen as a performing arts center. [Privately owned. Closed.]

Terra cotta details on the Fox's exterior.

## KANSAS CITY

**■ Granada**
1015 Minnesota Avenue
Boller Brothers
1929

The blocky archwork and striped window awnings originally decorating the Granada's exterior reflected a popular Boller Brothers interpretation of Southwest Spanish Colonial Revival architecture. The auditorium is a Spanish villa atmospheric treatment, with a mock-stone bridge for a proscenium arch. The plaster au-

The Granada during its first year of operation.

The Granada's Spanish atmospheric interior, styled by the Boller Brothers.

ditorium walls, roughened to resemble stonework, continue the courtyard illusion around the 1,040 seats of the main floor and balcony. Shuttered in 1970, the theater was reopened in 1986 by a civic group, which also installed a vintage 1931 Barton pipe organ to replace the lost Robert Morton original. [Granada Theatre Historical Society. Performing arts center.]

## WICHITA

The Orpheum is the oldest surviving Eberson theater to show any traces of his popular atmospheric style. Ornamental curved sounding boards above the front of the house give way to a plaster "sky" above the balcony, with a wooden trellis spanning the rear of the auditorium. The Spanish-courtyard decorative scheme of the auditorium is continued in the original trompe l'oeil asbestos curtain. Equally noteworthy are the fancy ceiling and pinwheel-patterned tile floor of the carriage lobby. Eberson's "Garden of Andalusia" serves as the fulcrum of his career, balancing elements seen earlier in opera house designs such as his Austin Majestic (1915) and a few decorative touches destined to play a major role in his later courtyard atmospheric designs. NR. [Orpheum Center for the Performing Arts. Stage shows.]

■ **Orpheum**
200 North Broadway
John Eberson
1922

Box office lobby in the Orpheum.

■ ■ ■ ■ ■ ■   MICHIGAN   ■ ■ ■ ■ ■ ■

### ANN ARBOR

■ **Michigan**
601 East Liberty Street
Maurice H. Finkel
1928

The Michigan, with its brick and stone Romanesque Revival exterior, was built as the Ann Arbor flagship for the W. S. Butterfield theater chain. The stately barrel-vaulted lobby features a semicircular balcony promenade atop a split grand staircase. The auditorium was re-painted in the late 1970s in maize and blue, the school colors of the nearby University of Michigan.

The Michigan Community Theater Foundation leased the theater in 1979 for operation as a performing arts center. By 1982 the nonprofit organization had convinced Ann Arbor voters to buy and restore the theater. Restoration work has included regilding auditorium and lobby decorations, re-covering the Michigan's 1,800 seats and returning the original bronze drinking fountain, long in storage, to its place in the grand lobby. The theater was rededicated in January 1987 after a $5 million invest-ment. The original Wurlitzer pipe organ again operates on all three manuals. NR. [City of Ann Arbor. Movies and stage shows.]

Left: The Michigan's marquee advertising air conditioning.
Right: Grand foyer in 1981.

### DETROIT

■ **Fisher**
Grand Boulevard and
Second Avenue
Graven and Mayger
1928

From an impossibly wonderful Mayan temple movie house, its auditorium walls coated with ancient symbols and its lobby filled with mock-primitive furnishings, the Fisher was transformed into a very modern concert hall in the 1960s. Sound baffles replaced the auditorium stencilwork. Gone is the Temple-of-Doom exoticism, and now the Fisher more closely resembles such monuments to midcentury American culture as the Kennedy Center for the Performing Arts in Washington, D.C. [Michigan Opera Company. Concerts.]

The Fisher's Mayan-turned-modern lobby and entrance hall.

Theater historian Ben Hall tagged this theater and its twin Fox (1929) in St. Louis as "Siamese-Byzantine" temples. Attending a show at the Fox, with its exotic atmosphere of the Near and Far East, is like going to the circus. Eagles, monkeys and Chinese lions cavort in plaster along the temple fronts forming the side walls of the auditorium. A golden elephant's head dominates the proscenium arch. A great plaster tent forms the ceiling, with a huge illuminated stained-glass globe hanging at its center. The Fox had the rare good fortune to house an organ in its grand lobby to supplement the mighty four-manual Wurlitzer in the orchestra pit. The lobby model is a three-manual Moller, its presence explaining the fake pipes rendered in plaster above the theater entry. The actual organ chambers are two stories higher up the foyer

■ **Fox**
2211 Woodward Avenue
C. Howard Crane
1928

Views of Detroit's Fox toward and from the stage.

walls. The 5,000-seat auditorium of the Fox has not been substantially altered through more than 60 years of movies, vaudeville and, more recently, music concerts. NR. [Privately owned. Movies and stage shows.]

■ **Grand Circus (Capitol)**
Grand Circus and Broadway
C. Howard Crane
1922

Engaged Corinthian columns of terra cotta grace the exterior of the office building containing the former Capitol, now known as the Grand Circus. This theater was originally the flagship of the midwestern chain of Kinskey theaters. Crane gave the Capitol a small outer lobby that opens into a three-story grand foyer, designed to curve around the rear of the auditorium. A mezzanine bridge above this space is one of the most elegant spaces ever created by Crane. Its low ceiling is studded with illuminated glass-paneled octagons that are flush with the ceiling. This motif is carried over inside the auditorium on the underside of the balcony and, again, in the cove-lighted octagons curving above the proscenium. NR district. [Privately owned. Concerts.]

■ **Grand Riviera**
9222 Grand River Avenue
John Eberson
1924

This early atmospheric design was meant to suggest an Italian garden setting, with a serene mix of small temples and classical statuary in quiet repose. The atmospheric "sky" extended only halfway above the balcony, at which point a great pergola spanned the space, complete with hanging vines. Cloud projection machinery was concealed behind a small rounded shrine along the left side wall. The dominant feature of the exterior was a hexagonal tower designed to house the grand lobby rotunda. The interior was illuminated in part by the high arched windows encircling the top of the rotunda, at least on the street side; the window openings on the auditorium side held mirrors. The initial success of the 2,800-seat Grand Riviera prompted construction just down the street of a smaller Eberson atmospheric design, the Riviera Annex (1927), which was torn down for parking in 1949. The older theater, now known simply as the Riviera, has been shuttered and deteriorating for years. NR. [Privately owned. Closed.]

Exterior and interior of the Grand Riviera, one of the first of Eberson's atmospheric designs.

Originally known as the State, this theater owes its current name to its location in the downtown Palms Building. This early Crane design includes some Empire-style decorative patterning. The coffered divisions of the auditorium ceiling are offset by the attractive vaulting above the inner foyer. The last movie at the Palms-State was shown in 1981. Restoration of the interior begain in 1986. NR. [Privately owned. Concerts.]

■ **Palms-State**
2111 Woodward Avenue
C. Howard Crane
1921

Foyer of the Palms-State, one of Crane's early works.

## FLINT

■ **Capitol**
140 East Second Street
John Eberson
1928

The exterior decorations of the theater and the surrounding office block were referred to in original publicity material as "15th-century Hispano-Italian style." The auditorium has a simple Roman-courtyard atmospheric design, one of several Eberson created for Col. Walter S. Butterfield's theater chain around the state. The Capitol has seen infrequent use in recent years. NR. [Privately owned. Concerts.]

## JACKSON

■ **Michigan**
124 North Mechanic Street
Maurice H. Finkel
1930

Built for the Butterfield chain, the Michigan has an interior treatment caught somewhere between Renaissance and Art Deco. The lower walls of the auditorium are formed by baroque and Renaissance compositions in plaster, contrasting with the more innovative orange and green plasterwork spanning the hall. The narrow entry facade is slightly purer in its origins, with its Moorish–Spanish colonial terra cotta tower. The Michigan's original Barton pipe organ remains in place. NR. [Michigan Theater Preservation Association. Performing arts center.]

Above: The Michigan's interior. Right: Moorish-style exterior of the State.

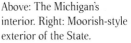

## KALAMAZOO

■ **State**
404 South Burdick Street
John Eberson
1927

The design of the State shows Eberson in full mastery of the atmospheric style he originated in the Majestic (1923, demolished) in Houston. The auditorium of the State is like a romantically illuminated Spanish courtyard open

The State's Spanish castle courtyard.

to the sparkling electric constellations of a blue plaster "sky." Plaster Renaissance-like statues fill every niche; one figure is even positioned on the short balcony atop the rampart that spans the proscenium opening. Patterned terra cotta trim gives the brickwork exterior a Moorish flavor. Past the wrought-iron box office, termed "quaint" in the opening program notes, is the tile-floored lobby done in the style of a small Spanish patio. Although the theater was closed in 1981, its fancy asbestos curtain and the original Barton organ remain intact. [Butterfield Theaters. Closed.]

## MUSKEGON

The former Michigan and its surrounding office block are encased in ornamental terra cotta. The Spanish colonial design of the auditorium is particularly elaborate in the arched bays of the side walls. Baroque ornamentation frames these bays enclosing draped niches filled with classical figures, set above the exit doors. This 1,800-seat theater was adopted by the local community in the late 1970s to be reopened as a performance hall bearing its current name, the Frauenthal Center. [Muskegon County Community Foundation. Performing arts center.]

■ **Frauenthal Center (Michigan)**
407 West Western Avenue
1928

## ■ ■ ■ ■ ■ ■    MINNESOTA    ■ ■ ■ ■ ■ ■

## AUSTIN

The main facade of the Paramount was loosely modeled on Spanish and Italian baroque church architecture. A Spanish theme also rules the mock-adobe atmospheric interior, designed to resemble a small Spanish town. Built to showcase the new talking motion pictures, the 1,000-seat Paramount survived as a movie theater until 1975. The building was subsequently converted into a

■ **Paramount**
125 Fourth Avenue, N.E.
Ellerbe and Company
1929

nightclub, with the main-floor seats of the auditorium removed and a freestanding bar constructed in the center of the leveled area. NR. [Theater Night Club. Nightclub and bar.]

## LUVERNE

■ **Palace**
Main Street and
Freeman Avenue
W. E. E. Greene
1915

A simple Classical Revival exterior yields to Art Nouveau murals and drapery inside the Palace. The original owner, Herman Jockims, added a pipe organ to his downtown theater in 1926, installing Vitaphone equipment two years later for the new "talkies." Otherwise, little has changed inside this early movie theater. NR. [Privately owned. Movies.]

The Palace, an early picture theater.

## MINNEAPOLIS

■ **Hollywood**
2815 Johnson Street, N.E.
Liebenberg and Kaplan
1935

This neighborhood movie house has the sweeping lines of Moderne architecture. Simply patterned sandstone panels sheathe the exterior. Metallic paint accents the patterned tile of the auditorium. Other Minneapolis neighborhood theaters designed by Liebenberg and Kaplan include the Varsity (1938) and the Uptown (1939). [Privately owned. Movies.]

■ **State**
805 Hennepin Avenue
J. E. O. Pridmore
1921

The last intact picture palace in the downtown area, the State sports an exuberantly ornamented, glazed white terra cotta facade. The dominant style, inside and out, is Italian Renaissance. After the 1976 sale of the 2,400-seat theater to the Jesus People Church, classical statues of the theatrical muses atop the ornate organ screens were

The State's auditorium and orchestra pit in the 1920s.

draped for modesty. A half dozen crystal chandeliers were left suspended above the balcony seating.

A controversy arose in mid-1986 when new owners announced plans to dismantle the interior and reuse some of the ornament to decorate a 450-seat recital hall in a planned 32-story tower. One local preservationist likened the proposal to performing a cut-and-paste reduction of the *Mona Lisa* to 8-by-10 size. Following a threatened lawsuit, the developer — with the support of the mayor and city council — found that the theater could be accommodated in the new building. Left to be determined was whether to leave the State unaltered for road shows or shrink it for music, dance, theater and films sponsored by local groups. [The Palmer Group. Closed.]

Recent view of the State's auditorium.

Liebenberg and Kaplan were known primarily for their 1930s Moderne theaters built in the neighborhoods of Minneapolis and across the Dakotas. This early design, opened as the Granada, followed a Spanish-Churrigueresque theme inside and out. The heavily ornamented sandstone veneer of the street facade was altered somewhat in 1966, when the tall vertical sign was removed. Although interior alterations stripped the lobby of its 1927 decor, the romantic Spanish-courtyard atmospheric auditorium was left largely untouched. [Cinema Land. Movies.]

■ **Suburban World (Granada)**
3022 Hennepin Avenue
Liebenberg and Kaplan
1927

The original Granada auditorium ringed with plants.

## ROCHESTER

The Chateau features a fascinating one-of-a-kind variation on the atmospheric style pioneered by John Eberson. The simulated side wall architecture is a crenellated medieval castle, complete with turrets, battlements and a fake stonework bridge for a proscenium arch. The exterior is unique, too, with zigzag-patterned brickwork and a trio of illuminated sunbursts added to the marquee.

■ **Chateau (Chateau Dodge)**
15 First Street, S.W.
Ellerbe and Company
1927

The Chateau, Rochester. Auditorium with crenellated walls and sun-ray motif on the marquee.

Since the recent closing of the Chauteau, at least one proposal has been made to convert the theater space into a shopping mall. NR. [Minnesota Amusement Company. Closed.]

## ST. PAUL

■ **Grandview**
1830 Grand Avenue
Myrtus A. Wright
1933

Glass bricks and Vitrolite panels, both popular in Moderne designs, give added character to the banded brickwork exterior of this neighborhood movie house. The interior of the Grandview was altered significantly in 1973 when the theater's balcony (added in 1937) was walled off as a second auditorium. The theater takes its name from its location, one-half block west of the intersection of Grand and Fairview avenues. [Privately owned. Movies — twin.]

■ **Highland**
760 South Cleveland Avenue
Myrtus A. Wright
1939

The ziggurat form of the Highland's primary facade strangely calls to mind Prairie School architecture — as if Frank Lloyd Wright had a hand in the Moderne design. The materials and overall appearance share a great deal with the architect's earlier Grandview (1933). [Privately owned. Movies — twin.]

■ **World (Shubert)**
488–94 North Wabasha
Street
Marshall and Fox
1910

Certainly not the fanciest theater in the state, the World has become nationally famous as the home base of the "Prairie Home Companion" radio show. Opened as the Sam S. Shubert, the old vaudeville palace was renamed the World in 1933. The remodeling that prompted the name change included sealing the second balcony with a false ceiling. A 1985 rehabilitation of the Beaux Arts interior was carried out in part from the proceeds of the sale of shirts with the slogan, "I Saved the World." Preservationists hope that Garrison Keillor's departure from the show in 1987 will not be the end of the World. [Minnesota Public Radio. Broadcasts.]

The World, saved to host "Prairie Home Companion."

■ ■ ■ ■ ■ ■    MISSOURI    ■ ■ ■ ■ ■ ■

### COLUMBIA

The monumental facade planned for the Missouri Theater Building was ultimately reduced to a modest neoclassical entryway, with concrete urns topping a low parapet of terra cotta. The Missouri's 1,000-seat auditorium received a more developed ornamental treatment, categorized locally as "Louis XV Rococo." The elegant side bays and baroque-style organ screens are constructed primarily of plaster, with a few elements of solid walnut. Stained-glass soffit lighting was included in the final interior design.

One Missouri state official has observed that in 1967 the exterior was "transmogrified," giving this downtown theater an appearance more common for shopping center multicinemas of the period. A large concave panel of concrete, decorated with the theater name in fancy script lettering, has four matching plain-faced panels above the adjoining shops to the south. Despite the drastic exterior changes, the interior remains largely intact. NR. [Commonwealth Theaters. Movies.]

■ **Missouri**
201–15 South Ninth Street
Boller Brothers
1928

### KANSAS CITY

The Midland shows Lamb at the height of his picture palace career. Only his design for the San Francisco Fox (1929, demolished) exceeded the powerful scale and wealth of detail to be found here. Legend has it that this 4,000-seat showplace, opened as Loew's Midland, was the personal favorite of Marcus Loew, owner of the vast theater empire. On entering the Midland, patrons may ascend a carpeted marble staircase to a lavishly appointed promenade, designed like a Roman loggia. Those who proceed instead to the grand lobby find a

■ **Midland**
1228–34 Main Street
Thomas W. Lamb
1927

Grand staircase at the Midland.

Marquee of the Midland, Kansas City.

■ **Plaza**
Country Club Plaza
Boller Brothers
1929

Exterior and marquee of the Plaza.

second grand staircase on the left. Above walls of mahogany and a row of plasterwork cherubs and cartouches, the mural-covered vaults are illuminated by a pair of original Czechoslovakian crystal chandeliers. Lamb would later use this masterful lobby layout, with an East Indian motif, for Loew's State (1928, now the Landmark) in Syracuse, N.Y. In the balanced composition of its baroque and rococo elements, the Midland's auditorium possesses a beauty unsurpassed in all of Lamb's work. The draped plaster organ screens have a deep brown tone suggesting fine woodcarvings. The proscenium composition rises to a crescendo, with a great plaster crown, which in turn supports a fully modeled armor helmet. The $4.5 million price tag for the Midland included construction of a basement ladies' smoking lounge from salvaged portions of the Oriental Room in the demolished New York town house of William K. Vanderbilt.

Despite a temporary conversion into a bowling alley in 1961, as well as partitioning carried out for multiple movie screenings, the palatial decor of the Midland has survived largely intact. In 1977, just one month shy of its 50th anniversary, the theater was designated a National Historic Landmark. NR. [American Multi-Cinemas. Movies.]

The Plaza sits along the edge of Country Club Plaza, known internationally as one of the first planned shopping centers. The Boller Brothers used this setting to create one of their finest theater designs. The principal facade of the Plaza is entirely in keeping with the Spanish-style tile-covered towers and sculpture-laden fountains of the surrounding retail center. A two-tiered bell tower is perched above the richly detailed cornice. The lobby has the feeling of a Spanish patio visited in the cool evening twilight. The similarly styled auditorium has been divided in half with minimal disruption of the decorative effects. [J. C. Nichols Company. Movies — twin.]

The Renaissance Revival exterior of the Uptown Building, with its lantern-topped corner dome, was built in
1926 according to the plans of local architect Robert
Gornall. The Universal Film Company brought in movie
palace architect Eberson a year later to produce an
auditorium with his popular Italian-garden atmospheric
treatment. A low ceiling kept Eberson from reaching his
usual flamboyant heights in the side walls of the
auditorium. Still, the capacity crowd at the Uptown's
1928 unveiling was more attracted by Eberson's stars-
and-clouds effects than by the less-than-stellar opening
picture, *The Irresistible Lover.* A 1973 conversion into the
Palace Dinner Playhouse replaced the main-floor seats
with terraced seating levels but left Eberson's side wall
creations and fake shrubbery intact. NR. [Uptown Office
and Theater Building Investors. Cabaret.]

■ **Uptown**
3700 Broadway
John Eberson
1928

The Uptown's exterior.

### ST. JOSEPH

Architect Robert Boller, working with his older brother,
Carl, designed this 1,400-seat Persian picture palace for
his hometown of St. Joseph. Portions of the striking
exterior, executed in polychrome terra cotta, were removed in 1960, but the remaining decorative features
convey the flavor of the original appearance. The carriage
lobby of the Missouri is a fantasy of Near Eastern
tilework. The enclosed spaces are equally exotic in their
origins. The ruins of Persepolis served as the basis for the
decoration of the walls alongside the balcony. The overall
effect of the auditorium is of sitting beneath a canvas tent,
outdoors in some faraway desert kingdom. Enhancing
the illusion are a few decorative motifs borrowed from
Babylonian and Assyrian originals. NR. [Town Hall
Center. Performing arts center.]

■ **Missouri**
Edmond and South
Eighth Streets
Boller Brothers
1927

### ST. LOUIS

In their design for the Ambassador, the Rapp brothers
first began to experiment with the new Art Deco style.
The grand lobby of the Ambassador was decorated in a
pure French baroque never bettered by any picture palace
architect, along the lines of the former Palace (1926) in
Chicago, also by Rapp and Rapp. Inside the auditorium,

■ **Ambassador**
411 North Seventh Street
Rapp and Rapp
1926

The Ambassador, St. Louis.
Auditorium stage and lobby
staircase.

familiar baroque elements were modified by a flattening
and compression of the decorations in a manner that
foretold the Rapps' later Renaissance–Art Deco hybrid
designs.

The continued survival of the Ambassador is now in
doubt. In 1986 plans were announced to gut the 3,000-
seat auditorium and build a 350-car garage within the
shell. Another Rapp and Rapp picture palace, the
Michigan (1926) in Detroit, was similarly disemboweled
in the 1970s. Discussion continues about the Ambassador's fate. Will it become a parking lot? Will it be
returned to theatrical uses? Or might it be converted into
a condominium apartment complex? NR. [Ambassador
Building. Closed.]

■ **American (Orpheum)**
416 North Ninth Street
G. Albert Lansburgh
1917

Lansburgh designed this French Renaissance showplace
for the Orpheum vaudeville circuit. A vaulted auditorium
space encloses several balcony levels, with tiered opera
boxes stepping down either side. The Beaux Arts

stonework exterior was fairly ornate for its day, with classically modeled figures sculpted by artist Leo Lentelli. After several decades as a movie theater, the American returned to use as a playhouse in the mid-1970s. NR. [Privately owned. Playhouse.]

A virtual twin of the deteriorating Fox (1928) in Detroit, the so-called "Fabulous Fox" of St. Louis survived a near-fatal closing in 1978 to rise again in all its exotic Siamese glory six years later. In marked contrast to its Detroit sibling, this Fox has a beautiful baroque terra cotta street facade to complement the unceasing display of decorative magic within. The grand lobby is a towering space, its encircling colonnade topped by capitals of golden vultures. A staircase, flanked by seated lions with flashing electric eyes, rises to a landing furnished with four high-backed red velvet throne chairs, each with armrests in the form of camels. Dozens of monkeys and elephants decorate the walls of the inner lobby and promenades. Passing through lobby doors designed to replicate Burmese shrine doors, patrons approach the imposing 4,000-seat auditorium. It was described in typically florid newspaper accounts of 1929:

The ceiling is swathed in Indian fabrics draped circularly from the center to the sides, while the canopied dome of the theatre is studded with brilliant stones. Suspended from the center is a massive chandelier, a monstrous globe 12 feet in diameter and 34 feet in circumference. It is fashioned of aluminum, wrought iron, and gold leaf and is illuminated by 20,100 watts of electrical current.

In fact, the globe was even larger than reported, measuring more than 41 feet around.

■ **Fox**
527 North Grand Boulevard
C. Howard Crane
1929

Exterior of the "Fabulous Fox" in 1929 and the auditorium, a twin of Detroit's Fox.

Clockwise from left: The Fox's lion-lined entry hall, the central lobby entrance, deities along the auditorium walls and "The Spirit of St. Louis" in the lobby.

After decades as the premier showplace in town, the Fox began to slide downhill in the late 1960s, apparently doomed after vandals damaged the interior in 1979. Fortunately for the Fox, a group of local investors could still see the beauty of the theater despite the darkness and destruction. Through careful repair work and the infusion of more than $2 million, the Fox was brought back to life. The original Wurlitzer organ was also resurrected, largely through volunteer efforts. Today, gold-plastered "grim warriors," brandishing their scimitars on either side of the grand staircase landing, once again survey full houses at the Fox. NR. [Fox Associates. Stage shows, concerts and classic films.]

The old Loew's St. Louis might have faded away, remembered only as a middling Rapp and Rapp design, if the St. Louis Symphony had not decided to take up residence here. This decision is a pioneering event in the conversion of movie palaces into concert halls. Architecture critic Ada Louise Huxtable called the 1968 reclamation an "intelligent re-use of an old structure that was, and is, a stagily theatrical setting." The original decor — Huxtable called it "Silver Screen Versailles" — was largely painted over in the course of the conversion. The new color scheme shows golden and crimson highlights against a backdrop of cream white. Still, the essence of the motion picture palace survives in this successfully renovated orchestra hall. [St. Louis Symphony. Concerts.]

■ **Powell Hall**
**(Loew's St. Louis)**
718 North Grand Boulevard
Rapp and Rapp
1925

Powell Hall's auditorium and lobby.

## SPRINGFIELD

The Landers was designed as a playhouse by Carl Boller, an architect who would later rule the theater-designing business in the Southwest and Plains states, in conjunction with his younger brother, Robert. The street facade is a particularly elegant Beaux Arts composition, perfectly balanced in its ornamentation. The 830-seat auditorium has the flavor of a late Victorian opera house, with a full complement of side boxes. Light globes line the arches looping overhead at the front of the house.

A wintertime fire in 1920 gutted the stage area, but the remainder of the theater was spared by the asbestos curtain. The Bollers were called to assist in repairing the damage in 1921. A new marquee was added in the course of a general conversion for movie showings. The Landers, like many theaters in the South, originally restricted blacks to the upper balcony. This policy reportedly was discontinued after the 1921 renovations, when the off-street box office and a back stairway to the second balcony "For Negroes" were removed. NR. [Springfield Little Theatre. Stage shows.]

■ **Landers**
311 East Walnut Street
Boller Brothers
1909

■ ■ ■ ■ ■   NEBRASKA   ■ ■ ■ ■ ■

### HASTINGS

■ **Rivoli**
532 West Second Street
1927

After fire destroyed the downtown Princess in 1926, a group of local promoters decided that their new Rivoli would not suffer this fate. The theater shares its fire-resistant concrete and masonry walls with the adjoining Carter Hotel. Opening one year after the Princess fire, the Rivoli offered a combination of vaudeville and motion pictures. Equipment was added in 1929 for sound pictures, with movies remaining the main attraction until the theater closed in 1984.

Although still shuttered, the 860-seat auditorium is in good condition, with elements of the original modified Palladian decorative treatment visible along the walls and ceiling. The lobbies and lounges of the Rivoli have light fixtures made of copper and frosted glass, as well as painted floral designs dating from an Art Deco remodeling in 1939. The marquee hanging from the brick exterior is the Rivoli's third, having replaced the Art Deco version in the 1950s. A nonprofit citizens group, Rivoli Performing Arts, Inc., would like to reproduce the original marquee as part of its plan to adapt the theater as a performing arts center. [Privately owned. Closed.]

### NORFOLK

■ **Granada**
110 South Fifth Street
Watson and McCracken
1927

A newspaper headline from 1927 summarized the character of this new theater: "Interior of Granada Gives Patron Picture of Spanish Patio." The atmospheric effects of the Granada were reported to be on a par with those at the new Riviera (1927) in Omaha by master palace architect John Eberson. Baroque castle facades climbed to the blue plaster "sky," enclosing the Granada auditorium, which seated more than 1,100 patrons. The exterior is more restrained, with just a few terra cotta details along the brick facades. The Spanish mood was broken only once, by what the newspapers called "an English Gothic vestibule." The Granada came to national attention briefly in 1981 when former usher Johnny Carson paid the theater a visit during the taping of his TV special, "Johnny Goes Home." Closed in 1977 because of a dispute over liability for a leaky roof, the Granada bounced back to life the year after Carson's return. [Privately owned. Stage shows.]

### NORTH PLATTE

■ **Fox**
301 East Fifth Street
Beck and Henninger
1929

Former Nebraska Gov. Keith Neville joined with builder Alex Beck to build this Plains State outpost of the Fox West Coast theater chain. A boxy exterior is brightened considerably by the crisscross patterns of the inset brick bays, each topped by a terra cotta grotesque. Additional terra cotta ornament caps the entry bay and forms a ruffled cornice. The fan-shaped auditorium received a more elaborate Spanish–Moorish Revival treatment. A touch of local color was added in the painted house

curtain, which depicts travelers setting up camp beside their covered wagons along the route west to the Oregon Territory. In 1981 Keith Neville's four daughters deeded the 700-seat Fox to a local group, which currently operates the theater as the Neville Center for the Performing Arts. NR. [North Platte Community Playhouse. Performing arts center.]

The Fox's painted curtain and surviving vertical sign.

## OMAHA

Built as the Riviera but quickly renamed the Paramount, this theater benefits from one of the most elaborate Moorish exterior treatments among all Eberson designs. Only the Loew's (1928, now the Carpenter Center) in Richmond, Va., can rival the Astro (as it is currently known) in its exotic terra cotta tracery. Tiered loggias grace the facade above a marquee that wraps around the corner entry tower. The crowning balustrades of this tower enclose the largest of three metallic domes. Construction figures for the theater demonstrate the efforts that went into providing both safety and entertainment in the motion picture palaces of the 1920s. A solid foundation was created using 353 concrete piles, each encased in steel tubing and driven to a depth of 57 feet. Erecting the theater required 750 tons of steel; lighting it took 50,000 light bulbs. The courtyard atmospheric interior, labeled Hispano-Italian by Eberson, did temporary duty as a bowling alley, but returned to movie showings before closing in the 1980s. NR. [Privately owned. Closed.]

■ **Astro
(Riviera/Paramount)**
2001 Farnam Street
John Eberson
1927

The Astro in the 1930s, then known as the Paramount.

■ **Orpheum**
407 South 16th Street
Rapp and Rapp
1927

The Rapp brothers designed this combination vaudeville and motion picture house with a simplified French baroque treatment similar to their earlier Orpheum circuit designs. For decorative effect they relied heavily on crystal chandeliers and wall sconces, with ornately framed mirrors along the walls of both the grand foyer and the theater balcony. The entry hall of the Orpheum tunnels through the 17-story City National Bank Building (1910, Holabird and Roche), the first skyscraper in Omaha. The Orpheum was among the earliest theater conversion projects, embarking in 1975 on a new career as a performing arts center and principal home of the Omaha Symphony Orchestra. The house was redraped in rich brocades and repainted in the original ivory and gold. A new sound baffle, positioned directly beneath the proscenium arch, was painted in a pattern roughly equivalent to Rapp and Rapp's Versailles-inspired decorative scheme. The Orpheum's Wurlitzer has been restored for occasional organ concerts. NR. [City of Omaha. Performing arts center.]

Auditorium of Omaha's
Orpheum.

■ ■ ■ ■ ■   NORTH DAKOTA   ■ ■ ■ ■ ■

### FARGO

■ **Fargo**
314 North Broadway
Buechner and Orth;
Liebenberg and Kaplan
1926, 1937

One of the most startlingly original Moderne auditorium spaces ever built is concealed by the classical exterior of the Fargo. The street facade presents a Renaissance Revival appearance, executed in brick and accented by stone trim. The auditorium was rebuilt in 1936, by Jack Liebenberg of the Minneapolis firm of Liebenberg and Kaplan, in keeping with the forward-looking designs of the period. Just before the theater's reopening in 1937, Liebenberg told the *Fargo Forum* of his goal in the makeover: to immerse "an architectural ogre of the ancient hierarchy of the baroque [in a] fountain of architectural youth, commonly called international or modern style." Liebenberg's experiment is probably unmatched in the United States for its boldly sweeping lines, having more in common with the Odeon theaters of Great Britain. The auditorium walls are striped with blue

The Fargo after its Moderne remodeling in 1936.

neon, each stripe punctuated at its balcony end by a trio of golden light cones. The multilayered curves of the ceiling form the architectural tour de force of the Fargo, each curve originating in the blocky geometric element that crowns the picture-frame proscenium arch. Lieben-berg's flamboyant lobby design was altered in the 1950s to a relatively characterless state.

Through all the changes, the Fargo has played a major role in the cultural life of the city. A central figure was the organist, the Incomparable Hildegarde, who accom-panied silent films in the late 1920s and spent 28 years playing for WDAY radio's live broadcasts from the Fargo stage. Hildegarde officially retired only in 1976, with a tribute from the Red River Chapter of the American Theatre Organ Society. This group has restored the original Wurlitzer built especially for the Fargo in 1926 by the Rudolph Wurlitzer Pipe Organ Company in North Tonawanda, N.Y. The theater remains in use with a mix of classic film revivals, organ concerts and special events. NR. [Fargo Theater Management Corporation. Perform-ing arts center.]

## MARMARTH

A rare timber-framed theater just a few steps removed from its nickelodeon predecessors, the Mystic survives in this once-prosperous Badlands boomtown. The chief attractions of the stuccoed streetfront are the stud-lighted archivolt and the attached decorative cornice of painted metal. Inside the recessed entry, a ticket booth boasting the last original globe light fixture projects out from between the doors to the theater. Wooden wainscoting and patterned fabrics cover the interior walls. Although its population now numbers fewer than 300 (less than a quarter of its 1910 census total), the Missouri River town of Marmarth pulled together to renovate the 200-seat Mystic as a 1976 Bicentennial project. NR. [Marmarth Historical Society. Entertainment center and town meet-ing hall.]

■ **Mystic (Marmarth)**
Main Street
Guy Johnson
1914

■ ■ ■ ■ ■ ■   OHIO   ■ ■ ■ ■ ■ ■

### AKRON

■ **Civic (Loew's Akron)**
182 South Main Street
John Eberson
1929

At a cost of just over $2 million, Eberson provided master showman Marcus Loew with one of his finest atmospheric designs in the Civic. Eberson's auditorium side walls are especially notable, with antiqued polychrome plasterwork that is both powerfully massed and minutely detailed. The crowning beauty of the space is a statue-filled niche at the center of the vine-draped proscenium arch. Initially, Eberson had to face some site-related problems that contributed to the unusual layout of this theater. Principal access to the Civic is by way of a one-lot-wide entry that Eberson clad with stonework decorated in the style of the Italian Renaissance. An extremely long and narrow hallway, leading from the main entry to the grand foyer, is actually a bridge that spans the Ohio Canal on stilts of poured concrete. Once across the canal there is a sudden explosion of space. Within the foyer Eberson has re-created a great Moorish banquet hall, with tasseled wrought-iron chandeliers, Spanish tapestries and spectacular plaster ornamentation. Hanging beneath an archway on the left of the grand staircase to the balcony is a stuffed parrot, considered an Eberson trademark. The Moorish theme of the foyer was continued throughout the lounges to the uppermost of the antiques-lined lobbies.

The theater and its three-manual Wurlitzer organ were rescued in 1965 by the local Jaycee Foundation, after having been threatened with destruction for parking space. NR. [Community Hall Foundation. Performing arts center.]

The Civic's stately auditorium and its grand foyer.

### BELLEFONTAINE

■ **Holland**
127 East Columbus Avenue
Peter Hulsken
1931

The atmospheric styling of the Holland is a delightfully novel adaptation of the format popularized by movie palace architect John Eberson. The Dutch theme is readily apparent from the start in the stepped gabling of the brickwork street facade. Royal lions and operable windmills are included among the faux architecture of

the auditorium side walls. These side wall constructs remain essentially intact despite the conversion of the 1,400-seat auditorium into four smaller viewing spaces. [Privately owned. Movies — quad.]

Dutch and Flemish side walls and stepped gables of the Holland.

## CANTON

Eberson adopted a particularly emphatic Churrigueresque style in the terra cotta–trimmed exterior and atmospheric garden interior of the Palace. The semihexagonal ticket booth received a Moorish treatment. A tall vertical sign rising above the cornice line has its own Churrigueresque ornament. A tile-floored outer lobby leads to the grand foyer, with its staircase to the balcony and doorways to the blue-domed auditorium. Somewhere amid all the plaster ornamentation is a panel decorated with the giraffe trademark of Tonseline, the sore-throat remedy of local businessman Harry H. Ink. Profits from this medicine enabled Ink to commission Eberson to design this theater. NR. [Canton Palace Theatre Association. Performing arts center.]

■ **Palace**
605 Market Avenue, North
John Eberson
1926

The Palace's walls, ringed with plants and flying birds.

CLEVELAND

■ **Allen**
1501 Euclid Avenue
Playhouse Square
C. Howard Crane
1921

In the 1920s a stretch of theaters along Euclid Avenue was dubbed Playhouse Square. This Pompeian picture palace now is the only unrestored theater in the Playhouse Square group, comprising the Ohio (1921), the State (1921), the Palace (1922) and the Allen, although it too has been reported as "restoration prone." The Allen's auditorium is contained within the eight-story Bulkley Building. Its Euclid Avenue entry originally featured a fanciful half-dome canopy marquee. Crane was said to have used the Villa Madonna near Rome as the model for his 45-foot-tall lobby rotunda. Both the rotunda floor and the entry hall were used in the early 1980s as a restaurant and bar. NR. [Playhouse Square Foundation. Planned performing arts center.]

■ **Capitol**
West 65th Street and
Detroit Avenue
Prack and Prack Associates
1920

The Capitol is the oldest surviving theater in Cleveland designed for motion pictures. Located in the Detroit Shoreway community, the 1,235-seat theater is built into the Gordon Arcade. This red brick three-story building housing a variety of shops and businesses is the focal point of redevelopment efforts in the neighborhood. The theater was redecorated in the 1930s, its classically ornamented walls covered with draperies and trimmed with Art Deco–style wooden moldings. Used only occasionally for foreign films and special events, the Capitol is due to be rehabilitated, in part with architectural elements salvaged from the old downtown Hippodrome (1907, demolished). [Friends of the Capitol Theatre. Movies.]

■ **Ohio**
1511 Euclid Avenue
Playhouse Square
Thomas W. Lamb
1921

The year was 1972, and three adjacent 50-year-old theaters in Playhouse Square were set to be replaced by what preservationist Diann Scarwelli ironically called "a grand parking lot." Instead, redevelopment got under way as the Junior League of Cleveland sponsored a drive to raise $25,000 to rescue the Ohio, the adjoining State (1921) and the Palace (1922). The Ohio was built as a playhouse, only to be absorbed into the Loew's movie theater chain the year after it opened. Lamb designed the theater with a supremely elegant grand lobby and an Adam-style auditorium. The auditorium decor was given a terraced Moderne look during its years as the Mayfair Casino nightclub in the mid-1930s. A fire in 1964 gutted the lobby and damaged the auditorium. Both spaces were fully renovated in 1982 to serve as the home of the Great Lakes Shakespeare Festival. NR. [Playhouse Square Foundation. Performing arts center.]

■ **Palace**
1615 Euclid Avenue
Playhouse Square
Rapp and Rapp
1922

The Palace was the most lavishly appointed and the last to open of the Playhouse Square theaters. Vaudeville king Edward F. Albee dedicated the theater to his partner, Benjamin Franklin Keith. The theater is entered at the base of the 21-story Keith Building, which was originally topped by the largest electrical sign yet built, advertising "B. F. Keith Vaudeville." Movies became part of the theatrical fare at the Palace in 1926. The theater shut down its movie showings in July 1969, the last to close of

Playhouse Square along
Cleveland's Euclid Avenue.
Top: The Allen by C. Howard
Crane. Center: The State by
Thomas W. Lamb. Below:
The Palace by Rapp and
Rapp.

Clustered theaters of the
Playhouse Square group. The
Allen, the Ohio and the State
all opened in 1921. Below:
The State's grand lobby in
the 1920s.

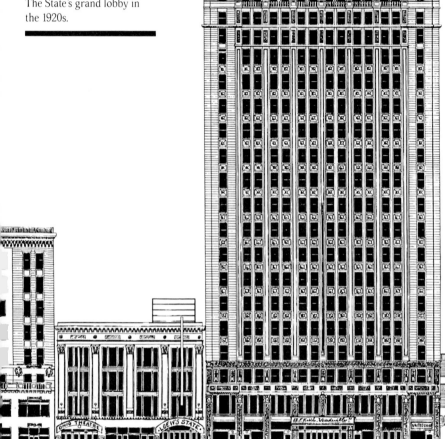

— OHIO THEATRE —      — LOEW'S STATE THEATRE —      B.F. KEITH PALACE THEATRE —

the Playhouse Square group. Rapp and Rapp decorated with crystal chandeliers and rich brocades along with true and faux marbre in the fancy Second Empire–style grand hall. The auditorium, with its elliptical ceiling dome, is a Palladian vision filled with more than 3,000 seats. A Cole Porter revue staged in 1973 in the grand hall helped draw the attention and funding necessary for the eventual rehabilitation of the entire theater. NR. [Playhouse Square Foundation. Stage shows and concerts.]

The State is the "middle child" of Playhouse Square. The theater was built well off Euclid Avenue, its only means of access provided by a tremendously long and narrow hallway wedged between the Ohio (1921) and the side of the Palace (1922), then still under construction. The ornate decorations lining the walls of the grand lobby serve to frame the colorful modernistic murals by James Daugherty. One of these panels, the *Spirit of Cinema America*, graced the cover of *Life* for an article on nostalgia in the 1970s. Cabaret performances were held in the lobby in 1973 during the initial effort to promote the rejuvenation of Playhouse Square. Prominent among the impressively restored areas of the State are the half dome above the semicircular mezzanine promenade at the back of the auditorium and the Adamesque organ screens. Preservation efforts culminated in a grand reopening of the State in 1984 as a stage for ballet, opera and live theater. [Playhouse Square Foundation. Performing arts center.]

■ **State**
1519 Euclid Avenue
Playhouse Square
Thomas W. Lamb
1921

## CLEVELAND AREA: SHAKER HEIGHTS

The Colony is among several Moderne designs built late in Eberson's career. The grand foyer of the theater has a broadly sweeping ceiling that appears to grow out of the walls of the stairway to the balcony. Aside from this decorative flourish, the Colony maintains a low architectural profile at the corner of the main square in Shaker Heights. [Privately owned. Movies.]

■ **Colony**
13116 Shaker Square
John Eberson
1937

## COLUMBUS

The Ohio has served as a showpiece for picture palace preservation since the citizens of Columbus rallied to save the former Loew's theater from demolition in 1969. Careful restoration of the interior, supervised by the Rambusch Company of New York, has been in progress since 1971, even as the Ohio has held a full schedule of events.

Lamb previewed his opulent designs for the Ohio in a 1928 issue of *Motion Picture News:* "The side walls are divided into bays . . . in the center of each is an elaborate shrine [and] rising above . . . there is one vast dome of gold culminating in a star formation of rich relief ornamentation." Lamb exulted over the "Mexican baroque" character of the auditorium sounding board, "a vast surface of deep red, completely covered with stars of innumerable sizes and shapes." He planned his overall

■ **Ohio**
29–39 East State Street
Thomas W. Lamb
1928

The Ohio, Columbus. The auditorium has been restored to its original appearance.

design to dazzle patrons with "the sumptuousness of Spain . . . and the intricacy [of] our modern art." Among the original features still visible in the restored auditorium are the glass Pegasuses of the central chandelier and the white-paneled Morton pipe organ. NR. [Columbus Association for the Performing Arts. Stage shows, movies and organ concerts.]

■ **Palace**
50 West Broad Street
Thomas W. Lamb;
C. Howard Crane
1926

The Adamesque Palace opened as a combination house featuring movies and Keith-Albee vaudeville acts. The 55-story American Insurance Union Citadel, which houses the Palace, was the work of Crane, Lamb's fellow palace architect. Now called the Leveque-Lincoln Tower, the building was hailed in 1926 as "the world's most beautiful skyscraper." Near the top of the Art Deco building Crane included a statuary group portraying a 26-foot-tall giant holding a pair of children in a protective grasp. The theater space, threatened with demolition in the 1970s, was reopened in 1979. Restoration of the interior has continued into the 1980s. NR. [Privately owned. Performing arts center.]

■ **Southern**
South High and
East Main Streets
Dauben, Krumm and Riebel,
with Menno G. Detweiler
1896

This late 19th-century showplace was built in conjunction with the Great Southern Hotel. The exterior bears a strong resemblance to earlier designs by Louis Sullivan. The Southern's auditorium shows a similar reliance on

The Southern's auditorium, with its Sullivanesque detailing.

Sullivan's interiors for the Schiller (1892, demolished) and the Auditorium (1889), both in Chicago. This is most apparent in the concentrically arched rings forming the proscenium sounding board. The Southern, which remained open until 1979, was the last operating movie theater in downtown Columbus. [Privately owned. Closed.]

## DAYTON

The exterior of the Classic, largely Georgian in character, is built of brick with stone trim. The theater was planned for use primarily by the black population of Dayton, which was restricted to back balcony seating in the other city theaters. Builders Anderson and Giles booked classical recitals to precede the feature films. The marble and plaster decorations of the interior are mostly gone. But belated recognition of the historical importance of the town's first black-owned theater has prompted efforts over the past decade to rehabilitate the Classic. [Privately owned. Planned cultural center.]

■ **Classic**
815 West Fifth Street
Carl Anderson and
Goodrich Giles
1927

## LIMA

Representatives of the state government rescued the shell of this one-time nickelodeon from its sad theatrical end as an "adult" movie theater. Offices now fill the gutted interior. The principal surviving elements from the original design are the buff-colored terra cotta cornice and the concentric arches over the new entry doors. [Bureau of Workers Compensation. State offices.]

■ **Sigma**
69 Public Square
c. 1910

The Sigma, before and after being converted for office use.

## LORAIN

This theater, billed as the "Temple of Amusement Dedicated to the Future Progress of Lorain," opened with the first motion picture shown in Lorain with the new Vitaphone sound device. The Renaissance Revival terra cotta exterior and palatial 2,000-seat interior included work by such 1920s craftsmen as the Venetian Art Mosaic Company, the Italian Fresco and Paint Company and the Cleveland Plastering Company. Features of note are the two-story Venetian Gothic grand lobby and the sunburst proscenium arch. NR. [Civic Center Committee. Planned performing arts center.]

■ **Palace**
Sixth Street and Broadway
1928

## MANSFIELD

■ **Ohio (Renaissance)**
136 Park Avenue West
1928

This theater, rechristened the Renaissance in 1985, was the beneficiary of a $2.25 million restoration, including the addition of a Wurlitzer organ. The principal design motifs are neoclassical on the broad terra cotta exterior, with baroque-inspired ornament decorating the 1,500-seat auditorium. NR. [Privately owned. Performing arts center.]

## MARION

■ **Palace**
272 West Center Street
John Eberson
1928

The palace boasts a Moorish exterior in brick and terra cotta to match the exotic Spanish castle appearance of the walls inside the atmospheric auditorium. Fabric doves and other stuffed birds still "fly" from roosts atop the organ screens and hover about the classical statuary lining the balcony walls. The source of the statuary was the Caproni Studios of Boston, known for providing similar life-size figures to schools of fine art. The Palace, built near the close of Eberson's atmospheric period, is unmatched for the romantic intimacy of its courtyard and auditorium. The theater came equipped with a Page pipe organ. Restoration efforts were spearheaded by a preservation group formed in 1976 and informally known as the Palace Guardians. NR. [Palace Cultural Arts Association. Performing arts center.]

Rehabilitated interior and exterior of the Palace.

## PORTSMOUTH

■ **Columbia**
832 Gallia Street
C. C. Taylor
1910

The Columbia started life as an arch-fronted nickelodeon with just over 300 seats. A 1921 expansion allowed for more than 1,000 paying customers. Aside from a few temporary closings for alterations or cleaning, the Columbia has enjoyed more than three-quarters of a century as a functioning movie house. The original Beaux Arts street facade is now covered by a false front, but the current owners hope to restore the 1910 appearance when funds permit. [Privately owned. Movies.]

### TOLEDO

A neoclassical temple forms the central entry facade of the State Theatre Building. The Adamesque style of the auditorium is most apparent in the broad ceiling dome with its inset cove. The city of Toledo purchased this property (part of the Old West End National Historic District) in 1982 for future development. NR district. [City of Toledo. For sale.]

■ **State**
2476 Collingwood Boulevard
1927

This playhouse opened on Christmas Eve 1895, advertised as the "Greatest Showplace West of the Alleghenies." The Louis XIV auditorium was remodeled for movies by Loew's in 1918. Rapp and Rapp performed a second set of alterations in 1942 in a floral Moderne motif flavored by the Orient. The theater is housed within a four-story office building. Originally the Valentine Building, this one-time city hall and hotel was renamed the Renaissance Building in 1971. [City of Toledo. For sale.]

■ **Valentine**
Adams and St. Clair Streets
Edward O. Fallis;
Rapp and Rapp
1895, 1942

### YOUNGSTOWN

The surviving founders of Warner Brothers Pictures commissioned Rapp and Rapp to design this theater as a hometown memorial to their parents and their late brother, Sam Warner. The 2,500-seat auditorium, opening off the lobby Hall of Mirrors, was designed with a French Renaissance theme strongly influenced by the prevalent Art Deco style. The Warner was among the first picture palaces to be rescued from urban blight for new use as a concert hall. The rechristened Powers Auditorium opened in 1969, with panels positioned throughout the auditorium side walls and ceiling to enhance the acoustics. NR. [Youngstown Symphony Society. Concerts.]

■ **Warner**
**(Powers Auditorium)**
266 West Federal Plaza
Rapp and Rapp
1931

■ ■ ■ ■ ■ ■    SOUTH DAKOTA    ■ ■ ■ ■ ■

### YANKTON

This turn-of-the-century opera house was the recipient of a wonderfully unique Art Deco facelift in 1941. The pattern of the ceramic tiles suggests a yellow Indian blanket, bordered in brown with red and blue highlights.

■ **Dakota**
328 Walnut Street
D. W. Rodgers, builder
c. 1900, 1941

The shiny silver marquee, with its pair of red neon "Dakota" signs, adds to the colorful effects. The Dakota closed its doors for good in the early 1980s. [Privately owned. Closed.]

■ ■ ■ ■ ■   WISCONSIN   ■ ■ ■ ■ ■

## BARABOO

■ **Al Ringling**
136 Fourth Avenue
Rapp and Rapp
1915

Albert C. Ringling, one of seven brothers, commissioned the two Rapp brothers to build this small-scale picture palace in the town that had served since 1907 as the winter home of the Ringling Brothers circus. Foremost among the magnificent spaces, decorated by the Rapps using French and Italian Renaissance models, is the auditorium. As a basis for their design the architects chose the 18th-century opera hall in the Palace of Versailles. Above the elliptical main floor of the Ringling auditorium, designed to seat 772, was a ring of 17 boxes with seating for an additional 102 patrons. The boxes, each illuminated by a hanging fixture, alternate with Corinthian columns finished in Dutch metal leaf. The boxes nearest the proscenium are more elaborately framed and are capped with sculpted ornament in an arched pediment. Al Ringling commissioned his own box at the back of the house, but by opening night he was too blind to see. He died shortly thereafter. The name "Al Ringling Theater" appears, carved in stone, directly beneath the fancy archway crowning the entry bay of the Beaux Arts exterior. The first of the lobby spaces encountered is the most special, an elliptical room decorated by pastel-shaded floral patterns under a cherub-filled ceiling mural. The high-relief frieze ringing the room was copied from an original by Luca della Robbia that once decorated the choir gallery of the old

Top: The Al Ringling's original exterior. Above and right: Facade of the theater today and the auditorium.

sacristy in the Cathedral at Florence. The side foyer directly above the entry lobby has a marble staircase cascading into it from the ladies' parlor, raised to one side.

Built to showcase live performances, the Ringling was remodeled for motion picture screenings in 1928. At that time the original Wurlitzer pipe organ was replaced by a three-manual Barton. Restored to its 1928 condition in the late 1970s, the Ringling still presents its asbestos fire curtain, entitled "Serenade au Petit Trianon," before each movie. NR. [Privately owned. Movies.]

## MADISON

The Capitol was built directly across State Street from the popular Orpheum (1927), designed by Rapp and Rapp the year before. The original decorative effects along the walls of the Capitol's lobby and auditorium were a blend of Spanish baroque and Art Deco. The mixture could be seen in the baroque arches around the edge of the auditorium ceiling, each archway outlined with boldly painted borders. Spanish noblemen coexist somewhat uneasily with Art Deco patterns on a baroque theme. These jarring effects were subdued substantially, however, in the course of a mid-1970s renovation carried out by Hardy Holzman Pfeiffer Associates. Renamed the Oscar Meyer for Madison's hot dog king, the 2,200-seat theater is now the centerpiece of the Madison Civic Center, an arts complex fashioned inside the theater lobby spaces and the former Montgomery Ward building next door. The Spanish cathedral front of the Capitol survived this transformation largely intact. Also in place is the original Barton organ, now restored. [City of Madison. Performing arts center.]

■ **Capitol (Oscar Meyer)**
211 State Street
Rapp and Rapp
1928

The Capitol and the Orpheum framing the view on Madison's State Street.

Yet another of the elegant French Renaissance vaudeville houses that Rapp and Rapp had been building for the Orpheum circuit since the early 1920s, this 2,200-seat theater was so successful in its first year that the

■ **Orpheum**
216 State Street
Rapp and Rapp
1927

architects returned for an encore, the Capitol (1928) across the street. The earlier Orpheum was more purebred in theme, however. Both theaters operated as combination houses, offering movies and stage shows. In 1969 the stage area of the Orpheum was cut off from the auditorium to house a second screening area, the Stage Door. [Privately owned. Movies.]

## MILWAUKEE

■ **Avalon**
2473 South Kinnickinnic Avenue
Russell B. Williamson
1929

The sole survivor of Milwaukee's three atmospheric theaters, the Avalon has a Spanish courtyard for its auditorium. The walls along the sides of the balcony stand out as vine-draped pergolas. Mock-wooden beam-work serves to shelter the Spanish patio lobby. Blending Art Deco and Egyptian Revival, the street facade is composed of brick and stone. The theater features regular performances by members of the Dairyland Theatre Organ Society at the console of a three-manual Wurlitzer. [Privately owned. Movies.]

■ **Oriental**
2230 North Farwell Avenue
Dick and Bauer
1927

Lobby and auditorium of the Oriental, with their Near and Far Eastern motifs.

The 2,100-seat Oriental is about as fine a neighborhood theater as one could want. Architect A. H. Bauer was probably within his rights to tell the *Milwaukee Sentinel* that it was "the most beautiful, the most artistic temple of Oriental art to be found in America," as long as the term "Oriental" is broadened to include East Indian. Ogee arches encircle the onion-domed minarets atop the glazed white terra cotta street facade. A tile-floored carriage lobby leads to a great hall, its colonnade reportedly modeled after Hindu pillars at Kankali, Mathura and Maravoti. The eight black porcelain lions guarding the stairs to the balcony were, according to Bauer, "symbolic of spiritual protection of the Buddhist temple." Indeed, continuing the temple motif are holy figures seated on each of the three principal bays along each wall of the auditorium. The Oriental remains in remarkably good condition, with fancy drapery and Barton organ intact, as a shrine for foreign and classic films. [Landmark Theatres. Movies.]

This combination vaudeville and movie theater fills the lower portion of the high-rise Empire Building. The interior decor is French baroque, its 2,500-seat auditorium covered by a recessed golden cove ceiling. Elaborate chandeliers hang like Christmas ornaments in front of the organ screens. [Privately owned. Stage shows.]

■ **Riverside**
116 Wisconsin Avenue
Kirschoff and Rose
1928

For all the changes of name and ownership, and despite having its auditorium sliced horizontally in two in 1973, this theater is in remarkably good shape. The decorative work of the former Warner has its own split personality. The three-story grand lobby is an Art Deco showstopper. Here, huge mirrors are set within radiating bands of silver-leaf plaster, fluted in a manner blending Renaissance and Moderne styling. The murals along the curved surfaces of the lobby staircase show ethereal maidens

■ **Warner (Centre/Grand)**
212 West Wisconsin Avenue
Rapp and Rapp
1931

artistically frozen between French palatial and French Deco styles.

The division of the 2,500-seat auditorium into upper and lower theaters left in the downstairs space the huge golden trophy urns at the bases of the former organ screens. Blue cove lights give this theater an underwater feeling, although what one really is under is the balcony floor. In the upper theater, a carpeted section stretches from the balcony rim to the screen. On either side are the upper portions of the organ screens, each capped by a regal eagle set against an illuminated plaster sunburst. Murals "after Fragonard" fill the side bays, with a lattice-bordered recessed ceiling above. Under new management since 1966, the theater was renamed the Grand in 1982. [Marcus Enterprises. Movies — twin.]

The Warner's facade and French palatial auditorium.

## WAUSAU

A Palladian-inspired arrangement of five bays with a crowning parapet dominates the exterior of this designated Wausau landmark, which has recently reopened. The column-framed organ screens are centered by niches filled with classical statuary. The renovated interior still houses a Kilgen Wonder Organ. [Grand Theater Committee. Performances, conventions and movies.]

■ **Grand**
415 Fourth Street
Wayne Schoupke
1928

# SOUTHWEST

The Majestic, San Antonio.
Moorish elements decorate
the auditorium's atmospheric
walls.

■ ■ ■ ■ ■ ■ ■   ARIZONA   ■ ■ ■ ■ ■ ■ ■

## CASA GRANDE

■ **Paramount**
418 North Florence
Boulevard
Harry Nace, builder
1929

The impressive main facade of the Paramount reflects both the influence of the early Spanish colonial architecture found in the region and the prominence of the theater as the long-standing entertainment center for the town. A red tile overhang shelters the marquee, above the doors to the lobby. Towers rise on either side of the marquee, each capped by a pyramidal clay tile roof. The interior was remodeled in 1942 and again in 1967. [Long Theatres. Movies.]

## DOUGLAS

■ **Airdome**
555–59 10th Street
H. C. Trost
1925

Although a remodeling of the lower-story shopfronts has erased signs of the theatrical origins of the building, the architectural highlights of the upper portion remain intact. Details include terra cotta trim, a checkerboard stripe on each column and a pair of winged statues atop the central columns. [Everett J. Jones Management. Offices.]

■ **Grand**
1139–49 G Avenue
Eugene Durfee
1919

The Grand was built for Greek-born Nick Diamos as part of a chain of road-show and vaudeville houses run by his family's Lyric Amusement Company. The theater quickly acquired a second role as a movie house. Fronted by a terra cotta Beaux Arts facade, the Grand has been empty since the late 1960s. NR. [Council on Arts and Humanities. Closed.]

## PHOENIX

■ **Palace West (Orpheum)**
209 West Adams Street
Lescher and Mahoney
1927

A curved marquee, bordered in neon, marks the entry to this Spanish baroque-style theater. Clad in cast-stone block and stucco, the Palace West has a fanciful cornice arrangement, with alternating masks of Comedy and Tragedy interrupted at regular intervals by a small figure of Pan playing his pipes. The auditorium is designed to suggest a Mexican marketplace. At one time stars and clouds were projected onto its plaster ceiling. NR. [City of Phoenix. Spanish-language movies.]

The Palace West, Phoenix's last downtown movie theater.

## TUCSON

The oldest theater left downtown, the Rialto has a rich theatrical past. During the height of the vaudeville era, 16-year-old Ginger Rogers appeared on stage here. When sound pictures first came out, a sign above the canopy marquee announced, "Our Screen Talks." Aside from a few bits of stone trim around the windows of the brick exterior and the comfortable furnishings in the lobby areas, the decorative effects of the Rialto are concentrated in the 1,300-seat auditorium. The walls were painted to resemble huge tapestries depicting lives of European nobles from the era of the Enlightenment. The four panels of the flat ceiling were brightened by an attractive repeating border pattern. The Rialto still has its ornate grillwork proscenium arch. Beginning in 1963, X-rated movies were presented, but the current owners took over in 1973 and changed to Spanish-language films. [Privately owned. Spanish-language movies.]

■ **Rialto (Paramount)**
147 Congress Street
1919

The Rialto's subdued exterior and its more elaborately decorated auditorium.

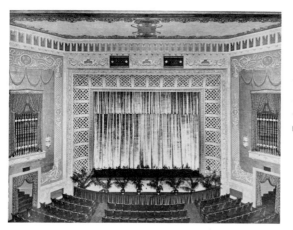

## YUMA

This theater was acclaimed at its opening as outfitted "to place Yuma on the theatrical map in a manner not surpassed by any town in the Southwest." The building no longer houses its original Francis Sullivan pipe organ, but the 1927 projectors are still in place. [Arizona Community Foundation. Planned cultural center.]

■ **Yuma**
254 South Main Street
Harry Nace, builder
1926

■ ■ ■ ■ ■    NEW MEXICO    ■ ■ ■ ■ ■

## ALBUQUERQUE

In their most inspired creation, the Boller Brothers blended indigenous southwestern Indian themes with early Art Deco motifs to decorate the KiMo inside and out. The name KiMo is derived from a native dialect, translating as "King of Its Kind." This pueblo picture palace is best known for its eerily dramatic buffalo-skull light sconces. The eyes of the lobby skull lamps shine a bright yellow, while the rows of skulls inside the auditorium are illuminated by hidden blood-red cove

■ **KiMo**
421 Central Avenue, N.W.
Boller Brothers
1927

The KiMo, Albuquerque. Replicas of cow skulls and southwestern Indian themes dominate the lobby, refurbished exterior, auditorium and tearoom.

lights. The original ceiling light fixtures, modeled after Indian farewell canoes, were lost in a fire that destroyed the original KiMo stage and its skull-lined proscenium arch.

In 1977 the KiMo received a 50th-birthday present when voters passed a bond issue to begin renovation. A new rope-sand proscenium arch was cast, and backstage areas received a technical upgrading. A replica of the original canopy marquee now projects over the sidewalk in front of the KiMo. The striking handpainted patterns of the carriage lobby ceiling were retouched. Inside, the metalwork birds forming the balustrade of the balcony promenade have been repaired by Roger Gilbert, son of the original artist. Trompe l'oeil pueblo murals by painter Von Hassler have been cleaned of a half century's grime, and plans have been made for further conservation work. The whitewashed mock-adobe exterior, with its Navajo-derived medallions of polychrome terra cotta, now occupies a position of honor among preserved examples of the newly classified Pueblo Deco architecture of the region. NR. [City of Albuquerque. Performing arts center.]

## CLOVIS

■ **Lyceum**
411 Main Street
Eugene F. Hardwick, builder
1920

This early combination vaudeville and motion picture theater was built to be "the best performing stage" west of Kansas City and east of Hollywood. The focal point of its classically styled 500-seat auditorium is the baroque arched proscenium opening. After 50 years of movies and stage shows, the Lyceum was closed. Sensing that the old place still had some life left, a group of citizens banded together to "Save the Lyceum," purchasing and reopening the refurbished theater in 1982. The theater still has its Indian-symbol vertical sign, added sometime after 1933. [Old Lyceum Theater. Performing arts center.]

The Lyceum's facade in 1933.

### GALLUP

The El Morro and the less elaborate Chief, located just down Coal Avenue, are the theatrical showpieces of this historic town bordered by a Navajo reservation and the Zuni Pueblo. The El Morro's stucco facade was designed in a richly embellished Spanish Colonial Revival style. A large heraldic shield, framed by a pair of porthole windows, figures prominently in the ornament above the updated theater marquee. Plans were announced in 1985 to replace this modern marquee with a replica of the original and to repaint the fancy facade in a bright mix of colors. [Privately owned. Movies.]

■ **El Morro**
205–09 West Coal Avenue
1928

### SANTA FE

The terra cotta ornament of the Lensic, cast in a Spanish Colonial Revival style, matches the decor of the cathedral-like interior. The most drastic alteration to the theater has been a modern marquee added in place of the 1930 original. [Privately owned. Movies.]

■ **Lensic**
211 West San Francisco
1930

■ ■ ■ ■ ■ ■    OKLAHOMA    ■ ■ ■ ■ ■ ■

### FREDERICK

Just before this Spanish Colonial Revival theater was completed, the stock market crashed on Black Tuesday and bankrupted the builder. A local financier, James Beard, stepped in to help underwrite the remainder of the work on the theater, later named for his daughter, Ramona. Decorative highlights along the buff-colored brick of the main facade include stone urns and scalloped transoms, highlighted with patches of bright blue tiles.

■ **Ramona**
114 South Ninth Street
George Kadane, builder
1929

The 1,000-seat Ramona hit the skids in the past decade, ultimately closing before a local arts council decided to purchase and restore the theater. NR. [Frederick Arts and Humanities Council. Community center.]

## MIAMI

■ **Coleman**
First and Main Streets
Boller Brothers
1929

Local zinc magnate George L. Coleman spent in excess of a half million dollars to build this showplace for motion pictures and touring Orpheum circuit vaudeville acts. The Boller Brothers decorated the exterior with an exuberant mix of baroque and Spanish Colonial Revival elements. Rising at the corners of the southern facade are a pair of bell towers, each capped by a red tile hipped roof. The Coleman's canopy marquee was moved from the main entry around the corner to a position above the theater doors on this facade. A newer marquee on the east side dates from the 1950s and serves as a platform for the Spanish cathedral front dominating this facade. The interior decor is a surprising change from the stucco-coated exterior, its richly appointed lobbies and draped auditorium reflecting a French Renaissance styling.

The local Masonic order has its lodge hall on the theater's second floor. The Wurlitzer organ was removed from the Coleman in the early 1980s, but the theater continues to serve the Miami area as a movie house and occasional performance space. NR. [Video Theatres and private owners. Movies and stage shows.]

The Coleman, just after its 1929 opening.

## NORMAN

■ **Sooner**
101 East Main Street
Harold Gimeno
1929

The 820-seat auditorium of the Sooner looks as if it had been conceived as the stage-set for some Hollywood epic about the Spanish Inquisition. Pendulum-like chandeliers hang between the decorated beams of the ceiling trusses. The exterior is a Moorish Revival concoction of tile and rough brick, presenting a replica of the original marquee that replaced a late Moderne version. The Sooner was the first theater in Norman to show "talkies," which were supplemented with regularly scheduled Orpheum vaudeville acts. In the mid-1980s, the University of Oklahoma produced its Filarmonica Concert Series here. NR. [Sooner Theater of Norman. Community center.]

### PONCA CITY

Dead center on the main facade of this showplace, a flaring sunburst molding rises above a slender arched window. This knockout piece of decorative artwork dominates the colorful Spanish Colonial Revival exterior of the Poncan. A late Moderne marquee, trimmed in zigzag neon, heightens the impact of the theater front. Inside, the mock-stucco walls and ornamentation are essentially intact although occasionally draped over. Architect Forsythe, who studied at the Sorbonne in Paris, also designed another Ponca City landmark, the Marland Mansion (1928); this Spanish castle masquerading as a modern residence was built for oil tycoon E. W. Marland. The mansion has been preserved as a tourist attraction, but Forsythe's theater is up for sale. NR. [Privately owned. Movies.]

■ **Poncan**
104 East Grand Avenue
John Duncan Forsythe
1927

■ ■ ■ ■ ■ ■ ■   TEXAS   ■ ■ ■ ■ ■ ■ ■

### ABILENE

Spanish Mission in style, outside and in, the 1,500-seat Paramount has an atmospheric auditorium whose walls are lined with mission buildings made of plaster to look like stucco. The romantic character of this peaceful space, with its basilica boxes and ornamented bell towers, was enhanced by the projected clouds and the electric stars set in the blue plaster ceiling dome. In the early 1930s, patrons were escorted to their seats by a corps of ushers militarily trained and garbed. Such rituals became but a memory by 1979, when movies were replaced by Abilene's own Paramount Opry. In 1986 the theater was temporarily closed for cosmetic repairs and backstage modifications designed to provide for general performance uses. NR. [Abilene Preservation League. Performing arts center.]

■ **Paramount**
352 Cypress Street
David Castle
1930

Detail of the Paramount's lighted marquee.

The Paramount, Abilene. Auditorium and marquee in 1930, complete with fighter airplanes in nose dives, used to promote the featured film.

## AUSTIN

■ **Paramount (Majestic)**
713 Congress Avenue
John Eberson
1915

For the first 15 years of its combined vaudeville and motion picture operations, this theater was known as the Majestic. Eberson designed the interior in a conventional opera house mode, showing none of the atmospheric flourishes he would develop in his later theaters. Far from being a shortcoming, the Old World theater design adds a significant measure of charm. Like the early theaters of Thomas Lamb and Chicagoans Rapp and Rapp, the Majestic served as a bridge from the elegant 19th-century European performance halls to the outrageously eclectic picture palaces of the 1920s. Renamed the Paramount in 1930, the theater still played host to live stage performances in addition to regular movie screenings.

Preservation specialists from Conrad Schmitt Studios were called in 50 years later to return the Paramount to its original opera house appearance. Restoration included reframing the tiered side boxes and repainting the

Descending side boxes in the Old World interior of the Paramount, Austin.

sounding board, its muse medallion bordered by gilded, classically inspired ornamentation. A new color scheme of pea green and burnt sienna, with gold coating on the ornamental bands, was introduced. NR. [Paramount Theatre for the Performing Arts. Stage shows.]

## BEAUMONT

The Jefferson Amusement Company commissioned Weil to design this 2,000-seat theater as the flagship of its east Texas chain. The cast-stone ornament of the exterior shows a light touch of the Italian Renaissance. A proliferation of area multicinemas forced the theater to close in 1972, but the Jefferson was reborn in the late 1970s. The original Robert Morton organ still holds forth from the orchestra pit. NR. [Jefferson Theatre Preservation Society. Performing arts center.]

■ **Jefferson**
345 Fannin Street
Emile Weil
1927

The Jefferson's auditorium, with its raised organ on the right.

## CONROE

■ **Crighton**
234 North Main Street
Emile Weil
1934

The Crighton is a Venetian variation on the Florentine atmospheric theme used by Weil in his design of the Saenger (1927) in New Orleans. Plaster balustrades top the make-believe palace walls that enclose the auditorium seating. Elegantly framed niches showcase replicas of urns and statuary of the Italian Renaissance. Weil designed this movie house for Harry Crighton, oilman and one-time mayor of Conroe. Crighton's heirs held onto the theater through its closing in 1967, but ownership passed in 1979 to a civic group that has restored and reopened the theater. [Montgomery County Foundation for the Performing Arts. Stage shows and movies.]

## DALLAS

■ **Majestic**
1925 Elm Street
John Eberson
1921

Early photographs of the Majestic's auditorium show just a few traces of the atmospheric concept Eberson would launch in the Houston Majestic (1923, demolished). The hanging vines of the Dallas auditorium are gone, but trelliswork is still visible around the edges of the recessed "open-sky" portion of the ceiling. Sets of opera boxes, framed by engaged Corinthian columns along both sides of the 1,800-seat auditorium, are more in keeping with preatmospheric designs by Eberson. The grand lobby, with its ornately framed mirrors and crystal chandeliers, is a definite throwback to more classically modeled European concert halls.

Five years after the Majestic closed in 1973, the city sponsored a "Light Up the Majestic" campaign. A bond issue passed on its second try in 1979, enabling general restoration of the theater for a grand reopening in 1983. One portion of the 1921 design not revived was "Majesticland," a supervised nursery room that once housed a carousel and a petting zoo. NR. [City of Dallas. Performing arts center.]

Postcard detail of Dallas's theater row with the Majestic's facade.

The Majestic's repaired
ceiling with chandelier,
auditorium and facade with
a replica of the original
marquee.

## EL PASO

Dunne gave the Plaza auditorium a Moorish castle atmosphere not unlike that of theaters designed by John Eberson. Departing from the Ebersonian versions, the Plaza included some stencilwork based on Aztec decorative motifs along its lobby walls. The focal point of this space is a Spanish landscape mural above the grand staircase landing. The Spanish Mission exterior includes a marquee spelling out "Plaza" in Art Deco lettering. The 2,400-seat theater began life as a deluxe vaudeville house, the "Showplace of the Southwest." Closed in 1973, the Plaza reopened five years later with Spanish-language films. Plans announced in 1984 to replace the theater with a parking garage sparked enough local interest to start the theater on the road to rehabilitation as a performance hall. NR. [Privately owned. Movies and concerts.]

■ **Plaza**
125 Mills Street
W. Scott Dunne
1930

### SAN ANTONIO

■ **Alameda**
314 West Houston Street
N. Straus Nayfach
1949

The curving auditorium walls of this late Moderne cinema are filled with brightly colored murals featuring such Texas sights and symbols as oil derricks, the Alamo and the five-pointed star. Like silver-colored molten lava that has recently cooled, the proscenium arch forms a sinuous border for the side wall murals. This 3,000-seat theater was built to present Mexican vaudeville acts along with Spanish-language movies. In recent years, live performances have again been added to supplement the movies. [Privately owned. Spanish-language movies.]

Top: The Alameda, with its multicolored vertical sign. Right: The Aztec.

■ **Aztec**
104 North St. Mary's Street
Meyer and Holler
1926

Among the handful of picture palaces decorated in a Meso-American theme, the Aztec alone was done in a full stars-and-clouds atmospheric style. The imposing fake-temple walls of the 3,000-seat auditorium are formed by plaster suggestive of heavy, carved stone blocks. Ornamental flourishes include colorful deity masks paired on the sides of the organ grilles and winding serpents balancing a great sun disk set at the center of the proscenium arch. The mystical grand lobby is equally foreboding, with each column capped by the stone-faced mask of Coyclaxiuhqui, the Aztec goddess of the moon. For the opening of the theater, native blankets were draped over the edges of the encircling balcony promenade. The eerie sacrificial altar chandelier, placed in the lobby some time after the opening, has been moved at last report to a San Antonio cafeteria specializing in Mexican food. The exterior of this theater is highly restrained, with only a handful of tribal chiefs looking down from the terra cotta cornice. Two minitheaters now fill the former balcony. [Privately owned. Movies — triplex.]

Above: Postcard views of the Aztec's Meso-American auditorium and grand foyer columns. Left: Sacrificial altar chandelier.

■ **Majestic**
214 East Houston Street
John Eberson
1929

Considered by many theater buffs to be the summit of Eberson's long career, the Majestic must certainly rate as the grandest of his Spanish-garden atmospheric designs. The great height reached by the "palace" walls enclosing the auditorium was necessitated partly by a second balcony, intended for blacks, at the upper reaches of the back of the house. As with the best of the Eberson atmospherics, the fanciful architectural forms of the side walls were asymmetrical, relying on the ruffled, cove-lighted proscenium arch for balance. No arch could strike a better balance than this, set between cathedral bell towers and a Moorish castle abandoned except for a few doves and some Texas turkeys. Other features of note include the jeweled oval ceiling above the split stairs to the balcony and the freestanding Moorish box office. The theater's switchboard was powerful enough to electrify a town of 15,000, even though only 3,700 could fit into the Majestic at one sitting.

The theater closed in 1974, but reopened as a venue for live theater a decade later. At present, with few traveling Broadway shows to book, the Majestic is threatened with demolition. NR. [Privately owned. Stage shows.]

The Majestic's marquee, extended the full width of its streetfront.

**SEGUIN**

■ **Texas**
314 South Austin Street
W. Scott Dunne
1929

This small-town theater has had its movie-showing career supplemented by brief appearances in two recent films, *The Great Waldo Pepper* and *Raggedy Man*. The Texas has a simple, boxy appearance brightened by patterned brickwork and its "Texas" vertical sign. Murals depicting scenes from the region's past cover the surfaces of its interior walls and ceilings. [Privately owned. Movies.]

Top: The Texas, with its lone-star marquee. Left: The Saenger's Palladian facade.

## TEXARKANA

Bas-relief ornament fills the auditorium walls of this former vaudeville house and movie theater. The Saenger, designed by the principal architect of the Saenger chain, had become known as the Paramount by the time it closed in 1977. Within a year of the shutdown, the city purchased the theater and hired Conrad Schmitt Studios to restore it. Substantial research went into the selection of the color scheme, cream and sky blue trimmed with 23-karat gold leaf. With its gleaming white and black marble, the floor of the lobby has its own richness. For its grand reopening in 1979, the theater was given yet another name, in honor of two lifelong Texarkana residents, Gabriel and Lulu May Perot. NR. [City of Texarkana. Performing arts center.]

■ **Perot
(Saenger/Paramount)**
219–21 Main Street
Emile Weil
1924

## WACO

This theater started life as the Hippodrome, promoting vaudeville acts on its stage. By 1918 the 1,300-seat Waco was part of the Hoblitzelle theater chain. A more visible change occurred in 1929, when the Sullivanesque exterior of the theater was remodeled along Spanish Colonial Revival lines. Now under consideration by the Junior League is a plan to acquire and refurbish the Waco as a center for the performing arts. NR. [Privately owned. Movies and stage shows.]

■ **Waco (Hippodrome)**
724 Austin Avenue
1913

Grauman's Chinese, Hollywood. The forecourt is illuminated for the 1933 premiere of *I'm No Angel*, starring Mae West and Cary Grant in his first major role.

■ ■ ■ ■ ■ ■ ■   ALASKA   ■ ■ ■ ■ ■ ■ ■

### ANCHORAGE

■ **4th Avenue**
630 West Fourth Avenue
Priteca and Porreca
1947

Construction of the Lathrop Building, which contains the 4th Avenue, began in 1941, but World War II and resulting supply shortages postponed the unveiling of the Art Deco movie house until May 31, 1947. Today, the theater presents a bright orange and yellow face to the street. The principal facade is split down the center by a full-height vertical sign. Both this sign and the carved panel above the entry doors spell out the name of the theater in distinctive Moderne lettering. Decorative touches in the 1,100-seat auditorium include floor-to-ceiling murals and elements trimmed with gold leaf and cut glass. Incorporated into the lobby is a wooden rendition of the city's mountainous setting, to scale, executed by renowned theater decorator Anthony Heinsbergen. The city began efforts to renovate the 4th Avenue in 1985. A plaque on the exterior details the preservation work and quotes the original vow of Austin E. "Cap" Lathrop to build "a Theatre especially for Alaskans . . . a Theatre unexcelled on the American Continent." NR. [Moyer Theatres. Stage shows.]

■ ■ ■ ■ ■ ■   CALIFORNIA   ■ ■ ■ ■ ■ ■

### BAKERSFIELD

■ **Fox**
20th and H Streets
S. Charles Lee
1929

The Fox's imposing clock tower and the Spanish courtyard interior.

With its massive corner clock tower, the Fox maintains a strong physical presence in town. Alterations to the whitewashed exterior have been few, aside from the addition of a splashy marquee. Lee's original atmospheric interior evoking a Spanish courtyard was supplanted by golden plaster curls, the so-called Skouras treatment popularized by the Skouras Brothers, who ran the Fox West Coast chain in the 1940s and 1950s. Sadly, the theater has not been used much in recent years. [Mann Theatres. Closed.]

As built, this theater had a conventional Beaux Arts-style facade. The Nile's exterior currently boasts an unusual blend of Egyptian and Art Deco design motifs, visible in its vertical sign and the rippling-wave neon border of its marquee. The interior has been divided and draped like many shopping center multiplexes. [USA Cinemas. Movies — twin.]

### ■ Nile
1721 19th Street
1926

Above: The Nile's Art Deco facade. Left and below: The Avalon on the water's edge and the theater's auditorium.

## CATALINA ISLAND

Located on Catalina Island, a two-hour boat ride from the California shore, the theater fills the first floor of the Avalon Casino Building, a posh complex that rises from a spit of land at the northern end of Avalon Harbor. The building was commissioned by chewing-gum tycoon William Wrigley, Jr., as the major nightspot of his island paradise. A grand ballroom on the upper level gives the

### ■ Avalon
Avalon Casino Building
Webber and Spaulding
1929

streamlined Spanish colonial casino building its distinctive circular shape.

"California as Paradise" might well be considered the theme of the theater's auditorium murals. Painted by John Gabriel Beckman, the vast canvas depicts a noble savage hunting deer with bow and arrow, as a few Franciscan monks arrive by galleon surrounded by stylized hillsides. The region along the back wall is even more unspoiled, populated only by birds and monkeys. To cap the scene, a re-creation of Botticelli's *Birth of Venus* appears directly above the rounded proscenium arch. The silver-leafed ceiling is made to glow in shades of pink and violet by colored floodlights, hidden behind a low wall curving around the auditorium. For theater curtain aficionados, few remaining asbestos curtains could match that of the Avalon. Entitled the "Flight of Fancy Westward," it shows a primitive "surfer boy" riding the crest of a wave, superimposed on a topographical projection of Catalina Island.

Polished wooden panels decorate the horseshoe-shaped lobby, which is covered by a red barrel vault decorated with gold-leaf stars. The outer lobby has a few Atlantis-inspired mural panels, painted by the artist directly onto the concrete surface but now being redone in polychrome tile under Beckman's supervision.

The casino building remains in the hands of the Wrigley family. Movies play at the Avalon every night during the summer and most nights the rest of the year. Daytime tours of the entire casino building are available. [Santa Catalina Island Company. Movies.]

## DUNSMUIR

■ **California**
5739 Dunsmuir Avenue
c. 1925

With more than 1,000 seats, the California appears oversized for the town. The theater owes its scale to the historical significance of Dunsmuir, which grew up along the West Coast railroad lines. Today, the tall vertical sign and marquee of the theater anchor the center of this quiet town. Although the screen is in place and original light sconces still line the auditorium walls, movies have not been shown here for years. Video machines fill the small lobby. Pool tables and air hockey games have taken over the front half of the orchestra floor. Reclamation for theater use is certainly possible. [Dunsmuir Masonic Lodge. Video arcade.]

## FRESNO

■ **Warnors (Pantages)**
1400 Fulton Street
B. Marcus Priteca
1928

Storefronts beneath panels of cast-concrete ornament, grouped under a red tile roof, combine to form an elegant Italian palazzo exterior that wraps around the theater proper. An octagonal tower, topped by a small lantern, hovers over the entry to the former Pantages. The fancy plasterwork of the box office lobby ceiling hints at the elaborate Spanish baroque decor within. The auditorium is a close cousin of the Priteca-designed Pantages (1926, now the Orpheum) in San Francisco. The resemblance is most prominent in the handling of the

Left and above: Exterior and interior of the Warnors. Below: The Liemert Park.

plaster decor along the side walls and the proscenium arch. A giant star pattern dominates the auditorium ceiling. Rehabilitation of what is now known as the Warnors was conducted by Seattle architect Richard F. McCann, successor to the Priteca firm. NR. [Privately owned. Performing arts center.]

### LOS ANGELES

This neighborhood movie house was designed in classic southern California streamlined Spanish colonial style. "Watchtower" has replaced the original theater name atop the steel frame perched above a lower, stucco-clad tower. [Jehovah's Witnesses. Assembly hall.]

Decked out in a luxurious rose and ivory French baroque treatment, the Los Angeles was Lee's crowning achievement. None of his more than 400 theaters could match the opulence of the Los Angeles, or the cost — $1.2 million. Lee added 30 new draftsmen to his staff to keep pace with a five-month construction schedule.

The terra cotta arch of the main facade, mounted above clustered Corinthian columns, finds echoes within the theater, in the plaster organ screens and the tri-

■ **Liemert Park**
3341 West 43rd Place
c. 1931

■ **Los Angeles**
615 South Broadway
S. Charles Lee
1931

The Los Angeles, showing the grand French baroque facade, lobby and auditorium in 1931.

umphal arch at the center of the three-dimensional stage curtain. This tapestry, depicting life at the French royal court, shows figures stuffed in billowy silks and velvets, complete with wigs. The mirror-lined lobby is equally majestic. From the landing of the grand staircase rises a triple-tiered crystal fountain, backed by a wispy mural painted "after Fragonard." Lee once described the interior as "Louis XIV adapted in a theatrical way." Years of heavy use and the intrusion of video games in the Versailles-inspired lobby have yet to seriously threaten the palatial character of Lee's masterwork. [Metropolitan Theatres. Spanish-language movies.]

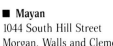 **Mayan**
1044 South Hill Street
Morgan, Walls and Clements
1927

Not one square inch of the Mayan's walls—inside or out—has been left devoid of ornament or bright color. The theater's most notable decorative feature is the row of seven Mayan warriors, in full headdress, above the marquee. The cast-concrete facade, originally a uniform gray, was given a gaudy paint job in the 1950s, using what the *Los Angeles Times* labeled "an authentic Mayan color scheme." As Mayan Revival specialist Marjorie Ingle has noted, architect Stiles O. Clements designed the theater with completely plain surfaces, to be clad later with ornamentation created by artist Francisco Cornejo.

Inside the Mayan, the auditorium is dominated by a replica of an Aztec calendar stone that serves as a central chandelier. Tableau stages, outfitted with drops depicting rituals, bracket the proscenium opening. Throughout the lobbies, including the Hall of Feathered Serpents, the Mayan patterns are unrelenting — on the wall brackets, the furniture, even the floor paving. Portions of this exotic interior can be glimpsed in the Jack Lemmon movie *Save the Tiger*. Seedy, yet still glorious to behold, the Mayan now survives by showing pornographic films. [Privately owned. Adult movies.]

Above and left: Warriors perched above the Mayan's marquee and the central chandelier over the auditorium. Below: The Million Dollar.

The Los Angeles theatrical career of Sid Grauman began at this early downtown movie theater. The sidewalk-to-rooftop ornamentation of the exterior is the real show at the Million Dollar these days. The style, most often classified as Churrigueresque, is an elaborate Spanish baroque composition in terra cotta. The building was the work of local architect Martin, with Woollett in charge of the interior. Here, Woollett followed Martin's lead, incorporating Spanish baroque elements into a fancifully lighted decorative pattern piled high along the organ screens and visible in the coffered ceiling. The current owners of the Million Dollar have stripped the lobby of its original decor and have given the 2,300-seat auditorium a gaudy paint job. NR. [Privately owned. Spanish-language movies.]

■ **Million Dollar**
307 South Broadway
William Lee Woollett
and A. C. Martin
1918

### ■ Orpheum
842 South Broadway
G. Albert Lansburgh
1926

Marquee of the Orpheum, designed by Priteca, and its elegant auditorium.

This was a Los Angeles encore by Lansburgh for the Orpheum circuit. His earlier vaudeville house, built two blocks up Broadway in 1911, was renamed the Palace when this theater opened. Lansburgh gave the new Orpheum a lavish French Renaissance treatment, with a marble-lined lobby, huge bronze and crystal chandeliers, damask wall panels and gold-leaf stencils on the ivory-colored auditorium plasterwork. The Orpheum featured two-a-day vaudeville until 1929, when RKO Pictures began to share the bill. Metropolitan Theatres took over four years later. Soon after, the mind-boggling neon marquee was added. Its design was attributed to Pantages circuit architect B. Marcus Priteca. [Metropolitan Theatres. Spanish-language movies.]

### ■ Pantages
South Hill and
West Seventh Streets
B. Marcus Priteca
1920

Starting in the 1920s, most downtown theaters were built at the core of office blocks. Priteca's Pantages Building was one of those rare cases where the beauty of the gleaming white terra cotta exterior matched the theater within. The marquee and theater entry are at the base of a rounded corner tower, topped by a shiny green dome. With the advent of sound films, the Pantages became a Warner Brothers movie house. A more recent conversion, into a retail jewelry outlet, has created the bizarre juxtaposition of a shopping mall–like main floor beneath the intact upper portion of the Priteca design, one of his so-called Pantages Greek treatments. A "Shower of Light" chandelier is the only major intrusion into the Beaux Arts composition of cove ceiling and column-framed proscenium. The balcony still has its red velvet seats. [The Jewelry Exchange. Retail store.]

### ■ State
703 South Broadway
Weeks and Day
1921

Opened as Loew's State on a prime corner of Broadway, this theater benefited early on as the primary downtown outlet for MGM pictures. New "Ideas" stage shows created every week by vaudevillians Fanchon and Marco added substantially to the draw. Visually, the theater suffers in comparison to the other picture palaces on

Broadway. One highlight, amid the restrained Spanish styling, is a futuristic "Ali Baba Goes to the Stars" asbestos stage curtain. The State was among the first of the Spanish-language movie houses, switching over to this specialty in 1963. [Metropolitan Theatres. Spanish-language movies.]

The Spanish-Moorish facade, with its corner clock tower, makes the most of a cramped 50-foot Broadway frontage. Lee was only 27 when he designed this theater for entrepreneur H. L. Gumbiner. The architect later told the *Los Angeles Times* that the Tower "was the first theater built for sound and I had tremendous problems because I didn't know how big the sound horns would be." Traces of the talent that would bring forth the French-inspired glories of the Los Angeles (1931) are already apparent in the Tower's interior features. Most noteworthy is the grand lobby staircase, rising between marble pillars to the shelf balcony of the narrow 900-seat auditorium. [Metropolitan Theatres. Spanish-language movies.]

When Charlie Chaplin, Mary Pickford, Douglas Fairbanks et al. decided to form United Artists film studios in the mid-1920s, they needed a new theater chain to showcase their movies. This flagship Los Angeles theater was the high point of Crane's Spanish Gothic variations. Here the treatment is complete, from the terra cotta tracery and enshrined statuary above the marquee to the powerful Gothic plasterwork of the proscenium arch and the organ screens. Capping it all is the three-story grand lobby, which resembles the nave of an old Spanish cathedral, with colorful murals decorating its groin vaults.

The involvement of Pickford in the design ensured that a few Hollywood touches would be included. Multi-colored cove lighting brings the gold and silver auditorium ceiling dome to life. Side wall murals depict

The State's ornate drapery pattern.

■ **Tower**
802 South Broadway
S. Charles Lee
1927

■ **United Artists**
933 South Broadway
C. Howard Crane
1927

Hollywood–Gothic Revival facade of the United Artists and wall detail from the auditorium.

cameramen filming Fairbanks in action, Chaplin's tramp and Pickford herself. Pickford's private screening room was built one floor below the auditorium. The United Artists opened with Pickford's *My Best Girl.* [Metropolitan Theatres. Spanish-language movies.]

### ■ Wilshire (Fox-Wilshire)
8440 Wilshire Boulevard
S. Charles Lee
1930

With its ornament heavily dependent on geometric patternwork, this former Fox theater was considered quite novel in its day. As Lee explained to the *Los Angeles Times.* "The Fox-Wilshire was Art Deco with a silver and black interior. It knocked everybody off their feet. At that time it was unbelievable." The theater was redecorated in 1980 by B. Marcus Priteca protege Richard F. McCann, to be used for live theater. [Nederlander Organization. Stage shows.]

### ■ Wiltern (Western)
3780 Wilshire Boulevard
Stiles O. Clements and
G. Albert Lansburgh
1931

Among theaters of the period, the Wiltern comes closest to the Oakland Paramount (1931) for wall-to-wall Art Deco splendor. Known in its early years as the Warner Brothers Western, this showplace was Lansburgh's last major theater design. Opening night was a klieg-lighted

Opening night at the Wiltern in 1931. Warner Brothers' "Bridge of the Stars" transported celebrities across Wilshire Boulevard.

spectacular. An illuminated bridge, festooned with electrified bouquets, spanned Wilshire Boulevard for the stars to cross before entering the theater. The highly visible green tile exterior of the theater and office tower was the work of Clements, the architect of the Mayan (1927) in downtown Los Angeles. When the Wiltern closed in 1980, original furnishings were stripped from the interior. A $4.6 million rehabilitation, completed in 1985, brought the place back to life. Notable views include the ceiling mural and frosted-glass fixtures decorating the two-story lobby rotunda, as well as the golden fan sunburst auditorium ceiling cove, its lights once again operational. NR. [Wiltern Associates. Performing arts center.]

The Wiltern's oval rotunda and inner lobby highlighted by ceiling murals.

### LOS ANGELES AREA: BEVERLY HILLS

This Taj Mahal of Beverly Hills entered its third life in 1986 as a bank. The original Indo-Chinese decor, with its Moongate proscenium arch, was replaced by a painted circus variation during a 1970s conversion into a retail boutique. In its most recent incarnation, the interior was gutted and rebuilt for use as a bank, leaving the white dome on the rooftop as the sole surviving ornamentation from the original design. [Israel Discount Bank. Bank.]

■ **Beverly**
206 North Beverly Drive
L. A. Smith
1925

### LOS ANGELES AREA: HOLLYWOOD

Looming alongside Hollywood Boulevard like a stage-set Oriental temple out of an exotic silent movie, Sid Grauman's last big theater is in many ways the biggest star in all of Hollywood. Even as the area has headed downhill, the Chinese still draws tourists by the busload. As described in a 1927 issue of *Exhibitors Herald*, the

■ **Grauman's Chinese**
6925 Hollywood Boulevard
Meyer and Holler
(Raymond Kennedy, designer)
1927

theater's entrance featured "a huge elliptical forecourt set with rare tropical trees," and the interior was "resplendent throughout in motifs of early Chinese dynasties."

Today, visitors come to match hand- and footprints with those of the stars. The tradition of leaving these marks began by happy accident when some famous stars —the names vary with the storyteller—were misdirected through a patch of wet cement on their way into the theater. Ringing the forecourt in place of the old cocoa palms are engraved plaques honoring Oscar winners. A gift shop awaits nearby.

Even with all the hoopla out front, the Chinese still shows a full day of movies. Marquees topped by neon dragons announce the show. The Chinese red, antiques-strewn interior was remodeled but not ruined in 1958. Later, two theaters were added to the building's east side. Since its grand opening with Cecil B. DeMille's *King of Kings*, the 2,200-seat Chinese has hosted a number of grand premieres, including one staged for Gene Kelly in *Singin' in the Rain.* The Chinese survives as a wonderful reminder of the kitsch and glamour that are Hollywood. NR district. [Mann Theatres. Movies.]

Grauman's Chinese, Hollywood. Appropriately dressed ushers spelling Sid Grauman's first name and the exterior as altered by current owners.

Just a few blocks away from the Chinese, one of the earliest of the exotic theaters sits virtually forgotten. A covered walkway clutters the long forecourt approach to this 1,800-seat Theban temple. Cast heads of the pharaohs are mounted on pylons to keep a watchful eye on the entry doors. Twin black plaster Dogs of Annubis sit in stately repose within the Egyptian lobby. Sad news awaits within the auditorium, where great lotus-capital columns and hieroglyph-stenciled beams that once formed the proscenium arch have been removed. Remaining decoration includes Tut mask wall sconces and a scarab whose grilled wingspan covers the ceiling. NR district. [United Artists Theaters. Movies — triplex.]

■ **Grauman's Egyptian**
6712 Hollywood Boulevard
Meyer and Holler
1922

Above: Section of the Egyptian's Theban temple facade. Left: The Pacific filling the core of an office block.

Tame in comparison to its exotic Hollywood neighbors, the former Warner is a stylish rendition of "Movie Palace Renaissance Rococo" design. The balcony has been turned into a piggybacked theater space and split in two, but the artistic integrity of the semicircular lobby is undisturbed. NR district. [Pacific Theatres. Movies — triplex.]

■ **Pacific (Warner)**
6423–45 Hollywood
Boulevard
G. Albert Lansburgh
1928

### ■ Pantages
6233 Hollywood Boulevard
B. Marcus Priteca
1930

In his last design for impresario Alexander Pantages, Priteca put on a dazzling display of geometric patterns. Heavily ornamented spokes radiate out from a frosted-glass chandelier at the center of the blue and gold auditorium ceiling. The coffered barrel vault of the grand lobby rises from the tops of fantastic golden zigzag column capitals. Heroes of the age (aviators and movie makers) are celebrated by golden statues placed beside the grand staircases at either end of the lobby. Despite complete chambers and almost frighteningly ornate grilles, the Robert Morton organ intended for the Pantages was never installed. Also eliminated was the 12-story office building for which the whitewashed Moderne theater was to serve as base. In addition to a mix of movie premieres and stage shows, the Pantages played host to the Academy Awards presentations for most of the 1950s. NR district. [Nederlander Organization. Stage shows.]

Above and right: Art Deco exterior and stairway of the Pantages. Below: The swan-shaped Loyola.

### LOS ANGELES AREA: WESTCHESTER

### ■ Loyola
8610 Sepulveda Boulevard
Clarence J. Smale
1946

The lyrical swan form of the Loyola rises to a height of 60 feet, facing the setting sun in this district near Loyola University. Despite a complete overhaul of the interior for use as medical offices, the silver-crowned box office and the terrazzo sidewalk were not removed. The marquee and the central portion of the facade have been stripped of their neon, but skeletal outlines of the original patterns remain, traced in red paint. [Loyola Professional Building. Offices.]

## LOS ANGELES AREA: WESTWOOD

The tall wedding-cake tower of this mixed Moderne and Spanish colonial theater is trimmed with neon icing. The whitewashed exterior gives way to a golden interior. A shiny feather motif, popularized by the Skouras Brothers, who managed the Fox chain, fans out along the auditorium walls. Atop the balcony stair landing rests a statue of golden maidens. A frieze along the top of the wall opposite shows scenes of the California gold rush. The Fox–Westwood Village is more modern than palatial but remains a must-see for neon buffs. [Privately owned. Movies.]

■ **Fox–Westwood Village**
961 Broxton Avenue
P. O. Lewis
1931

Above: The Fox–Westwood Village. Left: The Fox, Oakland. Both exemplify the Fox chain's elaborate building detail.

## OAKLAND

The auditorium of the Fox has a colorful East Indian Buddhist temple gloss applied over a standard squared-off Weeks and Day interior. The entry portion of the main facade takes the form of a polychrome mosaic-lined shrine, with smaller lantern-topped towers on either side. Trim with a Near Eastern flavor forms the cornice line for the remainder of the building. After years of misfiring plans, the Fox was set on the comeback trail in 1986. Plans called for the auditorium to be carefully divided into four small screening areas by the owner of the crosstown Grand Lake (1926). NR. [Renaissance Rialto Theatres. Planned movies — quad.]

■ **Fox**
1807–29 Telegraph Avenue
Weeks and Day
1928

■ **Grand Lake**
3200 Grand Avenue
Reid and Reid
1926

The Grand Lake rises in elegantly simple counterpoint to Oakland's glamorous Paramount (1931) and exotic Fox (1928). Its classically columned exterior turns a street corner not far from Lake Merritt. Inside, the landing of the grand staircase sports bouquet-filled urns, matching the springtime scene painted just above. Twinning of the theater in 1980 necessitated a wall more than two feet thick to enclose and soundproof the balcony. Only on the roof do things explode, visually if not audibly. The animated Grand Lake rooftop sign features electric fireworks, thanks to multicolored chaser lights. [Renaissance Rialto Theatres. Movies — twin.]

Facade of the Grand Lake.

■ **Paramount**
2025 Broadway
Miller and Pflueger
1931

In the Paramount, renowned Bay Area architect Timothy L. Pflueger performed a breathtaking high-wire design act, concealing sophisticated mechanical systems behind exquisite Art Deco ornament. The grand lobby ceiling composition, known as the Canopy of Light, glows a brilliant green, as a zigzag assemblage of galvanized metal strips is metamorphosed into a tropical rain forest. These 12-inch-high soldered "silver fins" (as Pflueger called them) were hung by steel cables from the solid roof above. The auditorium's ceiling grille, complete with rainbow lighting effects, is an even more elaborate series of these decorative metal panels. Each panel features the outlines of Isis, the Egyptian goddess of life. Both metal canopies make beautiful use of a novel scheme for indirect lighting and provide for full ventilation of the spaces below.

Under the guidance of Pflueger and chief designer Anthony Heinsbergen, several major artists worked to embellish this $3 million picture palace. The primary facade is dominated by Gerald Fitzgerald's tile portrayals of the god and goddess of cinema. Rising to a height of 120 feet, the panels are centered by a multicolored neon vertical sign. Inside, the designs for many of the smaller lounges are less monumental but equally spectacular. One wall of the ladies' smoking room downstairs is filled

Fountain of Light.

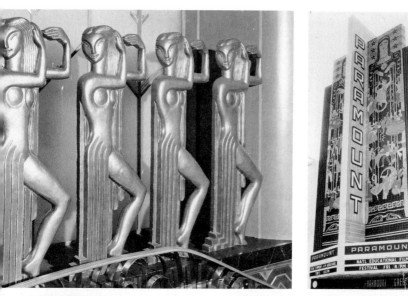

The Paramount's varied ornamentation, as seen in the ironwork staircase, mosaic facade, metal auditorium canopies, lobby interior and auditorium murals.

The Paramount in 1931.

by a Charles Stafford Duncan mural depicting a picnic scene, with sailboats plying a black lacquer sea. Dutch metal-leaf tableaux, by architect John Galen Howard, decorate the auditorium side walls with scenes suggestive of Paradise. The winged Poseidon of the proscenium sounding board was also by Howard. Uncredited marvels of the Paramount include the Fountain of Light, an illusionistic series of sandblasted glass panels that climb 50 feet inside the lobby doors. The lobby walls are lined with sets of plaster golden girls, attired as if they were Cleopatra's chorus line. The overall composition of the lobby is best seen from an oval porthole window, looking down from the upper balcony promenade.

The Paramount ended its days as a movie house in 1971. Portions of the theater in its dilapidated condition appear in the 1971 Warner Brothers film *The Candidate*, starring Robert Redford. The following year, the Oakland Symphony Orchestra made a commitment to buy and restore the Paramount to its 1931 appearance. The restoration, managed by Peter Botto in league with Symphony Director Jack Bethards, took nine months and $1 million to complete; seating was reduced from 3,476 to 2,998. Three years later, the building was resold, giving ownership to the city, with the symphony orchestra to remain as principal tenant. The orchestra folded in 1986, leaving the theater to house ballet, rock concerts and touring Broadway shows. The Paramount offers guided tours; for information, call (415) 893-2300. NR. [Paramount Theatre of the Arts. Performing arts center.]

## PASADENA

■ **Crown (Raymond)**
129 North Raymond Street
Cyril Bennett
1921

A quietly classical brick and stone exterior gives way to an auditorium based on French Empire models. A special feature of the Crown is its original curtain, showing an early model car posed before Half Dome in Yosemite National Park. The former Raymond, later Loew's Crown, has seen infrequent use in the past decade. [Privately owned. Closed.]

Jensen's Raymond before becoming the Crown.

## POMONA

Near the center of Pomona, a wedding-cake Moderne tower marks the location of the Fox. The silver and rose interior of the theater prompted picture palace historian Ben Hall to label this creation "Paris Comes to Pomona." Zigzags and a lotus motif dominate the auditorium grilles and stencilwork. The lobby clouds are blessed with visible silver linings, thanks to a recent paint job. Slightly worn and tattered, the Fox retains a stylish charm. NR. [Privately owned. Spanish-language movies.]

■ **Fox**
102–44 Third Street
Balch and Stanberry
1931

Above: The Fox, Pomona.
Left: The Fox, Riverside.

## RIVERSIDE

The auditorium of the Fox Building is wrapped inside a two-story Mission-style exterior. A deep arcade at street level supports a row of offices above. The theater spaces are fairly plain, except for stencils along the wide ceiling beams inside the auditorium. The Fox stakes its claim to fame on a plaque in front announcing that the first public screening of *Gone with the Wind* took place within its walls. [Privately owned. Spanish-language movies.]

■ **Fox**
3801 Market Street
Balch and Stanberry
1929

## SAN DIEGO

This imitation palacio was designed to honor the Spanish heritage of San Diego and came complete with Balboa in tile on the front sidewalk. Inside, a tapestry effect was used for the plaster side bays of the auditorium. In the 1920s the women ushers were dressed as bullfighters. During the Depression the Balboa operated as a Spanish-language movie house, serving the large Mexican-American population of the city. In the mid-1980s a huge post-Modern neo-Mediterranean shopping mall, Horton Plaza, was built around three sides of the theater. The Balboa's beautiful tile dome, set four stories above the corner entry, finds echoes in portions of the rooflines of the new retail center. [City of San Diego. Planned performing arts center.]

■ **Balboa**
648 Fourth Avenue
William Wheeler
1924

The Fox appears somehow impervious to the economic turmoil that has dogged it. Its opening festivities in early November 1929 coincided exactly with the start of the Depression. A more recent $4.75 million adaptation for

■ **Fox**
1245 Seventh Avenue
Weeks and Day
1929

use as a performance hall was completed just before the demise of the San Diego Symphony Orchestra in 1986. Designer Anthony Heinsbergen carried out the decorative scheme created by Weeks and Day, incorporating a few French design elements in the predominantly Spanish Gothic interior. Notes in the opening program boasted, "Surely no Croesus could have conjured—out of cold stone, warm silks, and gleaming gold — a castle of such compelling beauty." Standard Fox hype, it was accurate in this case. Not to be overlooked is the expert plasterwork used to suggest a finely detailed woodwork ceiling. [City of San Diego. Performing arts center.]

Right: The Fox, San Diego. Below: The Alhambra's exterior and interior in the late 1920s.

■ **Alhambra**
2330 Polk Street
Miller and Pflueger
1925

### SAN FRANCISCO

Timothy L. Pflueger, who would later design the Art Deco–style Paramount (1931) in Oakland, was responsible for this Moorish spectacle, just a few blocks south of the former Ghirardelli Chocolate Factory. In this quiet district, the corner minarets of the Alhambra glow a brilliant red in the night sky. Ogee arches pierce the main facade, matched inside by taller arches along the frantically busy auditorium walls. The glowing tail of a golden peacock spreads above the exit signs at either end of the main lobby. For the present at least, a full-height wall slices the auditorium in half for dual film presentations. [Blumenfeld Theatres. Movies — twin.]

The Castro presents a stylistic mix of design elements. For its exterior, it mimics a Spanish castle. Inside, classical ruins figure prominently in the side wall "tapestries" of the auditorium. A colorful plaster "tent" forms the ceiling. During the past decade, the Castro has put on several first-rate film series, complete with organ interludes. With a world-class refreshment stand to boot, the Castro is one of the best film venues to be found. [Landmark Theatres. Movies.]

■ **Castro**
429 Castro Street
Miller and Pflueger
1922

The Castro, the oldest standing theater designed by Pflueger in the San Francisco area.

After suffering harshly from modifications to house a piggybacked theater in its balcony, the auditorium of the Golden Gate was returned to its original layout in 1979. The interior decor is fairly restrained in comparison to the exterior, with its stepped-corbel balconies on the south face and a richly embellished dome above the corner. The highlight of the interior is the vaulted ceiling of the circular entry hall, which has a fantastically complex pattern of Gothic ribbing. NR district. [Nederlander Organization. Stage shows.]

■ **Golden Gate**
25 Taylor Street
G. Albert Lansburgh
1922

Theater expert Terry Helgesen identifies Priteca's inspiration for this design as the 15th-century Cantabrian Cathedral of Leon. The religious theme prevails throughout, including the altarlike organ screens. Cast ornament clads every inch of the Market Street facade, piled especially high above the central entry portion. Mock-medieval statuary and tapestries dominated the original lobby, now altered. Also gone is the velvet conquistador-themed house curtain, attributed to Priteca. Above the 2,500 seats of the auditorium, an illuminated lacework-plaster ceiling appears to hover on the backs of a great ring of plaster lions, each rendered in full and lighted from behind. Architect Richard F. McCann performed the renovation of this former Pantages showplace in 1976, at a cost of just under $2 million. [Nederlander Organization. Stage shows.]

■ **Orpheum (Pantages)**
1192 Market Street
B. Marcus Priteca
1926

### ■ Warfield
982 Market Street
G. Albert Lansburgh
1922

Lansburgh's exterior treatment of the Warfield was slightly less flamboyant than his design for the Golden Gate (1922) across the street. Such was not the case inside. From an ethereal mural-decorated sounding board, the auditorium ceiling of the Warfield spreads above the balcony like a broad peacock tail, with illuminated blue coves at the "feathertips." Once a Fox movie house, the Warfield has most recently promoted rock shows. NR district. [Privately owned. Closed.]

## SAN JOSE

### ■ Fox (California)
345 South First Street
Weeks and Day
1927

Opening as the California, this cathedral-fronted movie house spent most of its active life as part of the Fox West Coast chain. Spanish colonial was the order of the day for designer Weeks, including the balconies jutting into the shaded two-story box office lobby. Stencil designs highlight the beamwork ceiling above the entry foyer. A renaissance of San Jose's central district has raised hopes that a new theatrical use can be found for the Fox. [City of San Jose. Closed.]

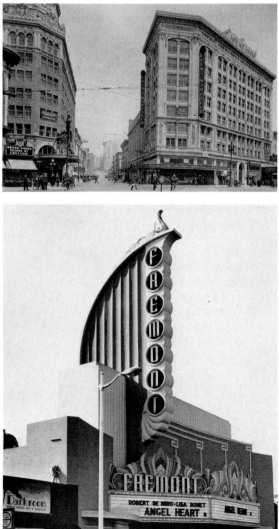

Clockwise from top left: The Fox in San Jose, the Warfield and Golden Gate in San Francisco and exterior and interior views of the Fremont in San Luis Obispo.

## SAN LUIS OBISPO

Themes from nature dominate the design of the Fremont. Conch-shell light sconces line the auditorium walls. Subdued purple lighting swirls around the painted ceiling, like seaweed in breaking ocean waves. The marquee soffit and the terrazzo floor below have swirls of their own. Above the marquee, the vertical sign rises like bird plumage, far above the roofline. The overall form of the building is matched by a freestanding swan-shaped box office, which faces directly across the street to the town's municipal office complex. [Mann Theatres. Movies.]

■ **Fremont**
1035 Monterey
S. Charles Lee
c. 1940

## SANTA BARBARA

With its glorious Spanish Mission atmospheric auditorium, the Arlington is what movie critics would call a "must see." The design, originally for the Fox organization, evolved from an Alcazar-inspired napkin sketch by architect Joseph J. Plunkett. The red-roofed tower, marked by soft lights at night, is the tallest structure for miles. Given the bulk of the Arlington's whitewashed exterior, the interior is surprisingly intimate, seating just over 2,000 on its main floor and shelf balcony. The lobby entry doors are well off the street, past the tiled box office and the Paseo fountain and under a mural of whirling Spanish dancers. Antique furnishings and tapestries (original and approximate) decorate the lobby areas. Crossing into the auditorium, patrons find themselves between two halves of a sleepy Spanish town, covered by a blue plaster "sky." Originally, the two sides were connected by a proscenium arch designed to resemble a stone bridge. The illusion was enhanced by a fire curtain that showed a river winding off into the distance. Alterations for wide-screen movies in 1955 covered the bridge with a flat, Mission-style facade. The unique side wall architecture of this atmospheric design still seems habitable.

On May 22, 1976, 45 years to the day from its original opening, a refurbished Arlington was celebrated as the home of first-run movies, classical music concerts and other live performances. [Metropolitan Theatres. Movies and stage shows.]

■ **Arlington (Fox-Arlington)**
1317 State Street
Plunkett and Edwards
1931

The Arlington's Spanish mission facade, iron gate entrance and scenic asbestos curtain and proscenium arch.

■ **Granada**
1216 State Street
Edward L. Mayberry
1924

Portions of the Granada were changed when the balcony was separated into two small theaters, but much of the Spanish decor survived. A divided grand staircase, just inside the entry doors, carries moviegoers to an upper lobby set under mock-timber beams. Still hanging in the main auditorium, the house curtain shows a broad Spanish landscape, entitled "Granada from Alhambra Hills." [Metropolitan Theatres. Movies — triplex.]

■ ■ ■ ■ ■   COLORADO   ■ ■ ■ ■ ■

### BOULDER

■ **Boulder**
2032 14th Street
Robert Boller
1936

Although closed for years, the Boulder Theater Building still presents a bright facade to the town square, just off Boulder's downtown pedestrian mall. The theater's name appears in fancy script along the top of the marquee. A symbolic fountain, in yellow and white tile with blue and green accents, rises behind the marquee to complete the composition. Historic Boulder, which owned the theater for three years following its last closing in 1982, holds an easement on the exterior, protecting it from alteration. With surviving Art Deco murals falling to pieces, the 1,000-seat interior may soon be hardhat territory. One development plan discussed for the Boulder would convert the auditorium into a boutique complex. [Privately owned. Closed.]

The Boulder's colorful marquee and tile fountain and the auditorium with Art Deco murals.

### DENVER

■ **Mayan**
110 Broadway
Montana Fallis
1930

The Mayan is slightly less excessive, less tomblike and more childlike in its decor than the Mayan (1927) in Los Angeles. The blocky temple form of the exterior is trimmed with polychrome terra cotta and centered by a warrior deity of the same material, with a one-foot-diameter ruby at the center of his forehead. A tall vertical sign reads "Fox-Mayan." The lobby and auditorium walls are covered with painted images taken from Mayan and Aztec originals. Mayan architecture specialist Marjorie

The Mayan's auditorium, decorated with replicas of Aztec images, and its terra cotta facade.

Ingle notes such elements as a Jaguar-god pattern derived from the Temple of the Sun at Palenque. The auditorium light fixtures appear to be made from ancient parchment. Mayan masks and seated figures, illuminated in bright colors from behind, border the stage opening.

Newspaper accounts in 1930 described how members of an Indian tribe were brought in from New Mexico to "exorcise" the theater just before its premiere, performing special chants and camping out on the roof. On opening day, they carried flaming torches through the theater. "Every corner and crevice will be gone over to rid the building of 'evil spirits' and implore the good ones to make it their abode," the *Denver Post* solemnly reported.

After closing in 1980, the Mayan appeared doomed despite its earlier exorcism. A yearlong battle by the Friends of the Mayan, carried out in 1985 to spare the theater from demolition, paid off thanks to an anonymous call to the office of U.S. Rep. Pat Schroeder. The phone tip provided information crucial in determining ownership of the theater, subsequently enabling the group to involve the city in the preservation efforts. Eventually a $700,000 restoration was carried out; the 900-seat auditorium was divided into three theaters, including two 140-seat theaters in the balcony. The Los Angeles–based Landmark Theatres chain took a 10-year lease to operate the new complex as a venue for first-run art and foreign films. [Landon Investments. Movies — triplex.]

The formal opening of the Paramount was clearly meant to be a "Depression buster." An August 1930 issue of *Paramount Parade* described "powerful searchlights playing hide and seek with airplanes, bombs exploding, [and] brilliant flares illuminating Sixteenth Street." A contest for opening night patrons was held to review the inaugural program, with a $100 diamond ring for the winner. The twin consoles of the Wurlitzer Publix One were "manned" by a pair of women organists. The opening film, *Let's Go Native*, featured Jeanette Mac-Donald, a Denver favorite.

■ **Paramount**
16th Street and
Glenarm Place
Rapp and Rapp
and Temple H. Buell
1930

The Paramount, Denver.
Facade and marquee, a
postcard view of the theater
on 16th Street and a detail
from the hybrid French
Renaissance–Art Deco
auditorium.

Buell is credited with the Glenarm entry facade, a
stylistic marriage of Gothic Revival and Art Deco in
gleaming white terra cotta. Chicago architects Rapp and
Rapp pioneered their distinctive blend of Art Deco and
French Renaissance in the auditorium. This stylistic mix
was perfected the following year for the Paramount (1931)
in Aurora, Ill. The walls of the 2,400-seat auditorium are
bordered by golden stencilwork. Fabric murals depicting
scenes of the French royal court fill symbolic bays along
the side walls. The bays are divided by modified column
forms, each topped by a light fixture hidden behind panes
of translucent red glass.

The original barrel-vaulted grand lobby has been
divided from the theater and reopened as the Paramount
Cafe. The theater survived arson damage in 1978. Renovation work on the auditorium began in 1985. NR. [His-
toric Paramount Foundation. Performing arts center.]

■ ■ ■ ■ ■ ■ ■ HAWAII ■ ■ ■ ■ ■ ■ ■

### HONOLULU

■ **Hawaii**
1130 Bethel Street
Emory and Webb
1922

The 1,700-seat auditorium of the Hawaii compares
roughly with that of its contemporary, the Chicago (1921).
Above a cove-lighted proscenium arch, the sounding
board bears an allegorical mural. On the sides, gilded
columns frame ornate organ screens. The inset ceiling
dome glows with multicolored cove lighting. Courtesy of
a 1936 facelift, a streamline Moderne marquee wraps
around the original neoclassical front. Glitzier theaters
would grace the islands in later years, but the Hawaii

remains a stately relic of early moviegoing days in Honolulu. A $2.4 million renovation is planned, to accommodate the Honolulu Symphony and other arts groups. NR. [Hawaii Theatre Center. Performing arts center.]

Throughout its history, the Toyo has showcased Japanese-language films for the island's Japanese-American community. Dickey, architect of the fabled Waikiki (1936, demolished), with its rainbow proscenium arch, decorated the Toyo with a blend of Hawaiian elements, such as the lanai, and Japanese temple forms. The primary model for the theater, according to the newspaper *Nippu Jiji*, was the Ieyasy Shrine in Nikko, a Buddhist temple from the Edo period in Japan. Although now absorbed into a shopping center, the Toyo maintains much of its original serenity. The theater doors are approached across raised walkways that skirt a central Japanese garden, with fishponds to the sides. The auditorium features painted screens along the sides and a stencil-covered gabled ceiling. [Consolidated Amusement Company. Japanese-language movies.]

**■ Toyo**
1230 College Walk
C. W. Dickey
1938

This Polynesian-Chinese pagoda theater was planned as a neighborhood movie house. Pointed corner towers rise at either end of the tiled roof, which is supported by coiled-snake columns. A massive central tower, with upturned eaves, covers the central theater entry. The Palama was renamed the Zamboanga when it began to show Philippine-language films. [Privately owned. Community center.]

**■ Zamboanga (Palama)**
709 North King Street
Louis Davis
c. 1930

Early view of the Zamboanga.

■ ■ ■ ■ ■ ■ ■    **IDAHO**    ■ ■ ■ ■ ■ ■ ■

### BOISE

Just a few blocks south of the domed Idaho State Capitol sits the Egyptian, with winged scarabs decorating the imitation-ashlar pylons and a pair of cast-stone sphinxes resting peacefully atop the south roof. Completing the composition are carnival-striped canvas awnings shading the second-story windows. Construction of this dream palace from the Nile caused quite a stir in Boise. A 1927 issue of the *Idaho Daily Statesman* marveled at the

**■ Egyptian (Ada)**
700 Main Street
Tourtellotte and Hummel
1927

theater's "sacred scarabs and holy hawks." Also drawing mention were the twin Theban figures of Memnon, seated cross-legged with illuminated bowls in their laps. These deities reside on either side of the stage between a pair of pillars "borrowed" from the Hall of Columns at Karnak. The forward proscenium arch shows a sun barge crossing the River Styx below a gold-leafed scarab, in a pattern taken from the ancient Book of the Dead.

In the early 1980s expansion of the candy counter into an adjoining office space was carried out with minimal alteration of the lotus-columned inner lobby. The original auditorium decor remains largely intact. This Boise showplace is one of a trio of Egyptian Revival theaters surviving in the northwestern states, joining the Egyptian (1924) in Coos Bay, Ore., and Peery's Egyptian (1924) in Ogden, Utah. NR. [Plitt/Cineplex Odeon. Movies.]

Above: The Egyptian, Boise. Right: Proscenium arch, featuring scenes from the Book of the Dead.

## POCATELLO

### ■ Chief
217-19 North Main Street
Walter Simon
c. 1937

The Chief's exterior and auditorium mural detail.

Denver architect Simon was hired by the Fox organization to build this unique movie house. Scenes of the old West were painted along the auditorium walls, with borders made of tribal symbols. Stenciled buffalo medallions loop overhead in rings on the ceiling above the balcony seating. A tall vertical sign, topped by an Indian chief in full headdress, dominates the street facade. [Privately owned. Closed.]

## SANDPOINT

The name of this theater pays tribute to the home of its patrons, the panhandle of Idaho. The bright blue and white exterior gives no clue to the Spanish-inspired mock-stucco interior. A large volunteer operation has kept the theater afloat since its purchase for public use in 1985. [Panida Theater Council. Civic auditorium.]

**■ Panida**
300 North First Avenue
1927

■ ■ ■ ■ ■ ■ ■   MONTANA   ■ ■ ■ ■ ■ ■ ■

## ANACONDA

A 1,000-seat Art Deco masterpiece, the Washoe was designed as the principal showplace for this copper boomtown in the Big Sky country of western Montana. With its patterned red brick exterior, the Washoe occupies a position of importance across from the town square. Seattle-based architect Priteca gave Anaconda a theater as elaborate and stylish as any of those he designed for the Pantages chain in coastal cities from Seattle to San Diego. Although the plans for the Washoe were drawn at about the same time as those for the Pantages (1930) in Hollywood, construction of the Washoe was delayed by the economic woes of the Depression. But when it was completed, the theater had a colorful design scheme with expressive Art Deco patterns uniquely evocative of the region's rich history. Entry doors, filled with etched-glass panels, lead to a lobby that

**■ Washoe**
305 Main Street
B. Marcus Priteca
1936

One of several murals in the Washoe's lobby.

The Washoe, Anaconda, Mont. Above: The 1,000-seat auditorium with Art Deco fixtures and trim. Right: Lobby carpet and furniture in 1936.

still contains some period furnishings, although it is without the original Art Deco carpeting with its swirling design. One lobby wall is covered with a delicately shaded mural depicting a long-tressed maiden and a bird of fantastic plumage. Twin murals atop the balcony stair landings show another maiden, Nocturne, rising into a pastel heaven.

In the auditorium, Big Sky themes predominate. Golden medallions of bighorn sheep rim the ceiling. The stage is framed by ornate copper-colored organ grilles. A tasseled valance hangs above the original house curtain, a rich silk composition with two great stags facing each other against a field of royal blue. The centerpiece of the Washoe is the ceiling mural, *Montana*, a pastel ode to the town's heritage, set in the recessed octagonal auditorium dome. Hollywood artist Nat Smythe described his "allegorical group of ornaments" as an attempt to "depict the dependence of our modern civilization on the copper which Montana produces in such abundance." Soft illumination is provided for the mural by a feathered central chandelier of frosted glass, with four smaller matching fixtures at the corners of the dome.

The Washoe has survived in near-mint condition, even as the town's fortunes have declined in recent decades. Manager Henry Lussey, grandson of one of the original owners, has kept the theater in business by supplementing the regular movie showings with local and traveling stage productions. No formal tours are given, but visitors are welcome. NR. [Washoe Amusement Company. Movies and stage shows.]

## BILLINGS

Built as part of the far-flung empire of the Fox West Coast chain, this theater included along with the standard Fox machinery a stereopticon that could produce simulated snowfall effects (presumably superfluous during Montana winters). Architect Reamer of Seattle entrusted the Art Deco treatment of the auditorium to designer Frank Kaslowski. Both the interior and the zigzag-patterned brick exterior of the Fox were dramatically altered during a 1986 adaptation as a new performance hall. The auditorium now is set at an angle within the shell of the old movie theater. A brick-encased pylon hovers above the corner entry, adding lobby space while contributing to a modified Moderne appearance for the exterior. [City of Billings. Performing arts center.]

■ **Fox (Alberta Bair)**
2801 Third Avenue, North
R. C. Reamer
1931

Early view of the Fox's auditorium.

## MISSOULA

The Wilma sits within the Hanson-Simons Building, at eight stories still the tallest building in western Montana. Architect Kirkemo fashioned the theater-office complex after the architecture of Louis Sullivan. Northwestern

■ **Wilma**
104 South Higgins Avenue
H. E. Kirkemo
1921

entrepreneur Billy Simons named the theater for his wife, Edna Wilma, a local star of light opera. The lobbies of the Wilma received a severe late Moderne updating in 1951, but the baroque paneling and the 1930s-vintage central chandelier in the auditorium were mostly undisturbed. The Wilma currently houses a Robert Morton pipe organ, salvaged from the Orpheum (1927, demolished) in Seattle. NR. [Hanson-Simons Company. Movies and stage shows.]

## RED LODGE

**■ Roman**
120 South Broadway
Anton Roat
1917

Adding this new 500-seat theater to his existing Alcazar and Royal theaters provided entrepreneur Steve Roman a long-standing monopoly over motion picture exhibition in this isolated town. The original electric-lightbulb sunburst over the entry doors gave way to a stepped Moderne marquee in 1935. A 1984 remodeling covered this marquee with white panels, decorated only at the ends with helmeted Roman warriors. [Privately owned. Movies.]

## ■ ■ ■ ■ ■ ■ ■   OREGON   ■ ■ ■ ■ ■ ■ ■

### ASTORIA

**■ Liberty**
1203 Commercial Street
Bennes and Herzog
1925

"Spawned from the ashes of the great fire of 1922, Astoria's Liberty Theater stands as a monument to the golden age of motion picture palaces," wrote Emmit Pierce of the *Daily Astorian* in 1979. The monumental Italian Renaissance front facade of the Liberty is angled at 45 degrees to the two street facades, directly facing traffic moving north on Commercial Street. The original lobby design was also classically decorated. A barrel-vaulted ramp provides access to the shelf balcony of the auditorium. Along the auditorium walls, paintings of Venetian scenes by Oregon artist Joseph Knowles "after Canaletto" fill the pilaster-divided bays. Despite several major alterations, the theatrical character of the Liberty is still largely intact. NR. [Privately owned. Movies.]

### COOS BAY

**■ Egyptian**
229 South Broadway
Lee Arden Thomas
1925

In a touch of poetic justice, the Egyptian *replaced* a parking lot. More precisely, the theater was built within the shell of a 1922 garage by the Coos Bay Amusement Company. The two opening night crowds at the Egyptian totaled just over 2,500 — about half the population of the town in 1925. Along with silent pictures and vaudeville acts, patrons were entertained by the fantastic decor, prompted by the 1922 unearthing of the tomb of Tutankhamen. In the auditorium, hieroglyphic patterns encircle the columns framing the stage. The propylon form of the stage arch is centered by a winged Horus disk. Twin organ grilles on either side of the stage were designed as great lyres, each played by a pair of bas-relief royal slaves. Slightly less flamboyant, the lobby features a pair of seated golden pharaohs. These eight-foot-tall royal fig-

ures guard the opposing staircases to a balcony, which currently houses a pair of small theater spaces, divided from the undisturbed main auditorium space below.

Despite alterations, the Egyptian is in remarkably good condition. A vaudeville show was produced locally to celebrate the 60th birthday of the theater in 1985. The original Wurlitzer–Hope Jones Unit Orchestra pipe organ is still called into service for special events and occasional concerts. [Luxury Theatres. Movies—triplex.]

The Egyptian, built within the shell of a car park.

## CORVALLIS

This theater, renamed the Varsity in 1949, opened as a combination vaudeville and motion picture house. The former Majestic has been closed since 1982, its neo-classical facade stripped of all theatrical signage. The Willamette Arts Council has sought to have the auditorium renovated for use as a community theater; funds for this work were appropriated in 1986. [City of Corvallis. Closed.]

■ **Majestic (Varsity)**
115 Southwest Second Street
1913

The Whiteside was one of seven theaters in this town operated by its namesake, Sam Whiteside. The Renaissance Revival brick exterior has a fanciful cornice line decorated by a trio of classical busts and a cartouche of cast stone. Spanning the front facade, a streamlined marquee features a neon script "W." The architectural treatment of the 1,000-seat auditorium is classical, with pilasters lining the side walls and framing the organ screens. Stencil designs decorate the ceiling dome around a central sunburst grille. [Moyer Theatres. Movies.]

■ **Whiteside**
361 Southwest
Madison Avenue
1922

## EUGENE

The McDonald retains its original form, but it has been altered in detail. The skyrocket vertical sign and the old marquee are long gone, leaving a nondescript terra cotta exterior. The showpiece auditorium murals, based on old Norse tales, have been painted and plastered over. The golden Oriental organ screens, set within archways framing the stage, are now hidden by drapes. Restoration remains within the realm of possibility. NR. [Privately owned. Movies.]

■ **McDonald**
1004–44 Willamette Street
Thomas and Mercier
1925

■ **Bagdad**
3702 Hawthorne Avenue
Bennes and Herzog
1927

Fan-shaped archways line the Bagdad's auditorium walls, and painted medallions and stencilwork patterns decorate the ceilings of the main lobby and the ramps to the balcony. These vaulted ramps were a favorite design device of Bennes and Herzog, who used them in the Liberty (1925) in Astoria and the Hollywood (1926) in Portland. The Bagdad is vaguely Spanish Colonial Revival in its exterior styling. A red tile hipped roof covers the corner carriage lobby, with a larger version atop the auditorium block. The Aladdin's Lamp vertical sign was a post-1930 addition. A wall now divides the balcony from the main auditorium. [Moyer Theatres. Movies — twin.]

The Bagdad's corner
entrance and a vaulted ramp
inside.

■ **Hollywood**
4122 Northeast Sandy
Boulevard
Bennes and Herzog
1926

The Hollywood is the fanciest of the Oregon theaters designed by Bennes and Herzog, with its heaped polychrome terra cotta ornament standing as a visual tour de force. The popularity of the theater was such that the surrounding neighborhood came to be known as the Hollywood District. The exotic exterior, with its twisting columns and Churrigueresque composition, remains a

Portland landmark. Original interior decorations included a wave motif painted on the curved ceiling of the lobby and Gothicized wrought-iron pendant chandeliers inside the 1,500-seat auditorium. In 1976 the balcony was cut off from the main floor and split in half. NR. [Luxury Theatres. Movies — triplex.]

The Hollywood's lobby.

When Rapp and Rapp built their two theaters in the Northwest, the consensus was that although the Portland Paramount had the better auditorium, the Seattle Paramount (1928) had a fancier lobby. Yet, since a 1984 conversion to make the theater home to the Oregon Symphony, the Portland Paramount's lobby can now bear comparison with its Seattle counterpart. Doors were added below the arched windows of the south wall facing a new performing arts complex under construction across Main Street. A new balcony-level overlook hovers above the grand lobby, matching the overhang extending

■ **Paramount (Schnitzer Hall)**
1037 Southwest Broadway
Rapp and Rapp
1928

Early view of the Paramount and the theater at night today.

Lobby of the Paramount,
Portland.

from the mezzanine level. Restored to the lobby was a remnant of the original design, the statue *Surprise*. The nude figure, discreet by today's standards, had to be removed after it provoked an outcry in Portland society following the theater's 1928 unveiling. The theatrical history of the Paramount includes another controversy: a 1965 legal action launched against Elizabeth Taylor in which the theater's management maintained that Taylor's off-screen romance with Richard Burton had hurt the box-office totals for *Cleopatra*. The suit was unsuccessful.

Public outcry later arose again over both plans to raze the theater for parking as well as the heavy abuse it suffered at the hands of rock-concert patrons. This eventually led to involvement by the city of Portland. Public donations gave the theater a second life, including a new "Portland" vertical sign added above the main entry doors and a uniform coat of soft lavender paint in the auditorium. NR. [Portland Center for the Performing Arts. Concerts and special events.]

## SALEM

**Capitol**
542 State Street
1926

A classical brickwork exterior gives way here to a golden-walled auditorium with seats for more than 1,100 patrons. Principal decorative effects are Palladian in style, with the two organ screens and the balcony walls framed by engaged Corinthian columns. The fan-shaped sounding board is unchanged, but the stained-glass ceiling dome was removed years ago. [Luxury Theatres. Movies.]

**Elsinore**
170 High Street, S.E.
Lawrence, Holford,
Bean and Allyn
1926

Named for the Danish castle in Shakespeare's *Hamlet*, the Elsinore possesses a brooding Tudor–Gothic Revival cathedral form. Just above the theater entry, stained-glass portraits of Portia, Lady Macbeth and Hamlet appear. Inside, murals in the aptly named Great Gothic Hall depict scenes from *Romeo and Juliet* and *Macbeth*. Gothic Revival features include miniature arches in the balustrades of the balcony stairways and mock-stone groin vaults of the lobby ceiling. The dominant Gothic image in the Elsinore is the magnificent ribbed sounding board arching above the front of the 1,300-seat auditorium. Hidden cove lighting illuminates this portion of the theater in 17 shades.

After a bond referendum to purchase the Elsinore was rejected by Salem voters in 1983, a local volunteer organization convinced the theater owners to allow them to restore the interior in exchange for producing 18 live stage performances each year. The restored theater celebrated its grand reopening in 1986. NR. [Luxury Theatres. Movies and stage shows.]

The Elsinore's Gothic facade and interior.

■ ■ ■ ■ ■ ■ ■   UTAH   ■ ■ ■ ■ ■ ■ ■

### OGDEN

The Peery brothers built and operated this Theban temple atmospheric theater along the main street of this town in northern Utah. The opening night program justifiably promoted the theater as "one of the few pure Egyptian structures of the western hemisphere." The principal facade is a superb example of Egyptian Revival

■ **Peery's Egyptian**
2439 Washington Boulevard
Hodgson and McClenahan
1924

Facade of Peery's Egyptian.

architecture rendered in polychrome terra cotta. Lotus columns articulate the bay divisions, supporting beams decorated with winged serpent scarabs. Bearded pharaohs, molded at life size, divide the recessed windows. The interior is a theatrical rendition of Egyptian architecture. Hieroglyphics of questionable origin and coherence decorate the panels above the proscenium. Seated deities at either end of the stage look out over 1,200 seats, all on one floor. During the theater's early years, the blue plaster ceiling was brightened by projected dawns and sunsets, or darkened to suggest a night sky. The theater was built with a Wurlitzer–Hope Jones pipe organ capable of reproducing string and percussion instrument sounds with booming effect. The Egyptian was closed, with no projected future, for health-code violations in the early 1980s. [Privately owned. Closed.]

## SALT LAKE CITY

■ **Capitol (Orpheum)**
46 West Second Street, South
G. Albert Lansburgh;
R. E. Powers
1913, 1927

Architect Lansburgh, trained at the Ecole des Beaux Arts in Paris, designed the exterior of the Orpheum in the style of the Italian Renaissance. Rich with overtones of Palladian architecture, the street facade features elaborate terra cotta trim around the windows and along the cornice line. This 1,800-seat vaudeville house was remodeled inside by Powers in 1927 and renamed the Capitol. The new decor was a modified Louis XVI style, with 400 seats and a Wurlitzer pipe organ added in the makeover. After 50 years as a movie house, the Capitol underwent a second conversion to serve as a public arts facility. NR. [Salt Lake City Redevelopment Agency. Performing arts center.]

The Capitol's recently remodeled palazzo-style exterior and auditorium.

■ ■ ■ ■ ■ ■ WASHINGTON ■ ■ ■ ■ ■ ■

## BELLINGHAM

■ **Mount Baker**
106 North Commercial Street
R. C. Reamer
1927

A tall, domed bell tower marks the location of this 1,600-seat theater in downtown Bellingham. The front face of the tower's hexagonal stucco shaft gives the theater name in large letters. Inside the Mount Baker, the decoration recalls Moorish castles. This influence is most apparent

The Spanish-style Mount Baker, with its mock bell tower.

in the golden organ grilles, beamwork ceiling and furnishings of the grand lobby. The domed ceiling of the auditorium is decorated with plaster busts of Spanish noblemen. The Mount Baker's original equipment matched the quality of its architecture. Most notable is the Hope Jones model Wurlitzer, still capable of speaking with the power of a 30-piece orchestra. NR. [Privately owned. Movies.]

## CAMAS

This wonderful small-town theater has more stud lights (540) decorating its marquee soffit than seats in its auditorium (411, including the shelf balcony). Arches with a Middle Eastern flavor and scallop-motif wall sconces highlight the interior decor. The light blue exterior has a central arch formed by twisting columns painted pink and lavender. In 1986 a reproduction of the original marquee was put in place, incorporating the red neon "Liberty" sign that dates from the 1930s. [Privately owned. Movies.]

■ **Liberty (Granada)**
315 Northeast Fourth Avenue
1928

## CENTRALIA

The simple brick exterior of the Fox is almost overwhelmed by its flashy marquee. The Art Deco interior has been divided, with two small viewing rooms filling the balcony. The screen of the main-floor theater is set within the radiating green and blue frames of the proscenium arch. [Privately owned. Movies — triplex.]

■ **Fox**
215 South Tower Avenue
B. Marcus Priteca, consultant
c. 1930

The Fox's eye-catching neon marquee.

## LONGVIEW

■ **Columbia**
1225–31 Vandercook Way
George B. Purvis
1925

In the mid-1920s a group of 40 local investors formed the Columbia Amusement Company to build a first-class entertainment hall for Longview. Purvis decided to take advantage of the Northwest's abundant supply of lumber to frame the Columbia in heavy timber. This approach, highly unusual for the time, was complemented by an equally unique system of interior decorations consisting mainly of painted patterns that effectively suggest mosaic tilework. This method was used to best effect to decorate the engaged side wall pillars and the inner rim of the proscenium arch. The organ screens, created by skillful jigsawing, have a floral motif in soft coral and green. A fan-vaulted sounding board originally concealed additional room for the organ swells of the departed Kimball pipe organ. Updates to the Columbia include the mica-paneled ironwork chandeliers installed in 1933 above the balcony and a marquee attached to the Classical Revival exterior in the 1940s. Since 1983 the Columbia Theater Task Force has managed the theater while seeking to upgrade the stage equipment and restore significant architectural features of the interior. NR. [City of Longview. Performing arts center.]

The Columbia, now host to classical concerts.

## OLYMPIA

■ **Washington Center
(Olympic)**
506 Washington Street
George B. Purvis
1924

What little remains of the old Olympic (opened as the Liberty) is encased in rough stucco to stand as exterior walls for a newly constructed performance hall. The stucco facade, trimmed in green, has a pair of post-Modern Palladian openings cut through it, out of belated respect for the 1924 design. The auditorium, with 1,000 seats on four levels, recalls the shape if not the appearance of the space it supplanted. [Washington Center for the Performing Arts. Performing arts center.]

## SEATTLE

■ **Coliseum**
Fifth Avenue and Pike Street
B. Marcus Priteca
1916

Clad entirely in terra cotta, glazed in creamy white, the Coliseum was among the earliest luxury movie theaters built west of the Mississippi. Situated on a prominent downtown corner, the two street facades of the theater were done in an elaborate Renaissance Revival style,

brilliantly illuminated at night by rows of stud lighting. A 1949 remodeling gave the exterior its revolving neon cylinder and curved marquee. Lost in the makeover was virtually all the interior ornament. City landmark designation protects the splendidly conceived exterior of the Coliseum, but some talk has been heard of replacing the altered 2,000-seat auditorium with retail operations. NR. [Luxury Theatres. Movies.]

Tucked away inside the Renaissance Revival–style Skinner Building, the Fifth Avenue magically transports its patrons to the ancient Forbidden City in China. Old gold highlights enhance the jade green and Chinese red color scheme of the ornate plasterwork walls, designed to suggest Oriental wood construction. The grand lobby reproduces the ancient Temple of Heavenly Peace, complete with ferocious royal guard dogs. Rich stencils cover the mock-timber beams and log roof of this great hall.

The auditorium of the Fifth Avenue is as magnificent

Interior of the Coliseum before a 1949 remodeling and the Renaissance Revival exterior.

■ **Fifth Avenue**
1308 Fifth Avenue
R. C. Reamer
1926

The Fifth Avenue's Oriental decor and a detail from the auditorium.

The Fifth Avenue, Seattle. Chandelier held above the theater's auditorium by a great dragon and a wall with an elaborate organ grille.

as any ever built. Its royal bearing can be attributed to the space it mimics, the Ming Dynasty audience hall of the emperor in the Forbidden City. The opening night program described the auditorium:

Its most imposing feature is the great dome. Coiled within an azure sphere and surrounded by glowing hues [rests] the Great Dragon, guardian genius of the place, his presence shadowed and multiplied in varying shapes and forms through the structure.

Indeed, five-clawed dragons, symbolic of the emperor, abound along the walls and ceiling beams, but none can match the bewhiskered giant of the dome. From his mouth hangs the Pearl of Perfection, the main chandelier, surrounded by eight smaller tasseled fixtures. Yet another dragon writhes "in scintillating coils" on the Fifth Avenue's asbestos curtain.

This magnificent 2,400-seat theater was the product of a collaboration between architect Reamer and Norwegian-born artist Gustav Liljestrom. Reamer is best known for his rustic Old Faithful Inn (1903) at the center of Yellowstone National Park. Liljestrom was a respected expert on Chinese art and architecture. Inspiration for the particular decorative patterns chosen by these two came from a contemporary sourcebook, Ernst Boershmann's *Chinesiche Architekture* (Berlin, 1925).

A restoration, highly respectful of the original architecture, was carried out in 1980 by Seattle-based architect Richard F. McCann. The reopening of the Fifth Avenue was credited with initiating a pronounced economic upturn in the surrounding business district. [UNICO Properties. Stage shows and concerts.]

The exterior of this former vaudeville theater was updated along Moderne lines in the 1930s. Whitewashed walls, trimmed with red rings, enclose the remodeled interior. The triangular marquee, added at the time of the modernization, is a particularly fine piece of neon signage. When a second Guild 45th addition was constructed to the west of the original in the mid-1980s, an equally colorful neon arrangement was incorporated into its red and white facade. [Privately owned. Movies.]

■ **Guild 45th**
2115 North 45th Street
1919

The Guild 45th, with neon "cooling rings" wrapping the exterior.

In its early years, the Moore served as a high-class vaudeville house. Patrons were welcomed in a Gothic-vaulted lobby space decorated with $40,000 worth of marble and onyx. The auditorium was more in keeping with Victorian opera house design, with a delicately patterned sounding board arching high above the stage. The oddly staggered collection of opera boxes, originally set on the walls near the stage, were stripped away during the Moore's lengthy run as a movie theater. A natural-colored terra cotta nameplate above the modern marquee differentiates the primary theater entrance from the doors of the adjoining Moore Hotel. NR. [Privately owned. Rock concerts.]

■ **Moore**
1932 Second Avenue
E. W. Houghton
1907

Once touted as the "Show Place of Seattle," the former Fox has been a hard-luck case in recent years. Its orchestra seats were replaced by terraced rows of fake-leather booths for a brief run as a dinner nightclub in the 1970s. The extremely busy exterior is concrete, cast in a Churrigueresque mold, and includes a row of arched windows filled with leaded glass. Developers, apparently anxious to rid Seattle of this gaudy leftover, have been pushing to have the city revoke its landmark designation,

■ **Music Hall (Fox)**
Olive Street and
Seventh Avenue
Sherwood Ford
1929

thus far to no avail. Just after St. Patrick's Day 1987, the barricades around the Music Hall were removed and new signs proclaiming the Emerald Palace started going up. [Privately owned. Planned dinner theater.]

Above: The suburban Neptune. Right: The downtown Music Hall.

■ **Neptune**
1303 Northeast 45th Street
1921

A seafaring theater by design, the Neptune features neon tridents on its marquee, portholes through each of its entry doors and a hull-shaped candy counter fully rigged for sail. Inside the marine green auditorium, golden masks of mighty Neptune line the top edge of the walls. Colored glass panels depicting scenes from Atlantis were placed on either side of the stage in the late 1970s. To supplement the Neptune's regular offerings of classic and foreign films in repertory, organ concerts are planned on a pipe organ installed in 1986 to replace the long-lost original. [Landmark Theatres. Movies.]

■ **Paramount**
901–07 Pine Street
Rapp and Rapp
1928

The golden highlights of the bas-relief ornament decorating every surface of the Paramount auditorium enhance the glow cast by cove lights hidden in the ceiling dome and along the edge of the proscenium arch. The basic decorative arrangement is strongly related to the standard French baroque designs used by Rapp and Rapp in

The Paramount's flashy marquee and the auditorium with bas-relief ornamentation.

their highly popular Orpheum chain theaters. With its ironwork railings and crystal chandeliers, the grand lobby has a particularly glamorous appeal. Glimpses of the lobby can be seen in *Frances*, the filmed life of hometown movie star Frances Farmer, portrayed by Jessica Lange. NR. [Privately owned. Concerts.]

Ornate drapes and fixtures on the Paramount's mezzanine.

## SPOKANE

A delicate butterfly pattern in green and beige runs along the cornice line of the Fox, lightening the blocky appearance of its concrete Moderne exterior. The huge grand lobby is a more lavish Art Deco arrangement with frosted-glass chandeliers and floral murals trimmed in silver. The highlight of the 2,350-seat auditorium is the cove-lighted sunrise spreading above the front of the house, similar to the sunburst ceiling of the Wiltern (1931) in Los Angeles. A wall divides the minitheaters in the balcony from the rest of the auditorium. [Luxury Theatres. Movies — triplex.]

■ **Fox**
1005 West Sprague Avenue
R. C. Reamer
1931

Far left: The Palace in 1980. Left and above: The Fox's facade and Art Deco details from the lobby.

A fan-shaped pattern of stud lights spreads above the theater doors on the arched street facade of this one-time nickelodeon. The straight-walled auditorium is entered through a narrow barrel-vaulted lobby. The Palace saw temporary service as a showcase for classic films in the early 1980s. [Privately owned. Closed.]

■ **Palace**
328 West Riverside Avenue
c. 1910

## TACOMA

■ **Pantages**
901–09 Broadway
B. Marcus Priteca
1918

This was among the earliest of the so-called Pantages Greek designs produced by Priteca for theater impresario Alexander Pantages. The designs are typically characterized by attached Corinthian columns framing the stage openings, high domed ceilings centered by allegorical murals in pastel shades and an overall classical arrangement rimmed by a denticulated cornice. The exterior of this theater is a throwback to the terra cotta–clad Renaissance Revival look of the Coliseum (1916) in Seattle. Built as a vaudeville house, the 1,300-seat Pantages survived until the late 1970s as a movie theater. The city then initiated efforts to rehabilitate it. Under the supervision of Richard F. McCann, a former colleague of Priteca, the auditorium was restored to its original appearance. The lobby spaces were modernized in a suitably elegant style to provide both comfort and improved access for patrons. NR. [City of Tacoma. Performing arts center.]

Below: Elegant classical elements, a Pantages trademark, on a row of balconies. Right: The Kiggins.

## VANCOUVER

■ **Kiggins**
1011 Main Street
Day Hilborn
1936

This comfortable small-town theater is housed within a whitewashed block of small shopfronts. A lively floral motif in cast concrete runs along the top edge of the Moderne street facade. The roomy auditorium has minimal touches of ornamentation, but Art Deco light fixtures, supplemented by hidden cove lights, make for a pleasant effect. Double features at bargain prices currently add to the pleasure of attending the Kiggins. [Privately owned. Movies.]

## YAKIMA

■ **Capitol (Mercy)**
19 South Third Street
B. Marcus Priteca
1920

Frederick Mercy, Sr., ran this theater (later the Capitol) as the entertainment center of this town. In the theater's early days, Pavlova and John Philip Sousa shared the stage with graduation exercises for local high schools. After attendance had dwindled to almost nothing in the early 1970s, the city purchased the building in 1974, only to see the Capitol burn to its outer walls the following year. The city council made the courageous decision to rebuild the theater as originally designed. Anthony Heinsbergen, the muralist and decorator who had worked with Priteca on the original design, returned to Yakima at age 83 to plan new murals for the Capitol's auditorium dome. By 1983 the Capitol had been resurrected to function in the role foreseen a decade earlier, as the showplace for local and touring stage presentations. NR. [City of Yakima. Performing arts center.]

■ ■ ■ ■ ■ ■ ■ WYOMING ■ ■ ■ ■ ■ ■ ■

### CHEYENNE

The Atlas was constructed in 1907 inside a three-story building opened 20 years earlier as a tea shop. The late Victorian theater space that has survived as the street-front portion of the Atlas Building has been turned into shops. The fanciest ornament of the auditorium is concentrated in a plaster band that forms the proscenium arch. As recently as a decade ago, the theater maintained a painted curtain showing a scene of a Venetian canal, with the artwork surrounded by ads for shops and hotels long out of business. [Privately owned. Status unknown.]

■ **Atlas**
213 West 16th Street
William Dubois
1887, 1907

Painted curtain of the Atlas, displaying advertisements and a Venetian scene.

### SHERIDAN

Still Roman-Byzantine inside, the Wyo's facade was altered in 1941, giving it a Moderne look complete with a neon-trimmed marquee. Efforts to rehabilitate the theater have been spearheaded by a group calling itself Save the Wyo Theater, Inc. [Privately owned. Movies.]

■ **Wyo**
42 North Main Street
Carl Berg, designer
1921

■ ■ ■ ■ ■ ■ ■ ■ ■ ■ ■ ■ ■ ■ ■ ■ ■ ■

# EPILOGUE:
## THE ONES THAT GOT AWAY

T he problem is really that the best are gone. Perhaps one could debate which movie theaters were the "best." But what the public — the real judge, in the end — liked best and tried to save were, in most instances, a select few of the thousands of theaters built primarily to show movies.

Survival was essentially a matter of economics. From early nickelodeon storefronts to the cinemas of the 20th century's teen years, through the development of the true palaces and on to the last few large examples — the Southtown (1932, Rapp and Rapp) in Chicago, Radio City Music Hall (1932, Donald Deskey) in New York City, the Los Angeles (1931, S. Charles Lee) in Los Angeles — money continued to be the name of the game. If a building could not function economically, it was viewed by its owners as a dinosaur; and the "dinosaurs" are gone. Not only were the owners slow to recognize the architectural treasures they had; so was the public. Scores of theaters succumbed before the rise of the preservation movement, which has shown that these landmarks can both be saved and provide unique economic and cultural returns to their communities. It took another generation to recognize the magic that was being sacrificed with the loss of each theater.

Theaters generally thrived in groups — at 42nd Street and Broadway in New York, on Randolph Street in Chicago or on Broadway in Los Angeles. Cinema operators now tell us they need at least two or more screens to break even; so what once covered several blocks is now compressed into one building. Today, film fans go to their favorite multiplex, even with a particular movie in mind, but can be swayed by crowds, timing and other factors to see a different movie. That is how the clustered — and much larger — movie palaces made money in the 1920s, 1930s and 1940s. Competition is a tonic to business; stagnation or deficit is fatal, as the following theatrical tales illustrate.

■ **Paradise**
Chicago
John Eberson
1928–56

Competition made the Paradise into the most costly theater per square foot in Eberson's long and distinguished career. The strong pressures of nouveau-riche exhibitors on the west side of Chicago pushed this theater's construction from the incapable ownership of a hotelier to an underfinanced exhibitor and then to the most successful theater chain of the era. Balaban and Katz seized the chance to challenge the larger and better-situated Marbro (1927, Levy and Klein; demolished) around the corner. Plans for the Paradise were redrawn, materials were upgraded, and the advertising department had a field day. What emerged was more than might have been; many of the craftsmen who had created cherubim and palm fronds for Eberson's theaters around the country lived and worked very near the Chicago Paradise. Instead of just chiseling out one more Venus de

Opposite: Chicago's Paradise lost, a Second Empire tour de force dubbed the "World's Most Beautiful Theater" by promoters Balaban and Katz.

Above: The Paradise's atmospheric auditorium with cherubim and seraphim adding to the elegance. Below: Lobby with marble-clad staircase and balcony.

Milo, the artists gave their best because they would be able to enjoy their work at close hand "for all time."

The exterior of the Paradise was a half-block-long Second Empire tour de force with stores adjoining a seven-story entrance tower. It was modestly tagged by Balaban and Katz as the "World's Most Beautiful Theater." The buff terra cotta, bronze and marble-framed shop windows and gold-leaf trim on a slate blue mansard roof were obviously costly. The marquee captured a slice of Paradise itself. Inside, a grand staircase ascended on the left and right into a soaring domed room with stars, clouds and zodiac signs in the "sky" above. And then, past the ticket taker and a second set of doors, a somewhat understated baroque-style lobby of modest scale was flanked by a luxurious foyer on the first and second floors. The vast atmospheric auditorium (entered through nine aisle doors) included so many gimmicks and details that many patrons may have been completely distracted from the stage or screen. Above the huge, bowed proscenium arch, three steeds galloped toward the audience pulling a chariot like Apollo's. Intermission started with a "sunrise" over the stage that lighted, as Eberson described it to the press, "a garden of a Louis . . . made for the merriment of the court." The lighting effects, stars, clouds and specially commissioned statuary (attributed to Lorado Taft) were copied in various ways for several other theaters.

The builders' challenge worked all too well. The competition quickly folded. Soon came the Depression; then staff shortages caused World War II closures. Television and Cinemascope forced John Balaban to say after a brief visit in April 1956, "Rip it down." Fortunately, blueprints and photographs survive to identify every fragment of this ultimate concept of Paradise.

Competitive factors led to the loss in 1963 of San Francisco's fabulous Fox, always advertised as the "Last Word." Here, an established architect, Lamb, was given a very large budget to create a West Coast showplace for the exhibition empire William Fox was completing. Drawing on experience and established sources (and keeping at arm's length the enthusiasm of the boss's wife and decorator, Eve Leo Fox), Lamb pulled together the largest and finest of three quite similar theaters; the other two — the Midland (1927, Thomas W. Lamb) in Kansas City, Mo., and the Jersey (1929, Rapp and Rapp) in Jersey City — still stand.

■ **Fox**
San Francisco
Thomas W. Lamb
1929-63

The Fox possessed an unusually fine arrangement of lounges and service areas amassed on a difficult and irregular site. The theater was to be part of a large commercial building, including shops, offices and a hotel; only the theater portion was built, however. An elaborate assortment of details surrounded a large faux window above an ornate marquee of light bulbs, neon and stained glass. Behind heavy brass doors, the foyers, lobby, lounges and auditorium were an orgy of gilded French details with a heavy Victorian feel of cherubim, frets and panels. The massive auditorium managed to appear elegant and luxurious with reportedly excellent sight lines and acoustics. A large mezzanine beneath the flowing balcony offered loge seating off a foyer overly decorated with fine antiques. The ornate dome would have pleased any of the Kings Louis of France.

Above: The Fox's facade. The theater was declared "irreplaceable" by preservationists who failed to save it. Left: Gilt lobby and staircase.

Auditorium of the Fox,
San Francisco.

The behemoth Fox was a little too far from the center of activities and a little too large for voters to understand and save in a special referendum. This great theater was demolished amid much fanfare and many auctions. A fitting epilogue — and a boon to preservationists elsewhere — is a poster showing the razing of the Fox and the word "irreplaceable."

■ **Paramount**
Times Square
New York City
Rapp and Rapp
1926–64

On a more sensible scale, Rapp and Rapp designed the Times Square Paramount in the base of the quasi-Deco building built to house the Paramount corporate offices. Turning to the French style that had worked so well for them previously, the architects created a luxurious theater that at some 4,000 seats managed to enfold the audience with the stage productions through careful and expensive staging and lighting effects.

The Paramount in New York City in the early 1930s. The theater was originally designed as part of an office complex, which remains today.

A stained-glass "Mount Paramount" medallion was the focal point of a two-story window in the base of the Paramount Building. An ornate, curved French marquee of modest scale protected the box office and front doors. A black marble rotunda preceded a low Hall of Nations with large display cases of stones from famous buildings of the world. The half-block-long lobby that came next terminated in a graceful staircase inspired by the Paris Opera. Each foyer had a distinctive design, custom Aubusson carpeting and enough statuary and antiques to furnish a museum. The somewhat narrow auditorium was surrounded by an arcade of cove-lighted arches on the main and mezzanine floors and covered by a rectangular dome with overlooks from an encircling lounge above.

This theater did not manage to survive far into the 1960s, despite the corporate wizards in adjoining offices. Altered many times to accommodate swings of taste, the Paramount disappeared relatively quietly in the pre-preservation early 1960s. The skyscraper, still a notable structure at 43rd Street and Broadway, remains sans theater.

Lobby and auditorium of the Paramount. Rapp and Rapp sought a French baroque environment in the Paramount's interior space.

A few blocks from Times Square, the nearly 6,000-seat Roxy did not have an attached skyscraper to share operating costs. Its understated entrance was at the corner of the still-surviving Taft Hotel. A nondescript corridor terminated in a large oval rotunda surrounded by green faux marbre columns and capped with a dome and monumental chandelier. A cartoon of the period shows a moppet and her mother staring into this room in awe as the child asks, "Mommy — does God live here?" Samuel L. "Roxy" Rothapfel, the entrepreneur who mounted this venture, did call his theater the "Cathedral of the Motion Picture." Several staircases and a foyer led

■ **Roxy**
New York City
W. W. Ahlschlager
1927–61

to the large oval auditorium, set at an angle to the street. A unique plan of mezzanine and balcony with a center cutout for the projection booth gave a good view of an expansive stage, flanked by stairs spiraling from mock pulpits and surmounted by an ornate pierced grille. A curious dome and side wall scheme was characteristic of Ahlschlager's style.

The architect's largest work, with a unique floor plan and fabled glitz, could not survive economically. After several attempts by knowledgeable showmen (even John Balaban, brought back from retirement) to re-establish the theater, the Roxy was razed in 1961.

The Roxy, New York City. Above: Oval rotunda with green faux marbre columns. Right: The theater's modest exterior.

These few key examples of the finest lost theaters serve as an epitaph for scores of buildings that survived for just a few decades. Now we have come full circle; simple, small cinemas, often boxed together, are the key to economic survival in the exhibition business. If any of the first nickelodeons had survived (I know of none), they would have much in common with today's scale and approach in the movie business.

## AN HONOR ROLL OF LOST PALACES

Together with the four departed masterpieces just described, the 38 theaters named below form at least a partial listing of the greatest of the picture palaces that have been demolished. Represented are a few of the earliest downtown palaces such as the Capitol in Manhattan and the Tivoli in Chicago. The Majestic in Houston, the first fully atmospheric theater by John Eberson, has been razed. Resort theaters, as far apart stylistically and geographically as the Warner in Atlantic City and the Waikiki in Honolulu, are now ghosts. Baltimore, Philadelphia and Minneapolis have been stripped of their best theaters. With such treasures as these now lost to us forever, the remaining pre-Depression theaters — palaces or not — should be valued all the more highly.

Joseph DuciBella

■ **Albee**
Brooklyn
Thomas W. Lamb
1925

■ **Albee**
Cincinnati
Thomas W. Lamb
1927

■ **Capitol**
Chicago
John Eberson
1925

■ **Capitol**
New York City
Thomas W. Lamb
1919

■ **Carthay Circle**
Los Angeles
Dwight Gibbs
1926

■ **Earle**
Philadelphia
Hoffman and Henon
1924

■ **Fox**
Brooklyn
C. Howard Crane
1928

■ **Fox**
Florence, Calif.
S. Charles Lee
1932

■ **Fox (Capitol)**
Washington, D.C.
Rapp and Rapp
1927

■ **Granada**
San Francisco
Alfred Henry Jacobs
1921

■ **Grand**
Atlanta
Thomas W. Lamb
1893, 1932

■ **Harding**
Chicago
Friedstein and Company
1925

■ **Hollywood**
Detroit
Graven and Mayger
1927

■ **Loew's 72nd Street**
New York City
Thomas W. Lamb,
John Eberson
1932

■ **Majestic**
Houston
John Eberson
1923

■ **Marbro**
Chicago
Levy and Klein, with
Edward Eichenbaum
1929

■ **Mastbaum**
Philadelphia
Hoffman and Henon
1929

Gloria Swanson amid the ruins of the Roxy, New York City.

■ **Metropolitan (Paramount)**
Los Angeles
William L. Woollett
1923

■ **Minnesota**
Minneapolis
Graven and Mayger
1928

■ **Norshore**
Chicago
Rapp and Rapp
1926

■ **Oriental**
Portland, Ore.
Thomas and Mercier
1927

■ **Orpheum**
Seattle
B. Marcus Priteca
1927

■ **Palace**
Rochester, N.Y.
Graven and Mayger
1928

■ **Pantages**
San Diego
B. Marcus Priteca
1924

■ **Paramount**
Toledo
Rapp and Rapp
1928

■ **Pekin**
Pekin, Ill.
Elmer F. Behrens
1928

■ **Picadilly**
Chicago
Rapp and Rapp
1927

■ **Regal**
Chicago
Levy and Klein, with
Edward Eichenbaum
1928

■ **Riviera Annex**
Detroit
John Eberson
1927

■ **RKO Roxy (Center)**
New York City
Reinhard and Hofmeister
1932

■ **Stanley**
Baltimore
Hoffman and Henon
1927

■ **Stanley**
Philadelphia
Hoffman and Henon
1921

■ **Texas**
San Antonio
Boller Brothers
1926

■ **Tivoli**
Chicago
Rapp and Rapp
1921

■ **Tower**
Chicago
Friedstein and Company
1926

■ **Triboro**
Astoria, N.Y.
Thomas W. Lamb
1931

■ **Waikiki**
Honolulu
C. W. Dickey
1936

■ **Warner**
Atlantic City
Hoffman and Henon
1929

# FURTHER READING

Bagley, Mary. *The Front Row: Missouri's Grand Theatres.* St. Louis: Gateway Publishing, 1984.

Bishop, Mary, ed. *The Ohio Theatre: 1928–1978.* Columbus, Ohio: Columbus Association for the Performing Arts, 1978.

Bowers, Q. David. *Nickelodeon Theatres and Their Music.* Vestal, N.Y.: Vestal Press, 1977.

Duncan, Alastair. *American Art Deco.* New York: Harry N. Abrams, 1986.

Francisco, Charles. *Radio City Music Hall: An Affectionate History of the World's Greatest Theatre.* New York: E. P. Dutton, 1979.

Freeman, Robert E. *Scene II: Re-Using Old Movie Theaters.* Providence, R.I.: Author, 1977.

Hall, Ben M. *The Best Remaining Seats.* New York: Bramhall House, 1961.

Headley, Robert K., Jr. *Exit: A History of Movies in Baltimore.* Baltimore: Author, 1974.

Ingle, Marjorie. *The Mayan Revival Style: Art Deco Mayan Fantasy.* Salt Lake City: Peregrine Smith, 1984.

Kaufmann, Preston J. *Fox — The Last Word.* Pasadena, Calif.: Showcase Publications, 1979.

Morrison, A. Craig, and Lucy Pope Wheeler, eds. *Nickelodeon to Movie Palace: Ten Twentieth Century Theatres 1910–1931.* Washington, D.C.: Historic American Buildings Survey, U.S. Department of the Interior, 1978.

Naylor, David. "Ticket to the World of Movies." *Historic Preservation,* May–June 1979.

_____. *American Picture Palaces: The Architecture of Fantasy.* New York: Van Nostrand Reinhold, 1981.

Pabst, Georgia. "Pizzazz, Inc." *Historic Preservation,* May–June 1987.

Pildas, Ave, and Lucinda Smith. *Movie Palaces: Survivors of an Elegant Era.* New York: Clarkson N. Potter, 1980.

Sexton, R. W., and Betts, B. F. *American Theatres of Today.* 1927, 1930. 2 vols. Reprint. Vestal, N.Y.: Vestal Press, 1977.

Sharp, Dennis. *The Picture Palace and Other Buildings for the Movies.* New York: Frederick A. Praeger, 1969.

Stoddard, Richard. *Theatre and Cinema Architecture: A Guide to Information Sources.* Performing Arts Information Guide Series, vol. 5. Detroit: Gale Research, 1978.

Stoddard, Robert. *Preservation of Concert Halls, Opera Houses and Movie Palaces.* Information Series No. 16, National Trust for Historic Preservation. Washington, D.C.: Preservation Press, 1978.

Stone, Susannah Harris. *The Oakland Paramount.* Berkeley, Calif.: Lancaster Miller, 1983.

Strauss, Mary, and David Naylor. *The Fabulous Fox.* St. Louis: Fox Theatre, 1985.

Theatre Historical Society. *A Pictorial Survey of Marquees.* Notre Dame, Ind.: Theatre Historical Society, 1980.

Valerio, Joseph M., and Daniel Friedman. *Movie Palaces: Renaissance and Reuse.* New York: Academy for Educational Development, Educational Facilities Laboratories, 1982.

### PERIODICALS

*Marquee,* quarterly journal of the Theatre Historical Society. South Bend, Ind., 1969–79; Hyattsville, Md., 1980–86; Columbus, Ohio, 1987–

*Motion Picture News,* monthly. New York, 1925–30.

Le Grand David, performing troupe appearing at the Cabot Street in Beverly, Mass.

# INFORMATION SOURCES

The following organizations and agencies can provide further information on architecture, historic preservation and related subjects covered in *Great American Movie Theaters*. In addition, state historic preservation offices are excellent resources.

American Institute of
Architects
1735 New York Avenue, N.W.
Washington, D.C. 20006

American Theatre
Organ Society
4633 S.E. Brookside Drive,
Suite 58
Milwaukie, Ore. 97215

B'hend and Kaufmann
Archives
P.O. Box 40165
Pasadena, Calif. 91104

League of Historic
American Theatres
c/o The National Theatre
1321 E Street, N.W.
Washington, D.C. 20004

Library of Congress
Prints and Photographs
Division
Washington, D.C. 20250

National Endowment
for the Arts
Design Arts Program
1100 Pennsylvania Avenue,
N.W.
Washington, D.C. 20506

National Park Service
U.S. Department of
the Interior:

Historic American
Buildings Survey
P.O. Box 37127
Washington, D.C. 20013-7127

National Register of
Historic Places
P.O. Box 37127
Washington, D.C. 20013-7127

Preservation Assistance
Division
P.O. Box 37127
Washington, D.C. 20013-7127

National Trust for
Historic Preservation
1785 Massachusetts
Avenue, N.W.
Washington, D.C. 20036

Regional Offices:

Mid-Atlantic Regional Office
6401 Germantown Avenue
Philadelphia, Pa. 19144

Midwest Regional Office
53 West Jackson Boulevard,
Suite 1135
Chicago, Ill. 60604

Mountains/Plains
Regional Office
511 16th Street, Suite 700
Denver, Colo. 80202

Texas/New Mexico
Field Office
500 Main Street, Suite 606
Forth Worth, Tex. 76102

Regional Offices Continued:

Northeast Regional Office
45 School Street, 4th Floor
Boston, Mass. 02108

Southern Regional Office
456 King Street
Charleston, S.C. 29403

Western Regional Office
One Sutter Street
San Francisco, Calif. 94104

Society of Architectural
Historians
1232 Pine Street
Philadelphia, Pa. 19107-5944

Theatre Historical Society
P.O. Box 767
San Francisco, Calif. 94101

■ ■ ■ ■ ■ ■ ■ ■ ■ ■ ■ ■ ■ ■ ■ ■ ■ ■ ■ ■

# PHOTOGRAPHIC SOURCES

Abbreviations used refer to collections maintained by the following institutions:
HABS — Historic American Buildings Survey, National Park Service
NTHP — National Trust for Historic Preservation
THS — Theatre Historical Society

**2** top and middle, Lake County Museum, Curt Teich Postcard Collection, 121933 and 8A-H 2862; bottom, THS. **7** top and bottom, Lake County Museum, Curt Teich Postcard Collection, 111097 and 3C-H963; middle, THS. **8** THS/Ben Hall Collection. **9** NTHP. **11** David Naylor. **14** Denver Public Library, Western History Department. **15** top, NTHP/Robert Truax; bottom, Peoria (Ill.) Library. **16** top, The Riviera/ Wright Photos; middle, The Rialto, Tucson; bottom, Minnesota Historical Society. **17** Smithsonian Institution. **18** top, NTHP; bottom, B'hend and Kaufmann Archives. **19** top, B'hend and Kaufmann Archives. **20** left, HABS; right, David Naylor; bottom, THS. **21** top, Raymond Brubacher; bottom, NTHP. **22** top left and bottom, Paramount Theatre; right, NTHP. **24** top, Dick Haden, Orpheum Theatre Restoration Committee/ Kansas State Historical Society; middle, Smithsonian Institution; bottom, B'hend and Kaufmann Archives/ THS Collection. **25** Smithsonian Institution. **26** Fred Lundy, *San Francisco Examiner.* **27** top left, David Naylor; top right, Manchester Historic Association and Gary Samson; bottom, HABS. **28** David Naylor. **29** David Naylor. **30** NTHP. **31** NTHP. **32** Walter Smalling, Jr. **33** top, Christiane Citron, Denver; bottom, David Naylor. **35** all, Saint Louis Symphony Society. **36** top, Paramount Theatre of the Arts, Oakland, Calif.; middle and bottom, Cathe Centorbe, San Francisco. **37** THS/Ben Hall Collection. **38** Columbus Association for the Performing Arts. **39** all, Aaron D. Cushman and Associates, Inc. **40** both, Aaron D. Cushman and Associates, Inc. **41** David Naylor. **42** top, David Naylor; bottom, NTHP. **43** R. F. McCann and Company. **45** Preservation of the Egyptian Theatre, Inc. **46** THS. **47** Richmond Newspapers, Inc./Carpenter Center. **49** Walter Anderson, Emporia, Kans./Kansas State Historical Society.

## NEW ENGLAND

**50–51** HABS. **52** David Naylor. **53** top, Torrington Historical Society; bottom, David Naylor. **54** both, David Naylor. **55** left, THS; right and bottom, David Naylor. **56** both, HABS. **57** top and bottom right, Steve Heaslip; bottom left, Smithsonian Institution. **58** left, David Naylor; right, Richard Longstreth. **59** top, both, David Naylor; bottom, THS. **60** left, B. Andrew Corsini/THS; right, Warren Jagger. **61** top, both, Lewis R. Brown/Latchis Corporation; bottom, David Naylor.

## MID-ATLANTIC

**62–63** ©Peter Aaron ESTO.   **64** left, David Naylor; middle, B. Andrew Corsini/THS; right, THS.   **65** top left, B'hend and Kaufmann Archives/Ron Downer Collection; top right, THS; bottom, Maryland Historical Trust.   **66** Herbert Striner.   **67** left, THS; right, David Naylor.   **68** left, THS; right, B. Andrew Corsini/THS.   **69** top left, THS; top right, David Naylor; bottom, THS.   **70** both, THS.   **71** top, THS/Ben Hall Collection; bottom, THS.   **72** both, THS.   **73** top, both, THS; bottom, both, THS/Ben Hall Collection.   **74** THS.   **75** both, THS.   **76** top and bottom left, NTHP; bottom right, THS.   **77** top, both, THS/Ben Hall Collection; bottom, THS.   **78** top, THS/Loew's Collection; bottom left, The Riviera/Wright Photos; bottom right, The Riviera/Randy Piazza.   **79** Louis Ouzer, Rochester, N.Y.   **80** top left, David Naylor; top right, THS; others, Chris Cummings.   **81** left, State Theatre; right, David Naylor.   **82** top, David Naylor; bottom, THS.   **83** THS.   **84** David Naylor.   **85** THS/Herbert Harwood.   **86** top, THS; left and right, NTHP; middle, THS.   **87** top, B'hend and Kaufmann Archives/Karl Bowers Collection; bottom, Gordon Mahan/Library Theatre.   **88** top, David Naylor; bottom, Lake County Museum, Curt Teich Postcard Collection, A-37883.   **80** top, Allen Carney; bottom, THS.   **90** both, Foto Studio, Huntington, W.Va.   **91** Michael Keller/West Virginia Department of Culture and History.

## SOUTH

**92–93** Birmingham Public Library.   **94** top and bottom right, Birmingham Public Library; bottom left, both, Robert Yuill.   **95** top left, Erik Overbey/Mobile Public Library Collection, University of South Alabama Photographic Archives; top right, Mobile Historic Development Commission; bottom, both, Heritage Commission of Tuscaloosa County.   **96** Roger Coley, *Pine Bluff Commercial.*   **98** THS.   **99** both, HABS.   **100** left, Walter Smalling, Jr.; right, Lake County Museum, Curt Teich Postcard Collection, 121516.   **101** top, THS; bottom, THS/Ben Hall Collection.   **102** top, both, Floyd Jillson, *Atlanta Journal;* right middle, HABS; left, NTHP.   **103** David B. Schneider.   **104** B'hend and Kaufmann Archives/Wurlitzer Company Collection.   **105** top left, THS/Loew's Collection; others, HABS.   **106** Charles Seale.   **107** both, THS.   **108** left, John A. Moore/City of Shreveport Department of Public Works; right, THS/Ben Hall Collection.   **110** Mississippi Department of Archives and History.   **111** left, Joann Sieburg-Baker/North Carolina Division of Archives and History; right, THS.   **112** Gwynne Taylor/North Carolina Division of Archives and History.   **113** top, David B. Schneider; bottom, C. C. Benton, Jr.   **114** left, Debra Allen/South Carolina Department of Archives and History; right, David B. Schneider.   **115** top, both, THS; bottom, Cumberland Heritage, Inc.   **116** THS.   **117** left, THS; right, David B. Schneider/Tennessee State Library and Archives.   **118** Bob Ander/Virginia Stage Company.   **119** top, Byrd Theatre; bottom, David W. Newman/Carpenter Center.

## MIDWEST

**120–21** B'hend and Kaufmann Archives.   **122** top, THS; others, NTHP.   **123** THS.   **124** HABS.   **125** both, THS.   **126** all, THS.   **127** THS.   **128** Bob Thall/Commission on Chicago Historical and Architectural Landmarks.   **129** THS.   **130** left, David Naylor; right, THS.   **131** both, THS.   **132** both, THS.   **133** left and middle, THS; right, NTHP.   **134** all, THS.   **135** top, THS; bottom, NTHP.   **136** left, Lake County Museum, Curt Teich Postcard Collection, A75934 (detail); right, THS.   **137** both, B. Andrew Corsini/THS.   **138** both, THS.   **139** top left and bottom, THS; top right, THS/B. Andrew Corsini Collection.   **140** left and bottom, HABS; right, Indiana Repertory Theatre.   **141** left, THS; right, Lake County Museum, Curt Teich Postcard Collection, 121933 (detail).   **142** all, THS.   **143** top, HABS; bottom, THS.   **144** top, Walter Anderson, Emporia, Kans./Kansas State Historical Society; bottom, B'hend and Kaufmann Archives.   **145** top, B'hend and Kaufmann Archives; bottom, Dick Haden, Orpheum Theatre Restoration Committee/Kansas State Historical Society.   **146** both, THS.   **147** both, THS/ B. Andrew Corsini Collection.   **148** both, Fox Associates, St. Louis.   **149** top, both, HABS; bottom, B'hend and Kaufmann Archives.   **150** top, Charles Ahronheim; bottom, THS.   **151** THS.   **152** top, Minnesota Historical Society; bottom, THS/B. Andrew Corsini Collection.   **153** top, Judy Olausen/NTHP; bottom, NTHP. **154** top left, B'hend and Kaufmann Archives; top right, Elizabeth M. Hall/Minnesota Historical Society; bottom, World Theater.   **155** Robert Noback.   **156** top, THS/B. Andrew Corsini Collection; bottom, David Naylor.   **157** Sherry Piland.   **158** all, THS.   **159** top, Fox Associates, St. Louis; bottom, NTHP.   **160** top left and bottom, Fox Associates, St. Louis; others, Aaron D. Cushman and Associates, Inc.   **161** both, THS.   **162** Steven Pondelis/Nebraska State Historical Society. **163** top left, Janet Jeffries Spencer/Nebraska State Historical Society; top right, Joni Gilkerson/Nebraska State Historical Society; bottom, THS/Ben Hall Collection.   **164** both, THS/Ben Hall Collection.   **165** top, Fargo Heritage Society; bottom, State Historical Society of North Dakota.   **166** both, THS.   **167** top, both, David Naylor; bottom, THS.   **169** top and bottom, THS; middle, Playhouse Square Foundation.   **170** top, HABS; bottom, Lake County Museum, Curt Teich Postcard Collection, R84524.   **171** D. R. Goff Quicksilver Photography.   **172** top, both, D. R. Goff Quicksilver Photography; middle and bottom, THS.   **173** both, THS.   **174** both, THS.   **175** John Rau/South

Dakota State Historical Preservation Center.   **176** top left, THS; bottom, both, HABS.   **177** State Historical Society of Wisconsin.   **178** all, THS.   **179** both, THS.

## SOUTHWEST

**180–81** THS/Hoblitzelle Theatre Arts Library, Humanities Research Center, University of Texas, Austin.   **182** David Naylor.   **183** both, The Rialto, Tucson.   **184** top left, THS; top right, Lake County Museum, Curt Teich Postcard Collection, 8A-H 2862; others, David Naylor.   **185** Old Lyceum Theatre, Inc.   **186** B'hend and Kaufmann Archives/THS Collection.   **187** top, B'hend and Kaufmann Archives; bottom, Paramount Theatre, Abilene, Tex.   **188** both, Paramount Theatre, Abilene, Tex.   **189** top, THS; bottom, THS/George R. Hockmeyer, Houston.   **190** Lake County Museum, Curt Teich Postcard Collection, 3C-H963 (detail).   **191** all, The Oglesby Group, Dallas.   **192** both, THS/George Hockmeyer, Houston.   **193** top, Lake County Museum, Curt Teich Postcard Collection, 110941; bottom left, THS; bottom right, Lake County Museum, Curt Teich Postcard Collection, 111097 (detail).   **194** THS/Hoblitzelle Theatre Arts Library, Humanities Research Center, University of Texas, Austin.   **195** THS/George Hockmeyer, Houston; bottom, NTHP.

## WEST

**196–97** THS/Terry Helgesen Collection.   **198** all, THS.   **199** top, both, David Naylor; bottom, THS.   **201** top and left, THS; right, HABS.   **202** top left, THS/Ben Hall Collection; others, THS.   **203** top, David Naylor; left, THS/Terry Helgesen Collection; right, THS.   **204** left, THS/Terry Helgesen Collection; right, THS/Ben Hall Collection; bottom, David Naylor.   **205** THS/Loew's Collection.   **206** all, THS/Terry Helgesen Collection.   **207** top left, THS/Terry Helgesen Collection; top right, California Society of Theatre Historians.   **208** top, THS/Ben Hall Collection; bottom, David Naylor.   **209** both, David Naylor.   **210** top left, THS/Ben Hall Collection; right, THS; left, David Naylor.   **211** left, B'hend and Kaufmann Archives/Ron Downer Collection; right, David Naylor.   **212** top, THS/Terry Helgesen Collection; bottom, HABS.   **213** top left, HABS; top right and middle, both, Cathe Centorbe, San Francisco; bottom, NTHP.   **214** top, Gabriel Moulin Studios, San Francisco; bottom, Tom Owen.   **215** top, both, David Naylor; bottom, THS/Terry Helgesen Collection.   **216** top, Fox Theatre; bottom left, THS; bottom right, THS/Terry Helgesen Collection.   **217** left, THS; right, THS/Terry Helgesen Collection.   **218** top, both, THS/Terry Helgesen Collection; bottom left, B. Andrew Corsini/THS; bottom right, David Naylor.   **219** right, both, David Naylor; left, B'hend and Kaufmann Archives/Dave Bowers Collection.   **220** left, B'hend and Kaufmann Archives; right, Historic Boulder, Inc.   **221** left, Christiane H. Citron; right, Roger Whitacre/Historic

Denver, Inc.    **222** all, THS.    **223** Robert K. Headley
Collection.    **224** top, David Naylor; middle, HABS;
bottom, both, B'hend and Kaufmann Archives/Myers
Brothers Collection.    **225** HABS.    **226** top, HABS;
bottom, THS.    **227** B'hend and Kaufmann Archives.
**228** David Naylor.    **229** all, David Naylor.    **230** all,
THS.    **231** top and bottom left, THS; bottom right,
David Naylor.    **232** Oregon Historical Society.    **233**
Michael Lloyd, *The Oregonian;* right, THS; bottom, Utah
Historical Society/Friends of the Egyptian Theatre,
Inc.    **234** left, THS; right, David Naylor.    **235** top,
Richard Longstreth; bottom, David Naylor.    **236** David
Naylor.    **237** top, THS; bottom, David Naylor.    **238**
top, both, David Naylor; bottom, NTHP.    **239** David
Naylor.    **240** top left, David Naylor; others, THS.    **241**
all, David Naylor.    **242** left, NTHP; right, David
Naylor.    **243** HABS.


**244** THS.    **246** top, Clarkson N. Potter, Inc.; bottom,
THS.    **247** both, B'hend and Kaufmann Archives/John
J. McNamara Collection.    **248** top, B'hend and Kauf-
mann Archives/C. E. Macdonald Collection; bottom,
THS.    **249** both, THS.    **250** top, Smithsonian Institu-
tion; bottom, THS.    **249** both, THS.    **250** top,
Smithsonian Institution; bottom, THS.    **252** Smithso-
nian Institution.    **254** Cabot Street Cinema.

# INDEX

■ ■ ■ ■ ■ ■ ■ ■ ■ ■ ■ ■ ■ ■ ■ ■ ■ ■

# AUTHOR

David Naylor, a writer and lecturer, first became fasci-
nated with movie theaters on a visit in 1977 to the
restored Paramount in Oakland, Calif. Since then he has
written and lectured widely on the subject of historic
theaters. He is author of *American Picture Palaces,* a
history of movie theater architecture. An extensive
traveler, Naylor organized an exhibition for the Smithsonian Institution's Cooper-Hewitt Museum in New York
City presenting drawings, photographs and memorabilia
on movie theaters. The exhibition led to the film *The
Movie Palaces,* produced by the Smithsonian's Office of
Telecommunications, for showing on public broadcasting stations. He also has written about theaters for
*Historic Preservation* magazine and has worked exten-
sively with the Theatre Historical Society of America on
its annual publication.

Joseph DuciBella is an interior design consultant who
has written about theaters for *Marquee* and *Theatre
Organ,* both magazines about theatrical history. Duci-
Bella also has published booklets on theaters in and
around Chicago. He has been a consultant on numerous
theater restoration projects in New York, Indiana and
Illinois and most recently advised on restoration of the
Lake in Oak Park, Ill.

■ ■ ■ ■ ■ ■ ■ ■ ■ ■ ■ ■ ■ ■ ■ ■ ■

# OTHER BOOKS FROM
# THE PRESERVATION PRESS

## BUILDING WATCHERS SERIES

**What Style Is It? A Guide to American Architecture**

John Poppeliers, S. Allen Chambers, Jr., and Nancy B. Schwartz, Historic American Buildings Survey. One of the most popular, concise books on American architectural styles, this portable guidebook is designed for easy identification of 22 styles of buildings at home or on the road. 112 pp., illus., biblio., gloss. $7.95 pb.

**Master Builders: A Guide to Famous American Architects**

Introduction by Roger K. Lewis. Forty major architects who have left indelible marks on American architecture—from Bulfinch to Venturi—are profiled in this entertaining introduction. 204 pp., illus., biblio., append., index. $9.95 pb.

**Built in the U.S.A.: American Buildings from Airports to Zoos**

Diane Maddex, Editor. A guidebook-sized history of 42 American building types, showing how their forms developed from their functions. 192 pp., illus., biblio., append. $9.95 pb.

**America's Architectural Roots: Ethnic Groups That Built America**

Dell Upton, Editor. Ethnic groups from Africans to Ukrainians have shaped the way our buildings look. Highlighted here are 22 groups, featured in heavily illustrated chapters that document the rich ethnic diversity of American architecture. 196 pp., illus., biblio., index. $9.95 pb.

**The Buildings of Main Street: A Guide to American Commercial Architecture**

Richard Longstreth. A fresh look at architecture found along America's Main Streets. Building types are documented in this unique guide with 220 illustrations from towns and cities across the country. 156 pp., illus., biblio., index. $8.95 pb.

**All About Old Buildings: The Whole Preservation Catalog**

Diane Maddex, Editor. This fact-filled book offers a lively, readable mixture of illustrations, sources of help, case histories, excerpts and quotations on 15 major subject areas. 436 pp., illus., biblio., index. $39.95 hb, $24.95 pb.

**America's City Halls**

William L. Lebovich, Historic American Buildings Survey. Two centuries of municipal architecture are captured in this book featuring 500 photographs of 114 city halls in 40 states. 224 pp., illus., biblio., append., indexes. $18.95 pb.

**America's Country Schools**

Andrew Gulliford. Captures the historical and architectural legacy of country schools from soddies and frame buildings to octagons and provides ideas for preserving them. 296 pp., illus., append., index. $18.95 pb.

**America's Forgotten Architecture**

National Trust for Historic Preservation, Tony P. Wrenn and Elizabeth D. Mulloy. A pictorial overview of preservation, the book surveys in 475 photographs what is worth saving and how to do it. 312 pp., illus., biblio., append. Pantheon Books. $14.95 pb.

Photographs by Balthazar Korab. Presents a new way of looking at architecture — by searching for an alphabet in, on and around buildings. Juxtaposes dramatic photographs with quotations by architectural observers from Goethe to Wright. 64 pp., illus. $14.95 hb.

**Archabet: An Architectural Alphabet**

Drawings by Roxie Munro. An architectural ABC whose whimsical illustrations are paired with easy-to-understand definitions for architecture lovers young and old. 64 pp., 48 drawings, biblio. $8.95 pb.

**Architects Make Zigzags: Looking at Architecture from A to Z**

Ada Louise Huxtable. Foreword by John B. Oakes. These 68 pieces, most originally published by the *New York Times*, cover the classic urban confrontations of the 1960s and 1970s, analyzing the failures and successes and urging us to create more livable cities. 208 pp., illus., index. $14.95 pb.

**Goodbye History, Hello Hamburger: An Anthology of Architectural Delights and Disasters**

Katherine Cole Stevenson and H. Ward Jandl. A unique history and guide to nearly 450 precut house models — from bungalows to colonials — sold by Sears from 1908 to 1940, capturing the pride and memories of Sears house owners. 365 pp., illus., biblio., index. $24.95 pb.

**Houses by Mail: A Guide to Houses from Sears, Roebuck and Company**

Photographs by Jet Lowe from the Historic American Engineering Record. Introduction by David Weitzman. Some 120 color and duotone photographs are featured in this album of an industrial America that few people have seen — famous landmarks such as the Statue of Liberty as well as less celebrated bridges, power plants, windmills and dams. 128 pp., illus., biblio. $34.95 hb.

**Industrial Eye**

National Park Service. A "Dear Abby" for old buildings, this handy guide (now in an updated edition) answers 150 of the most-asked questions about rehabilitating old houses and other historic buildings. 200 pp., illus., biblio., index. $12.95 pb.

**Respectful Rehabilitation: Answers to Your Questions About Old Buildings**

To order Preservation Press books, send the total of the book prices (less 10 percent discount for National Trust members), plus $3 postage and handling, to: Mail Order, National Trust for Historic Preservation, 1600 H Street, N.W., Washington, D.C. 20006. Residents of California, Colorado, Washington, D.C., Illinois, Iowa, Louisiana, Maryland, Massachusetts, New York, Pennsylvania, South Carolina, Texas and Virginia please add applicable sales tax. Make checks payable to the National Trust or provide credit card number, expiration date, signature and telephone number.